BALANCING ACTS IN PERSONAL, SOCIAL AND HEALTH EDUCATION: A PRACTICAL GUIDE FOR TEACHERS

This book is designed for two types of reader: teachers trying out active learning methods and those with responsibilities for curriculum co-ordination and staff development. Its view of PSHE, and of the balance between personal and social values, is argued in relation to theoretical and practical questions which teachers can explore through a variety of exercises as they read. The authors offer four models of PSHE and a technique to help teachers identify these different approaches in practice. A framework is suggested for distinguished PSHE from other areas, including the pastoral curriculum, health education, moral education and careers education, and a procedure, using grids, is described to help identify which elements of PSHE are being taught and by whom. Given their commitment to a holistic view of health, in which both individuality and collaboration have a place, the authors argue for active teaching methods and include examples of a wide range of PSHE exercises and evaluation techniques for use in schools. The book also discusses the importance of 'healthy' whole-school organisation and suggests strategies for staff development.

Judith Ryder is Lecturer in Education at King's College, London.

Lesley Campbell is Advisory Lecturer in Health Education and Personal Development (ILEA) and Course Tutor for the Diploma of Health Education at King's College, London.

BALANCING ACTS
in personal, social and
health education

JUDITH RYDER AND LESLEY CAMPBELL

ROUTLEDGE
London and New York

First published in 1988 by
Routledge
a division of Routledge, Chapman and Hall
11 New Fetter Lane, London EC4P 4EE

Published in the USA by
Routledge
a division of Routledge, Chapman and Hall, Inc.
29 West 35th Street, New York NY 10001

© 1988 J. Ryder and L. Campbell

Printed in Great Britain
Filmsetting by Mayhew Typesetting, Bristol, England

British Library Cataloguing in Publication Data

Ryder, Judith
Balancing acts in personal, social and
health education : a practical guide for
teachers.
1. Life skills—Study and teaching
2. Health education
I. Title   II. Campbell, Lesley
370.11′5   HQ2037

ISBN 0-415-00537-X
ISBN 0-415-00538-8 Pbk

Library of Congress Cataloging-in-Publication Data
ISBN 0-415-00537-X
ISBN 0-415-00538-8 Pbk

Contents

List of Figures

List of Exercises

The authors waive their copyright to all the exercises.

Introduction

PURPOSE

Why a text on Personal, Social and Health Education? What is PSHE anyway? How does it differ from Personal, Social and Moral Education, Personal and Social Development, Lifeskills and the various other umbrella areas that have appeared in recent years — each occupying similar territory? Where does it belong in the curriculum: is PSHE a subject in its own right, a set of cross-curricular themes, an organising principle for work in social skills, or a new approach to pedagogy? Or is it all of them?

These are legitimate and important questions, which are addressed specifically in Chapter 1. As we shall see, though, the answers are not necessarily straightforward. Partly they depend on the individual teacher and his view of education. To some extent they depend on particular student groups and wider curriculum constraints: the nature of the timetable, patterns of assessment and so on. But untidy as this degree of variability may feel, it can also provide a potential source of richness, as we hope to show.

It would be unrealistic, then, to be prescriptive about PSHE. There are likely to be sound practical as well as personal and perhaps political grounds for differences. We shall not, therefore, be proposing a blueprint for a single ideal scheme of PSHE. In fact, we do not believe such a model exists. Part of the point of PSHE is, precisely, that it builds from the needs and starting points of those it aims to serve. Rather, we hope to provide a framework for teachers that helps in five main ways:

1. to describe the core of potential contents and methods which make up PSHE and to examine their relationship to some underlying values for society and education;
2. to recognise existing elements of PSHE work already being undertaken, to identify gaps and to devise co-ordinated strategies for whole-school curriculum planning and evaluation and for staff development;
3. to provide examples and schema for useful ways of working in PSHE, with a variety of student groups at different phases of learning;
4. to emphasise the importance of harnessing PSHE goals and approaches to those of the wider social life of the school and its surrounding community;
5. to encourage teachers to reflect purposively on their teaching in order to make the best use of the insights available from educational research and devise the most appropriate learning opportunities for students.

Balance — between aims, teaching methods and evaluation techniques and a healthy, whole-school approach — is perhaps the key feature of effective PSHE

Exercise 0.1: The General Aims of Education

Instructions: Read through the statements and mark any words or phrases which seem particularly important or contentious. Then, decide on the five aims which are most important to you. If you are working with others, compare your preferences and try to agree on three priorities. Alternatively, select the three priorities you feel your head or a group of students, or the governors, or particular parents would have chosen. Are there differences? If so, why?

1. to give children the experience of school as a caring, supportive community where life is enjoyable and where there is equal provision regardless of sex, race or culture ————

2. to enable all children to develop as fully as possible their abilities, interests and aptitudes and to make additional provision, if necessary, for those who are in any way disadvantaged ————

3. to allow children to develop lively, enquiring minds, to be capable of independent thought and to experience enjoyment in learning so that they may be encouraged to take advantage of educational opportunities in later life ————

4. to develop appropriate skills in literacy and numeracy ————

5. to develop a curriculum which ensures contact with those major areas of knowledge and experience which will help children to know more about themselves and the society in which they live ————

6. to work in ways which will enhance the self-respect and confidence of young people and encourage them to take responsibility for themselves and their activities ————

7. to establish a partnership between school and the community which it serves and to develop understanding of the wider community and of ways in which individuals and groups relate ————

8. to give children the skills necessary to respond effectively to social, economic and political changes and to changing patterns of work ————

9. to develop the social skills necessary to work successfully with other people ————

10. to equip children for their adult roles in society and help them to understand the responsibilities of being parents, citizens and consumers ————

11. to encourage appreciation and concern for the environment ————

12. to develop interests and skills which will continue to give personal satisfaction in the use of leisure time ————

for us. This is likely to be the product of judicious selection and a personal set of priorities for education. At relevant points throughout the book, we have introduced practical exercises to help readers think, if they wish, about their own practice and priorities. Most of these are designed so that they can be completed individually; others depend on feedback from a partner or are intended as workshop-based activities. Some are particularly useful in training sessions. In each case the instructions should make clear how to proceed and whether there are particular points to bear in mind about the specific level or processes required. Exercise 0.1, opposite, invites you to examine the general aims of education, as a context for considering the more detailed aims of PSHE. This list was compiled by teachers and LEA officers during an HMI enquiry in 1983 (see DES/Welsh Office (1983a) *Curriculum 11–16: Towards a Statement of Entitlement*).

Few teachers would dispute the place of such high-sounding purposes among the general aims of education. But, for some, there are no doubt omissions in the list. And perhaps many of us would feel unsure about how, in detail, to implement such aims for different groups of students. Whatever our priorities, what is of interest is to note how many of the aims refer to aspects of the personal and social development of students.

Is this appropriate? Were HM Inspectors, in fact, right to claim in *Aspects of Secondary Education* (1979) that, 'The personal and social development of the pupil is one way of describing the central purpose of education'? If so, does that mean all teachers are, or should be, involved in PSHE? We shall consider that issue more fully later. But whether or not it is a valid view, it is also the source of a problem. For if PSHE can be interpreted in such an all-embracing way it risks being taken for granted, as an obviously 'good thing' and rarely, if ever, planned in a deliberate and co-ordinated fashion. The consequence, as one writer has already warned, is that personal and social development 'though sounding grand' is 'no more than a pot-pourri of ... loosely connected skills, habits, bits of knowledge, attitudes, behaviours, feelings' (Pring, 1984).

Our challenge in this book is to bring life and definition to that pot-pourri. As a preliminary you may find it interesting to check your current perceptions of PSHE.

Please note that with Exercise 0.2, as with others that follow, there is a difficulty concerning reality and rhetoric (what PSHE actually consists of and what it might ideally be). We suggest you focus your immediate reactions on what you feel PSHE *ought* to be about and afterwards reflect on how you might be able to shift practice in your school closer towards that ideal. Before we continue, here are some notes about using the book.

Exercise 0.2: What is Personal, Social and Health Education?

Instructions: Consider each statement about PSHE and indicate whether you agree or disagree by ticking the appropriate column. If you are working with other people, compare your responses and discuss any that are particularly controversial.

	Agree	Disagree
1. PSHE is best carried out in educational establishments, given contemporary changes in family life.	____	____
2. PSHE includes the teaching of socially acceptable behaviour.	____	____
3. PSHE aims to foster positive social and personal relationships.	____	____
4. PSHE is mainly about teaching students to keep fit and feel good.	____	____
5. PSHE aims to lessen the dangers of over-indulgence by stressing the notion of balance.	____	____
6. PSHE involves groups of students taking political action to change their environment.	____	____
7. PSHE aims to change attitudes and behaviour.	____	____
8. PSHE helps young people to make responsible, realistic and informed decisions.	____	____
9. PSHE involves assessing local social and health services.	____	____
10. PSHE is concerned with preparing young people for life after school.	____	____
11. PSHE is effective only with methodologies based on active learning and student self-determination.	____	____
12. PSHE aims to encourage a healthier life-style: physically, mentally, spiritually and socially.	____	____
13. PSHE makes students more aware of the social and economic constraints on their lives.	____	____
14. PSHE should only be taught by those with expertise in health education, psychology or social studies.	____	____
15. PSHE gives information and advice on medical issues.	____	____
16. PSHE attempts to show the balance between students' responsibilities as members of society and their rights as individuals.	____	____
17. PSHE aims to stimulate and develop independent critical faculties.	____	____
18. PSHE depends on effective group work. It cannot be taught didactically.	____	____
19. PSHE gives students skills to challenge inequality.	____	____
20. PSHE encourages the practice of certain moral principles.	____	____

USING THE BOOK

1. Terminology and frames of reference

In view of our own background and experience, we have chosen to focus here on the 11–19 age range. When we refer to 'schools', therefore, unless we indicate otherwise, we shall mean secondary schools and colleges of further education. Similarly, we shall use the designation 'students' to mean both school pupils and FE students, and 'teachers' to mean both school teachers and FE lecturers. Only in Chapter 9 is the specific terminology of FE used. We have decided to respond to the problem of gender by using 'he'/'his' and 'she'/'her' in alternate chapters.

Since both of us have spent our teaching careers in London, we are more familiar with PSHE developments in the South East, and, in particular, in the ILEA, than with those happening elsewhere in the country. This is a regrettable gap and makes us ill-qualified to speak with authority on, for example, the place of PSHE in community schools, in modular curricula or in TVEI. However, we both belong to wider professional networks and have had opportunities to work in a variety of ways and at a range of levels.

2. Readership and routes through the book

We have had in mind two sorts of reader while writing: first, relatively newly trained teachers who want to experiment with more active ways of working. We hope such teachers, whatever their subject background, will be helped to clarify their ideas on PSHE and the contribution they might be able to make to its development. We also hope that they will be encouraged to find support for innovating in their own classrooms.

The second group of readers we have addressed are those in middle-management positions in schools or in training roles for LEAs who have responsibility for curriculum co-ordination, including the specific charge of PSHE and school-focused in-service development. Chapters 7 and 8 are specifically written for this second group of readers, while Chapter 9 is aimed at colleagues in Further Education. The Appendices provide a guide to resources, addresses of useful supporting agencies and professional training centres and a glossary of educational abbreviations and technical terms.

The flow chart in Figure 0.1 suggests some alternative ways through the book.

Figure 0.1: Routes Through the Book

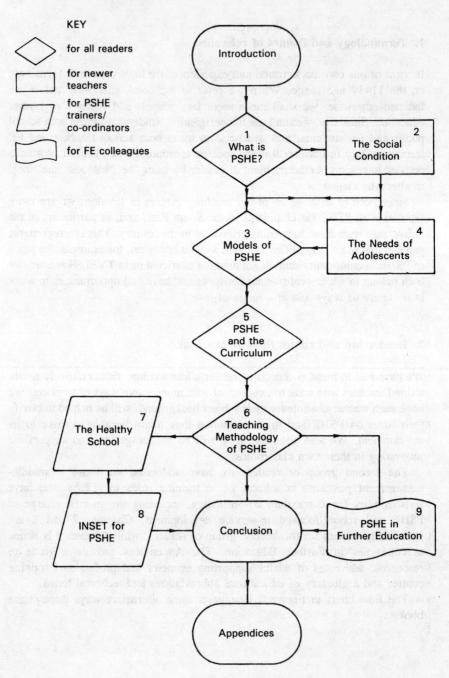

KEY

for all readers

for newer teachers

for PSHE trainers/ co-ordinators

for FE colleagues

Introduction

1 What is PSHE?

2 The Social Condition

3 Models of PSHE

4 The Needs of Adolescents

5 PSHE and the Curriculum

7 The Healthy School

6 Teaching Methodology of PSHE

8 INSET for PSHE

Conclusion

9 PSHE in Further Education

Appendices

3. Getting the most out of the book

We have tried to keep academic citation to a minimum in the text. This is because much of what we have to say is the product for us — as we hope it will be for you — of a genuine struggle to work things out from experience (often using the same exercises as those included here). We also believe that any learning which is truly significant is personal and must be personally owned. This does not mean we are simply pragmatists. On the contrary, we fully acknowledge the role of theory and research in shaping our thinking and beliefs and would like to make that available for readers who have the opportunity to take their study further. Much of this detail will be found in references and in the suggestions for further reading at the end of each chapter.

As will be evident from its form, we have conceived this as a practical book and as an interactive resource. We hope, therefore, that you will use it actively. In particular we should like to encourage you to work through the exercises — either on your own or with others. Ideally they repay discussion with at least one other person. Certainly they can be a lot of fun when shared. However, do not be put off if you cannot talk about them with a colleague; the exercises provide an opportunity for personal reflection and should offer a useful way of clarifying your ideas about PSHE. Nearly all of the exercises have been adapted specifically for this book, but we have used versions of them ourselves, in a variety of teaching and training contexts. We hope that you, in turn, will experiment with some of them in your teaching.

Before we proceed, we have just one word of caution. While many of the strategies for successful PSHE work are identical to those of traditional teaching: careful preparation; detailed advance planning of time and resources; clear instructions; appropriately designed tasks; attractive materials; sound evaluation, and so on, there is one area of skill in which many subject teachers have not been trained — group work. And effective group work is, for us, the foundation of successful PSHE. On its own, no book or video or set of exercises can supply the experience required to learn about the leadership and dynamics of groups. We strongly recommend, therefore, that PSHE teachers and in-service trainers try, if possible, to undertake some specific group work training. In some authorities this is possible on an INSET basis. Alternatively, there are opportunities via the various external agencies listed in Appendix 3. The rewards of such an investment will be well worth the time and effort. What is more, they will serve much wider personal and professional purposes than simply those related to PSHE. Training can enhance self-confidence; it also provides a source of professional support. In addition, it provides a framework of theoretical ideas which can illuminate and help refine practice — that of both individuals and teams.

4. Our view of PSHE

Having outlined our intentions and said a little about how the book might be used, it remains to account to readers for our particular perspectives on PSHE. We make no apology for taking a view of PSHE here which, perhaps unfashionably, sets it somewhat apart from the pastoral work of the school and which adopts a deliberately antagonist stance towards the competitive and individualistic values which have for so long dominated English education. As will become clear in the next chapter, our commitment is to a society in which attitudes of mutual esteem and respect are allied to the use of informed argument in order to create the possibility of healthier life-styles for everyone. Accordingly, this book does not set out to deal with management concerns such as crisis resolution, staff relationships, individual counselling, student disruption or discipline difficulties. Nor does it specifically address the issues raised by training and vocational preparation.

Lastly, a word about the title: *Balancing Acts*. Who needs balance? If balance implies woolly compromise and a juggling of 'ifs', 'buts' and 'maybes' rather than a firm and confident stance towards things, what is the point? Most teachers are only too well aware of the numerous balancing acts which they perform daily. Now is not the time for any more compromise and adjustment to 'reality', they may feel. Rather, what is needed is conviction and the courage to persist in spite of the constraints.

We ourselves are certainly persuaded of the need for commitment. Thus, in opting for the idea of balance we do not necessarily wish to advocate compromise or consensus — particularly if that means clouding difficult and sensitive issues of individual judgement. Our intention is to argue the case for the educational values and principles which seem relevant to PSHE and to recognise the tensions and contradictions which crop up when they are juxtaposed. Such a discussion inevitably raises questions of priority. We wish to acknowledge these openly and to be clear about the relative weight we give to different alternatives. Hence, balance, for us, is not a tendency towards acceptable norms; it is a rigorous assessment of different influences on the practice of Personal, Social and Health Education. Frequently, it is a question of choosing between relative advantages and disadvantages. It is never an easy option. The balance diagrams at the start of each chapter pinpoint the relevant balancing acts for discussion in that section of the book.

One of our explicit aims for this book is to help PSHE teachers by drawing attention to relevant theoretical debates, examining the underlying values and linking the emerging principles to current — or future — practice. We appreciate that educational theory is not readily accessible to all teachers (even if they had time to study it). However, all teachers share a commitment to helping students learn, and most expend considerable energy and thought in finding ways to do this well. What is so exciting about PSHE is the opportunity it provides to expand ideas about student learning, and to extend the range of teaching techniques. This is itself a balancing act!

ACKNOWLEDGEMENTS

As Chapter 6 will explain, a central tenet of PSHE is that our teaching approaches should model the values for which PSHE itself stands. We hope that the writing of this book demonstrates the same process. Although we were each responsible for drafting different parts of the book initially, the end result is very much a product of collaboration and shared authorship. We were also able to draw on the support of a very large number of colleagues, students and friends — as a source both of critical feedback and of detailed help with examples of good practice.

Among those whose encouragement and criticism we value most, we should like to thank our respective colleagues and team members at the Centre for Educational Studies, King's College and the HEPD Teachers' Centre: Gill Williams, Tony Mansell, Eileen Carnell, Jane Jenks, Barbara Patilla, Jan Mulreany and Ted Payne. We also owe an immense debt of gratitude to the many different groups of students with whom we have worked over the past two years: students on the 1986–7 PGCE course at King's, and especially the members of the Tutoring and Counselling short course; teachers on the 1986–7 Health Education Certificate course; and members of other in-service and Masters programmes with which we have been associated. While it is invidious to name some of these individually and not others, those listed below will each recognise the particular contribution they made: Roger Shortt, Susie Kennard, Moray Cooper, Janet Packer, Bill Bellew, Di Mattin, Anne Bannister, Sharon Ballingall, Stella Muttock, Linda Kelly, Blaine Stothard, Jan Balogh, Ian Marshall, John Bier and Dennis O'Sullivan. Their energy and imagination as practitioners was a source of inspiration to both of us. Another group of people who were important in ensuring the completion of the text are Joan Bliss, Brian Davies and Alison Reeves, who looked after Judith Ryder's administrative responsibilities at a critical stage in the research; Derek Potter, who helped with the graphics; Pam Thatcher and Diana Coke, who undertook some of the tricky bits of typing. Thank you to all of them and, especially, to our personal support group: Neil, Jake, Suke, John and Debbie. Without their faith that we could complete the task we might easily have given up. We hope the product justifies their optimism. However, for the inevitable errors and omissions, we take full responsibility. And we apologise in advance for any ideas which are inappropriately acknowledged. This has been an exciting and instructive book to write. We hope it will be just as stimulating for our readers.

Judith Ryder and Lesley Campbell
Health Education Unit, Centre for Educational Studies,
King's College, London University, 522 King's Road, London SW10 0UA

1

What is PSHE?

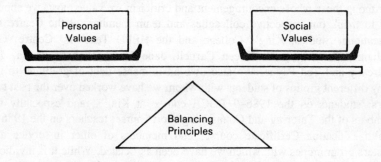

This chapter describes our values as teachers and explains how they relate to practice in PSHE. First, we tackle the question of what Personal, Social and Health Education means. There is a profusion of related and, frequently, overlapping areas: Moral and Religious Education, Political and Social Studies, Community and Development Education, and so on. Each of these can make a legitimate claim to independent existence. Yet each also supports and is supported by PSHE. Our conflation of Health Education with Personal and Social Education also needs explanation since, historically, the two areas have been seen as separate.

We begin with an example of PSHE in practice. There are other cameos in Chapters 5 and 6.

Cameo

It is mid-morning on a wet Wednesday in September. The 17 students (16–19 year olds) in a class on a City and Guilds Community Care course are milling around a visitor who has come to talk about adoption. The students have been studying adoption and fostering procedures during the previous two weeks and have decided that they need a more personal perspective. Their visitor and her husband have recently adopted a young child.

Jill, the visitor, is collected by two students from the foyer and then introduced by them to the rest of the group. Two other students serve tea and coffee to everyone. After five minutes or so, Jill is asked to sit in the middle of a semicircle of students and the more formal session begins. One girl welcomes Jill and explains that the class has prepared several questions for her. The questions, each posed by a different student, cover such areas as the duration of adoption procedures, the most painful or worrying moments, the rights of adopted children and parents, adopting handicapped children and Jill's recommendations for prospective adoptive parents. The exchanges are relaxed and good-humoured, the occasional silence or confusion being dealt with by the students themselves, without recourse to the teacher who is participating in the group.

After about half an hour, a student announces that 'time is up' and asks Jill if she would like to add anything. She is then asked a final question, 'How do you feel about the way the session went?' Jill admits that she was nervous initially but was soon made to feel comfortable. The whole group, including Jill and the teacher, then 'debrief' the session, using a prepared checklist as a framework. The students, prompted by the teacher, discuss what they have learned and make constructive criticisms of the session. At the end they thank Jill for coming and she is escorted to the dining room. The teacher stays a while to check that the students are all right. She then leaves them to rearrange the room. They work together efficiently and cheerfully (with one or two exceptions), chatting meanwhile about how pleasant Jill was and how much they enjoyed the discussion. One student wonders what they will do next lesson to 'follow it up'.

Do you recognise this as a PSHE lesson? If so, can you define its particular PSHE characteristics? If it is not a case of PSHE, in your view, where else does it belong in the curriculum?

As a starting point in defining PSHE, it is useful to acknowledge the wide range of potential ingredients it can embrace. The following brainstorm exercise is a method of doing this.

Exercise 1.1: Brainstorm: What is PSHE?

1. Draw a line down the middle of a large sheet of paper. Head one column 'PSHE IS …' and the other 'PSHE IS NOT …' Allowing yourself only five minutes to complete the task, write down whatever words or phrases come into your mind under each heading. Remember, in a brainstorming session, all ideas count. Do not waste time editing or refining what you have written at this stage.
2. After the five-minute brainstorm, briefly tidy up your list and compare it with a partner's or with our own list (next page).
3. Use the tidied list to reflect on similarities and differences. For example, use the list(s) to select your priorities for PSHE or use it as a checklist against current practice in your school. Grouping your ideas according to knowledge areas, values, methods and other categories can also be a useful clarification exercise.

We implied in the Introduction that there could be many valid interpretations of PSHE — even if, in our view, some are perhaps more valid than others! However, given that PSHE is still relatively uncharted territory, your brainstorm list — like the one in Figure 1.1 — is likely to be couched in very generalised terms. There is still the problem of defining PSHE rigorously, therefore, and of generating practical guidelines to help decide appropriate content and approaches. Some of the reasons why PSHE is such a tricky area to pin down and translate into practice are hinted at by Pring (1984 and 1987). He points to five main areas of difficulty.

DIFFICULTIES IN DEFINING PSHE

1. Conceptual

The very words 'personal', 'social' and 'health' education are contentious and invite an infinite number of interpretations. 'Personal' can mean individual but does that imply individualistic? 'Social' can be applied to a number of levels: the peer group, the school organisation, the community, the country, the world. But when does social equate with 'political' and how far should social education either reinforce the status quo or foster changes in society? If 'health', as we believe, incorporates physical, mental, social, emotional and spiritual aspects, how is it possible to weigh up what is healthy? And what of 'education'? Some argue that, in this context, the word is synonymous with development. But development towards what, and how? Does it involve familiarity with a body of knowledge, the acquisition of particular skills, or the development of attributes and qualities?

Figure 1.1: What is PSHE?

PSHE is ...	PSHE is not ...
hard work	just process
fun	counselling or pastoral casework
structured	indoctrination
dependent on certain skills	a fad or bandwagon
for everyone	just for the least able students
holistic	social and life skills
eclectic	playing games for the sake of it
contentious	a means of social control
based on a particular ideology	about good manners
about whole-school policies	just for 4th and 5th years
evaluative, using a variety of methods	about crisis management
about the 'new 3 r's':	a historical accident
relationships	
responsibility	
relevance	

---

2. Political

All the terms associated with PSHE can be, and are, used as a vehicle for values stemming from different educational ideologies. In fact, sometimes, the gap between rhetoric and reality opens up into a gulf under the influence of these processes. The impact of the 1986 Education Act is a case in point. Now, instead of teachers being able to negotiate appropriate sex education for different groups of students, they find themselves constrained by what governors determine students' needs to be. The fundamental question here is one concerning power. Who decides what goes on in school and, in particular, what goes on in PSHE?

For the record, we are both socialists and feminists and although we may argue over different interpretations we share educational principles which unquestionably derive from our political beliefs.

3. Ethical

Given that PSHE is permeated with values, how can teachers explicitly address ethical judgements without being accused of bias and indoctrination? We believe that there are ethical universals, such as keeping promises and not deliberately setting out to harm others, but perhaps more important is to encourage young people to recognise moral choices and their own criteria for deciding them. Is

13

this attention to moral reflection, itself, an ethical stance? A related, and arguably more problematic, concern is the nature of the implicit ethical messages carried by PSHE. Just as didactic teaching conveys notions of power, expertise and truth, so the group work methods which characterise practice in PSHE indicate attitudes to equality, collaboration and relativism.

4. Empirical

At present, there is little empirical evidence of 'successful' PSHE, nor are there many guidelines to good practice. As a relatively new curriculum area, PSHE still has to establish its paradigm, particularly in terms of evaluation. Case studies and illuminative descriptions, such as Rice (1981) and Brandes and Ginnis (1986), do exist but we would like there to be many more accounts available to teachers. There also needs to be a better forum for the exchange of ideas between committed practitioners and other interested parties, and more evident support from the Inspectorate and LEA advisory teams.

5. Organisational

Organisational difficulties are likely to confront PSHE teachers immediately, if only because the overlaps between PSHE and other areas of the curriculum are such a challenge. These exist in terms of content: for instance, between the moral issues that crop up in History, English and Religious and Moral Education and those that emerge in PSHE. There are also overlaps in terms of process: for example, between the approaches used in Pastoral Programmes, Social and Life Skills courses and Drama and those of PSHE. There is, in addition, a significant overlap with the para-curriculum. Effective participation in a school's decision-making process, for example, inevitably alters students' engagement with decision-making simulations in PSHE.

As with any curriculum innovation, PSHE teachers have to argue their case in the face of tough opposition, particularly from those whose subject empires seem most threatened. They also have to reassure those — colleagues, parents and employers — who genuinely fear a dilution of the overall curriculum offering. The issues are clearly complex. Small wonder, then, that we keep posing the question: 'What is PSHE?' There are a number of ways of proceeding. One way is to examine relevant curricula in practice and to identify what they have in common.

PSHE IN PRACTICE

The main difficulty of trying to define PSHE by reference to practice is that, given the diversity of teachers and schools, the names actually used for particular curriculum areas are often only labels of convenience. They can be totally unreliable guides to content and approach, as one researcher found (Lukes in Lee, 1980).

> Social education at M means the miscellaneous topics given to non-examinees, ranging from first aid to folksongs, while for example at D the same title refers to a two-year kind of anthropology to world religions course.

One reason for using the umbrella PSHE rather than any other is that both personal and social education (PSE) and health education (HE) are supported by recognised bodies of knowledge and share common aims. It is to a definition of these two fields that we turn initially, therefore. Among the broader definitions, David (1983), in a report for the Schools Council, suggests that Personal and Social Education includes:

> the teaching and informal activities which are planned to enhance the development of knowledge, understanding, attitudes and behaviour, concerned with:
> oneself and others;
> social institutions, structures and organisations;
> and social and moral issues.

Approaching the question differently and looking at the considerable diversity between schools in the actual provision for PSHE, the authors of the ILEA report, *Improving Secondary Schools* (1984a) were impatient to put the whole area in better order. They suggested that, over the five years of secondary schooling, PSE should include this rather ill-assorted collection of offerings:

- careers education
- citizenship
- community studies
- comparative religious education
- consumer education
- education for parenthood and family life
- health education
- industrial education and work experience
- mass media and leisure
- moral education
- political education
- social impact of science and technology
- economic education
- social and life skills
- information technology
- study skills

We would undoubtedly wish to argue about the specific components of this list (the inclusion of information technology rather than peace studies, for instance). What is particularly noteworthy, however, is the vast array of potential contents and approaches which is implied. These 16 headings include academic disciplines, skills, topics and issues, each with attendant methodologies. But in what sense do they belong to a core called PSE (or PSHE)?

The area with most consistency is probably that of health education, which, over the last 15 years or so, has been transformed from a fringe subject concerned with hygiene and fitness to a complex central theme incorporating all the dimensions of human-ness. Both the Schools Council Health Education Project: SCHEP 5–13 (1977) and the project: Health Education: 13–18 (1982) espouse the view that health education is to do with: making informed decisions, the development of self-esteem and the 'health career' (age and stage of development of the student related to health concerns). These teaching programmes have been widely used in schools and have contributed to a powerful rationale for health education practice, in spite of considerable variations in detail.

Cowley *et al.* (1981) make a clear connection between their field of health education and that of PSHE:

> health education is seldom nowadays seen as a narrow parade of physical matters; it is almost universally understood as an omnibus title for physical and mental attitudes to responsible health for the individual and the community, to well-being within a supportive family life and to lives lived positively and with some contentment. Curriculum terms such as 'personal and social education' correlate closely with this view of health.

For us, PSHE is more than just the common elements of these two areas. The integral nature of health education is threefold. First, health themes, ranging from physiological information to spiritual reflection, constitute important elements of personal and social knowledge. An essential component of knowing oneself is understanding one's individual health and an aspect of knowing others is the empathy that derives from an extension of such understanding. Second, the recent history of health education has incorporated methodological developments which have acted as models for practice in related fields. Lastly, health is a concept which underpins a particular approach to education based on enabling individuals to fulfil their potential. The multi-dimensional nature of health thus reinforces a holistic educational rationale. The fact that PSHE is a cross-curricular field — and even an extra-curricular activity in some instances — makes the task of clarifying a clear paradigm more hazardous than is the case for health education on its own. The same is true for the task of identifying common practice.

A further difficulty is that the few accounts of what we would count as schemes of PSHE are relatively fragmentary and highly context-dependent. For instance, the journal *Pastoral Care in Education* has carried articles describing a number of curriculum developments variously labelled: Social Education (Healey, 1984); Social and Personal Education (Clarke, 1984); Personal and

Social Development (Purnell, 1983) and Design for Living (Ribbins and Ribbins, 1986). And in the collection of papers edited by Thacker, Pring and Evans (1987), Plant describes how she set up a course in Personal, Social and Moral Education for fourth and fifth years. There are other manifestations of PSHE. For instance, from three Newcastle schools, we have an account of the work of a team from Northern MIND, the organisation for mental health, which experimented with Personal Education courses (Stewart and Brownlow, 1985). And from the ILEA Cockpit Cultural Studies Department, which collaborated with researchers from the London Institute of Education, we are offered an account of a radical experiment in pre-vocational education, based on drama and photography (Cohen, 1986a,b).

An alternative to looking at PSHE in practice is to examine the different sorts of aims outlined in established projects. This is the approach adopted by Lee in her survey of Social Education for the FEU (1980), by David for the Schools Council Report on Personal and Social Education (1983) and by Williams and Williams (1980) in their Health Education Co-ordinator's Guide. Attractive as this strategy may be on the theoretical level it does not take us much nearer to the reality of PSHE. Aims, after all, are fairly vague and general statements which, while acting as helpful signposts, cannot be taken as the final word on a scheme. In any case, there are many home-grown PSHE courses which have developed on the basis of only the most fleeting acquaintance with 'official' project aims.

CULTURAL ANALYSIS

Given the unreliability of the strategies outlined so far for determining the content and scope of PSHE, we have decided to adopt an approach based on Lawton's (1981) model of cultural analysis. This involves five stages as Figure 1.2 shows. Our INSET is a sixth.

Lawton argues that since no school can possibly teach everything there is to be known we have to have some principles of selection. He suggests that these can be derived by juxtaposing two sets of questions and judgements: those based on a philosophical consideration of what counts as 'really worthwhile knowledge' and those based on a consideration of the kind of society we live in. Once particular selections have been made by reference to these principles, Lawton suggests that an understanding of various theories of learning and personal development should next be brought into play to ensure that the chosen material is appropriately sequenced and presented to students. Lawton's system of cultural analysis and the questions it provokes provide a thoroughgoing approach to resolving some of our uncertainties — assuming we add, between stages 4 and 5, a consideration of the practical constraints on curriculum organisation. These stages also provide a framework for the organisation of this book. Thus:

Figure 1.2: Cultural Analysis Model: Questions for PSHE

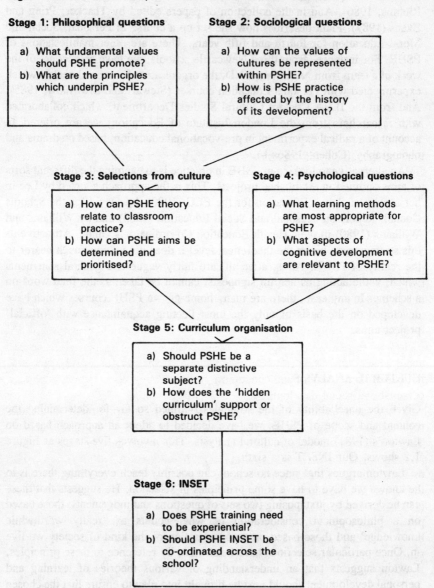

Stage 1: Philosophical questions

a) What fundamental values should PSHE promote?
b) What are the principles which underpin PSHE?

Stage 2: Sociological questions

a) How can the values of cultures be represented within PSHE?
b) How is PSHE practice affected by the history of its development?

Stage 3: Selections from culture

a) How can PSHE theory relate to classroom practice?
b) How can PSHE aims be determined and prioritised?

Stage 4: Psychological questions

a) What learning methods are most appropriate for PSHE?
b) What aspects of cognitive development are relevant to PSHE?

Stage 5: Curriculum organisation

a) Should PSHE be a separate distinctive subject?
b) How does the 'hidden curriculum' support or obstruct PSHE?

Stage 6: INSET

a) Does PSHE training need to be experiential?
b) Should PSHE INSET be co-ordinated across the school?

Note: This diagram shows examples of the sorts of question we feel PSHE planners would find it useful to ask. Obviously, there are many more. Perhaps a PSHE working party would find it useful to use this framework as a basis, posing questions they feel to be significant and then working out strategies for their solution.

Stage 1: Philosophical Questions   = Chapter 1
Stage 2: Sociological Questions   = Chapter 2
Stage 3: Selections from Culture   = Chapter 3
Stage 4: Psychological Questions   = Chapters 4 and 6
Stage 5: Curriculum Questions   = Chapters 5, 6, 7 + 9
Stage 6: Training Questions   = Chapter 8

AIMS AND IDEOLOGIES

For the remainder of this chapter we shall be concerned with Stage 1: a consideration of the philosophical questions relevant to PSHE. This brings us back to the formulation and interpretation of aims.

In spite of their grandiose tone, aims are actually only statements of intent, or guidelines for decision making. They are invariably high-minded and highly generalised. What is more, although educational aims tend to be the same for all students, 'their starting points are diverse, their speed and direction vary, and their destinations are even more diverse' (DES, 1981a). Patterns of implementation are also diverse, as are differences in outcome — at least in detail (which makes it all the more important that teachers are clear about what they are trying to achieve, for whom — and why). However, behind such diversity, there must be a degree of uniformity and consensus about the values and principles of the society for which young people are being educated. This includes judgements about what counts as worthwhile knowledge and what are the relative responsibilities of home, school and community in supervising young people's healthy personal and social development.

It is because teachers and curriculum developers interpret these values and responsibilities differently that there is such a profusion of teaching schemes. They do this because of the different educational ideologies they hold.

Let us look at what happens. Educational ideologies are built up on the basis of a set of beliefs about: knowledge, the learner and the society, and about how they interrelate. Exercise 1.2, which is adapted from an Open University text (1983), will help you identify the values and beliefs which underpin your personal ideology. When you have completed it, you might be interested to see how your beliefs and values relate to one or other of the educational ideologies set out for comparison in Figure 1.3.

Exercise 1.2: Views of Education

Instructions: In the column on the right tick all the statements with which you agree. Afterwards go back through your ticks and, for each section, try to decide on just one statement which you would regard as a priority. If you are working with other people, compare your priorities and discuss the ground for any differences or inconsistencies between sections. You may also wish to relate your answers to the table in Figure 1.3, to determine whether your views are consistent with a particular ideology.

A. Your view of the nature of knowledge
   1. There is an objectively real world and pursuing knowledge consists in trying to find out the truth about it.   ————
   2. Knowledge is essentially subjective and individual; what a person believes is his or her knowledge.   ————
   3. A sound grasp of the basic facts of a subject is an essential element in understanding it.   ————
   4. To understand a subject you need to grasp the relevant central concepts and general principles. Knowledge of facts is only important insofar as these provide concrete examples.   ————
   5. The main value of knowledge is in solving practical problems.   ————
   6. The main value of knowledge lies in the guidance it gives in deciding the difference between a 'good' and a 'worthless' life.   ————

B. Your view of the 'good' society
   A 'good' society is one in which:
   1. Individuals pursue their interests independently.   ————
   2. Social mobility depends on ability and willingness to work hard.   ————
   3. The rate of change is slower than it is in Britain now.   ————
   4. There are shared ideas and common values, rather than divisions based on class, race or religion.   ————
   5. Each community has distinctive values and habits and supports its members as far as possible from it own resources.   ————
   6. People are left to organise things for themselves, without being expected to fit into a national plan or system.   ————
   7. The state takes responsibility for ensuring a minimum working wage and minimum standards of housing and welfare.   ————
   8. Power and influence depend on what you inherit from your family.   ————

C. Your views of the learner
   1. Virtually everyone has a considerable capacity for learning if they wish to use it.   ————
   2. We usually underestimate what people can learn, especially in the case of 'low-ability' learners.   ————

Exercise 1.2 contd.

    3. The following capacities are important in motivating students
       to learn:

natural curiosity	—————
vocational needs/rewards	—————
peer interests	—————
fear of punishment or disgrace	—————
pleasing the teacher	—————
intrinsic interest of the subject	—————
self-confidence	—————
working independently	—————
working collaboratively	—————
variety of stimuli and activities	—————

D. Your view of the organisation of schools

    1. The following methods of teaching and learning should
       receive more time in the education of 5–16 year olds:

individual work	—————
group work	—————
whole-class instruction	—————
practice in basic skills	—————
creative work	—————
student-negotiated projects	—————
investigations	—————
residential courses	—————
work experience or job shadowing	—————
community service	

    2. The following approaches to curriculum organisation should
       receive more attention than they do now:

1. giving individual teachers greater autonomy as to what they teach and how	—————
2. making teachers collectively responsible for curriculum decisions in their schools	—————
3. providing stronger national guidelines on the curriculum	—————
4. providing the same basic objectives for virtually all learners	—————
5. building in opportunities for school-based team development and curriculum review	—————
6. insisting that all teachers are suitably trained and qualified to teach particular subjects	—————
7. modular structures and cross-curricular courses	—————
8. making student needs the starting point for any curriculum planning	—————

Figure 1.3: Some Educational Ideologies

Ideology	Views on the Learner		Views on Educational Content		Views on Society	Views on school organisation	
	Learning capacities	Dominant motivation for learning	Nature of knowledge	What should be taught		Classroom level	Other levels
Progressivism 1. individualistic	Considerable (and usually underestimated in all learners)	Natural curiosity Personal gratification	Essentially subjective/personal Knowledge is shaped by individual and cultural perceptions	What already interests the student, or what seems likely to do so	Individual autonomy and responsibility for others encouraged	Individual, heuristic, discovery methods Creative work	Integrated curricula and modular units Teacher and school autonomy
2. communitarian		Natural curiosity Peer interests Reciprocity/collaboration		Higher order skills e.g. problem solving and critical analysis	Distinct communities sharing values/power in national/international network	Group work Student negotiated projects Residentials Community service	Collective responsibility for curriculum decisions
Reconstructionism		Peer interests Social influences		Social and practical skills	Emphasis on shared ideals/principles	Group work Investigations Problem solving Work experience	Central curriculum control Teachers as managers Accountability
Instrumentalism 1. traditional	Limited according to prescribed social role	Peer interests and societal influences Vocational needs/interests	Relatively objective. Knowledge is worthwhile if it is useful to society and has practical applications	Vocational skills/role expectations Functional knowledge Practical problem-solving	Interlocking, stable system of sub-groups in efficient national system	Whole class and individual instruction and practice of basic skills Work experience	National guidelines. Increased influence for parents/governors/employers etc. Teachers subject specialists/trainers
2. adaptive	Sufficient to adapt to a complex changing society	Competitive instincts		Life-skills and social skills e.g. adaptability, practical problem-solving	Evolving sub-groups continuously adapting to circumstances	Group work Active learning Issues-based teaching. Community service	

Humanism							
1. classical	Very variable from student to student	Extrinsic e.g. teacher reward, fear of punishment/disgrace Coercion	Relatively objective Basic truths and conceptual structures	Fundamental intellectual disciplines for some Practical skills and aesthetic appreciation for others	Stratified according to inheritance Social mobility depends on ability and hard work	Demonstration Instruction Rote learning of facts	Dual system of curricula reflecting assessed abilities Teachers as subject specialists
2. liberal	Somewhat variable but often under-estimated (particularly in slower learners)	Intrinsic interest of subject matter and some extrinsic factors e.g. approval/dis-approval	Subject-specific methodologies Facts are tangible examples of concepts	Fundamental intellectual disciplines (+ some practical skills and aesthetic appreciation) for all	Nationally unified with core of shared principles and equal opportunities e.g. minimum wage but reward for different achievements	Critical analysis Investigations (teacher-instigated) Mix of individual work and whole-class instruction	Common core/ national curriculum as base but extensive opportunities for choice

VALUES IN PSHE

We now wish to declare *our* ideology and to describe the values and principles underpinning our view of PSHE. Figure 1.4 repeats the balance diagram which opened this chapter.

As you can see, we are weighing personal against social values. But this does not mean that they are mutually exclusive. It may be useful to view them as poles of a continuum, such as:

autonomy _____ collaboration

with preferred PSHE practice flexible, but in tension, somewhere between the two, according to the appropriate balancing principles.

In a practical book, it is not appropriate to explore the meaning of values like 'autonomy' or 'collaboration' at a deep philosophical level — even if we were capable! That is a task for another occasion. Our concern here is to give some concrete instances of what our preferred values might look like in practice. The summary in Figure 1.5 is therefore entirely pragmatic. For each value or balancing principle, we have simply tried to focus on a few examples of concrete teacher behaviours which exemplify their meaning in the school context.

For us, then, the aim of PSHE is to foster both personal and social values. We appreciate that, in reality, teachers constantly have to balance such ideals against expediency. However, the important thing is to be clear about priorities — especially where they concern student outcomes.

OUTCOMES

What kind of students, then, do we hope to see emerging at the end of courses in PSHE? It is important not to underestimate the other influences on young people's lives: their parents, peer group, the media and so on. Indeed, for some students, there may be a difficult clash of loyalties as the values of home, school and peer group meet and conflict. So, the potential outcomes we shall describe are not to be ascribed in a straightforward way to PSHE. However, an effective PSHE course should help to promote outcomes of the kind listed in Exercise 1.3 — with or without the support of other agencies and irrespective of students' different starting points.

Unlike many traditional curricula, the outcomes listed in the exercise are not expressed in terms of narrow, behavioural goals. Such objectives are inappropriate in PSHE because they assume norms which are overly simplistic and deny the uniqueness of individual development. Thus, while we advocate the improvement of communication skills, for example, we would not want to specify exact levels of proficiency for individual students. Within PSHE, perhaps more consciously than in any other curriculum area, we are concerned

Figure 1.4: PSHE Values and Balancing Principles

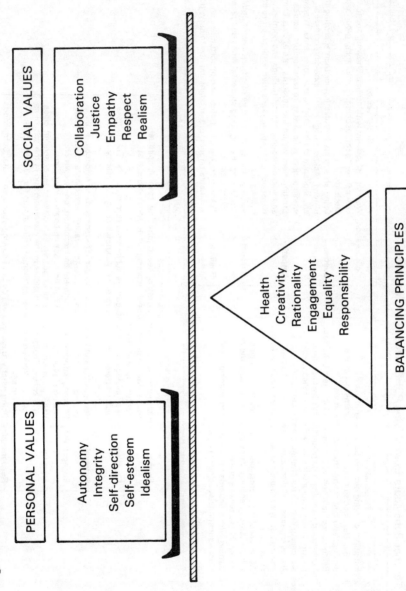

PERSONAL VALUES

Autonomy
Integrity
Self-direction
Self-esteem
Idealism

SOCIAL VALUES

Collaboration
Justice
Empathy
Respect
Realism

Health
Creativity
Rationality
Engagement
Equality
Responsibility

BALANCING PRINCIPLES

Figure 1.5: Teacher Behaviours Exemplifying PSHE Values and Principles

	Personal values
Autonomy	Initiating, carrying out and being able to justify independent decisions (within the parameters of the setting) and respecting students' decisions.
Integrity	Being honest and consistent (genuine) in one's behaviour. Reinforcing formal teaching approaches by appropriate informal interactions with students (and colleagues).
Self-awareness	Assessing one's own strengths and weaknesses. Managing personal disclosure appropriately. Dealing constructively with positive and negative feedback in the classroom.
Self-esteem	Acknowledging professional boundaries but not being falsely self-deprecating. Knowing when to 'pass the buck'. Being able to receive praise.
Idealism	Setting high standards for teaching and learning. Having clear educational/ideological goals.

	Social values
Collaboration	Working effectively with others. Showing support for colleagues. Team teaching. Encouraging group work methods.
Justice	Being able to justify rules (rather than accepting them blindly). Acknowledging and upholding contracts. Fairness and vigilance in challenging transgressions. Working for whole-school policies e.g. re sanction procedures.
Empathy	Starting from where the students 'are at'. Listening actively and acknowledging others' feelings and opinions. Not transposing/projecting one's own feelings on to students or colleagues.
Respect	Valuing others, irrespective of differences of opinion. Not pre-judging. Recognising students' limits and personal boundaries.
Realism	Acknowledging constraints and opportunities and setting attainable targets, e.g. recognising community, parental and media influences.

	Balancing principles
Health	Balancing the different aspects of health (physical, mental, spiritual, social, environmental). Openly working for personal, group and institutional well-being.
Creativity	Recognising diverse contributions/achievements in students. Taking risks. Using different teaching strategies. Acknowledging the validity of intuition.
Rationality	Recognising and knowing how to use different sorts of evidence, e.g. sorting out 'facts' and opinions. Demonstrating reasoning and reflection.
Engagement	Showing enthusiasm, commitment and resolve re one's own and students' projects. Being prepared to act on one's convictions.
Equality	Valuing the worth of students as people, especially re race, gender, class differences. Challenging inequalities in the classroom and in the school as a whole. Working for the recognition of equal status for all areas of the curriculum.
Responsibility	Doing what you say you will do but knowing your own limits. Complying with necessary external limits e.g. the law. Working out and adopting a professional role.

Exercise 1.3: Student Outcomes from PSHE

Consider each outcome below, rating its importance for students in your school: 3 = very important; 2 = moderately important; 1 = not very important at all. It will perhaps be helpful if you do this exercise in two stages: considering first the actual situation in your school and then the ideal ranking you would advocate for PSHE outcomes.

Outcomes   Rating

1. Increased competence in decision making, including the ability to assess risks, now and in the future. _____

2. Confidence to explore the balance between conformity and autonomy and to understand the effects of stereotyping so as to find a personal accommodation between the need to belong and the need to feel in control of one's own life. _____

3. Greater awareness of the relationship between attitudes, values and beliefs and of the bases from which personal attitudes and values, as well as those of wider social groups, are derived. _____

4. Increased confidence in the appropriate use of a variety of communication skills, including those concerned with self-expression and empathy towards others. _____

5. Skills of more realistic self-appraisal and a fuller awareness of personal strengths and weaknesses. _____

6. Greater knowledge of sources of information, support and advice and ability to deploy the assertion skills necessary to benefit from them and build on what students already possess. _____

7. Deeper understanding of their physical, mental and emotional needs and those of others. _____

8. An appreciation of and tolerance towards the religious and spiritual values that inform their own and others' lives. _____

9. Greater knowledge and know-how for informed and responsible political choices, including participation. _____

10. Increased self-confidence and self-esteem, alongside esteem for others. _____

11. Appreciation of the exchange of trust, concern and support within their learning group as a basis for future involvement in work, leisure and community groups. _____

12. Wider recognition of the health choices available to themselves (and others) and of their responsibility to make choices accordingly. _____

13. An appreciation of the advantages and disadvantages of working collaboratively as well as competitively and individually. _____

14. Greater awareness of the connectedness between individual decisions and those taken by groups — at family, community, local, national and international levels — and, hence, of the importance of personal and social responsibility. _____

15. Greater acceptance of the value of different types of relationship and awareness/understanding of the possible grounds for their acceptance. _____

> **Exercise 1.3:** contd.
>
> Outcomes   Rating
>
> 16. A capacity for the fullest possible enjoyment of life based on an
>   acceptance of self and a caring attitude towards others.   ─────
> 17. To develop links with the world of work.   ─────
> 18. To give information about various aspects of personal hygiene,
>   maintenance of health and fitness.   ─────

with the whole person: knowledge, attitudes, skills and behaviour. Although in some instances, like knowing certain scientific laws, objectives can be separately assessed, PSHE is about general outcomes and student-determined objectives which are not capable of standard measurement. This does not mean that PSHE is to be seen as a 'soft' option. It is neither 'soft' in terms of the challenges it poses to students nor in terms of the tasks it sets for teachers when they attempt to evaluate student achievement. Take an example: 'Wider recognition of the health choices available to themselves and others and of their responsibility to make choices accordingly'. For one student this might involve an analysis of statistics relating to mortality and morbidity in Third World countries; for another it might mean stopping smoking; for another a change in attitude towards abortion; for another involvement in a local campaign for improved home-help services. How can such diverse and individual responses be compared? For the teacher, the task is to help students negotiate their own programmes and evaluate their own progress, on both an individual and a group basis. This is much harder than giving marks out of ten but invariably much more rewarding!

Another point to notice about the outcomes listed in Exercise 1.3 is that they are outcomes for students. For some purposes, it may be important to specify aims and outcomes at other levels: for instance, for the school, for particular subject areas, or for particular year or class groups. Where such a hierarchy of aims and objectives is devised, as we suggest in Chapter 7, it is important to have consistency within the underlying values and principles.

Readers who wish to pursue the discussion of different educational aims and outcomes further are recommended to consult the suggestions at the end of this chapter. Pring (1984) is perhaps the best starting point but philosophical analyses of the concept of health, such as Seedhouse (1986), also provide invaluable insights.

PRIORITIES IN PSHE

Throughout this book, we want to encourage teachers to reflect on their own priorities for PSHE. We also hope to examine alternative models of teaching:

a process most initial teacher training courses neglect, in spite of the fact that it is the basis of everything we do. The diamond in the exercise which follows contains nine statements referring to different rationales for teaching PSHE. The priorities you decide for yourself will be an indication of your preferred model of teaching, a topic taken further in Chapter 3.

So far in this chapter we have attempted to clarify the principles and values underlying PSHE and to describe some of our hoped-for outcomes for students. We have assumed readers would accept the rationale for doing this on trust, either because they share our interest and commitment or because PSHE is so patently a 'good thing'! However, these are scarcely sufficient excuses, nor do they help any of you who have to defend PSHE against the arguments of those — colleagues, senior staff, governors and others — who are sceptical or less well informed. We hope the next three chapters will supply detailed arguments to support the case for PSHE.

To conclude this stage of the discussion we shall outline some general grounds for our belief in the importance of PSHE and, in particular for the urgency of its being taken up by schools NOW. We shall also outline some of the possible difficulties and some of the pay-offs it can bring.

Exercise 1.4: Diamond Nines: Why Teach PSHE? (from Richardson *et al.* 1980)

1. Photocopy and separate the diamonds so that you have nine pieces, each with a statement (see diagram overleaf).
2. Consider each statement in terms of the potential of PSHE to you as a teacher and rank them as follows (in the original diamond shape):

$$1$$
$$2 \ 2$$
$$4 \ 4 \ 4$$
$$7 \ 7$$
$$9$$

3. Discuss your diamond ranking with a partner or other members of a group and/or consider how your priorities tally with your practice.

N.B. Diamond nines is one of the most useful and versatile activities we know. This particular exercise is more individual but if the given statements were about aims, for instance, real negotiation with students (using snowballing techniques: $1 > 2s > 4s$ etc.) could follow. It is often useful to leave one diamond blank for participants to fill in themselves; this makes negotiation more difficult but more revealing! There is, of course, nothing sacred about the shape; some students or some topics, for instance, might work better with a triangle ten.

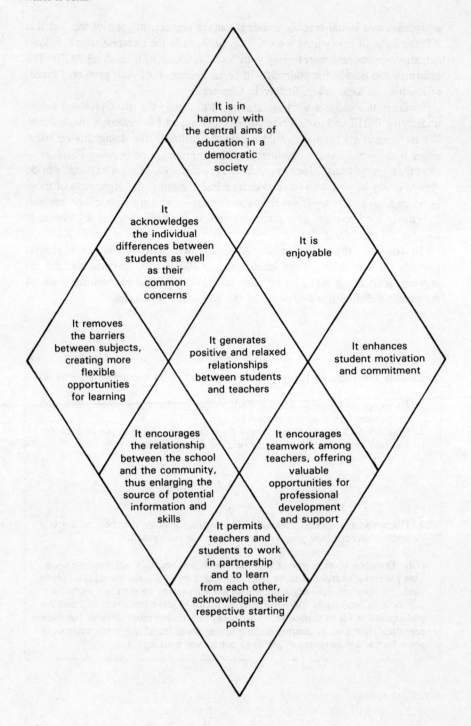

It is in harmony with the central aims of education in a democratic society

It acknowledges the individual differences between students as well as their common concerns

It is enjoyable

It removes the barriers between subjects, creating more flexible opportunities for learning

It generates positive and relaxed relationships between students and teachers

It enhances student motivation and commitment

It encourages the relationship between the school and the community, thus enlarging the source of potential information and skills

It encourages teamwork among teachers, offering valuable opportunities for professional development and support

It permits teachers and students to work in partnership and to learn from each other, acknowledging their respective starting points

ARGUMENTS FOR PSHE

Our general grounds for advocating PSHE relate to our ideological stance. Briefly, they include:

· a commitment to progress towards a more democratic and open society, with a more even distribution of power, greater accountability and increased engagement in decision making at all levels;
· a commitment to full comprehensive and community education;
· a belief in the necessity and justice of equal opportunities — in terms of both access and outcome, and in terms of the equal valuing of personhood;
· a response to our complex, rapidly changing, increasingly bureaucratic and technological society;
· the need to tip the balance from individualism towards collaboration;
· our responsibility to function in a pluralist society by making choices which reflect our values and our awareness of others.

That PSHE matters NOW rests on a number of developments happening elsewhere in the educational world. As we have already noted, there are a variety of closely related schemes in existence: Personal, Social and Moral Education; Personal and Social Development; Personal, Social and Religious Education; Social and Community Education, and so on. Some are complementary but some employ quite contradictory rationales to our own. Few have an integrated philosophy or training programme and few can boast teachers with co-ordinating responsibilities or local advisory teams. There is a major job of integration waiting to be done here.

The same is true of developments in the pastoral curriculum, especially in view of the overlap of teaching approaches and materials with those used in PSHE. Dialogue and co-ordination are vital to ensure that valuable staff energies are harnessed co-operatively and not wasted on duplication or competition.

While springing from a different source and supported by a different rationale, further overlapping developments exist in the various schemes for pre-vocational education and training. These include the CPVE, for instance, which incorporates core competencies like 'personal and career development', 'problem solving' and 'social skills'. Then there are City and Guilds Courses, such as the Community Care Course (C+G331) which features integrated assignments and student self-assessment, as well as specific content areas like Health Education. YTS schemes are also designed to acknowledge students' motivation and attitudes, as well as their recall of knowledge and skills. In this field as we shall see in Chapter 9, there are issues and ideals to be shared — including the field of assessment.

The GCSE, graded tests, profiling and records of achievement each have their own justification. However, they share a commitment to more flexible modes of examining which encourage higher levels of student motivation, negotiated project work and more peer- and self-assessment. All of these are in

31

harmony with PSHE approaches and demand personal and social skills which hitherto students have not formally required.

A final argument for taking action on PSHE now rests on the fact that teachers are, in fact, already experimenting in the field yet do not necessarily know where they are going or how to find the way. Many are struggling with problems of organisation and lack of training as well as having difficulty deciding on appropriate boundaries for PSHE. All this energy and enthusiasm will be threatened if we cannot clarify our thinking about PSHE.

CONSTRAINTS ON PSHE

The time is, therefore, ripe. But why are things not happening faster — and more confidently? What are the constraints? Some of these are a matter of teachers' personal hesitations and uncertainties, especially given competing demands (GCSE, profiles, pastoral and tutorial work, Information Technology, pre-vocational initiatives — and so on). Some, like the relatively low formal status attached to PSHE and the absence of any powerful subject associations to promote its cause, derive from wider factors and concerns. Some are more a matter of conceptual and organisational confusion: about where PSHE belongs, who should be responsible for it, and how it fits in with traditional curriculum areas. Figure 1.6 encapsulates many of the more typical criticisms and disadvantages of PSHE we have heard voiced — typically by teachers but sometimes by students, their parents or employers.

Notice the criticisms which are most problematic in your context. Some you may be able to counter immediately. After reading further, we hope you will be able to dismiss more (or all) of them! Remember, although this is quite a daunting and discouraging set of constraints, it is not so different from the criticisms advanced whenever innovations are proposed — especially innovations which threaten traditional subject empires and teacher identities. Consider the arguments that have been voiced, at different times, against comprehensives, mixed-ability teaching, integrated science or humanities, language across the curriculum, anti-racist and anti-sexist strategies. Like these, not all of the difficulties associated with PSHE are totally intractable.

In the remaining chapters it will be our job to persuade you that, in spite of the admitted tensions facing the implementation of PSHE, the arguments in its favour are so important — both for students and for society generally — that we have a responsibility as teachers, trainers or administrators to struggle for its acceptance and advance.

OPPORTUNITIES OFFERED BY PSHE

We end this chapter by listing what we believe to be the very positive advantages of PSHE. These, by the way, are real, not hypothetical — as many experienced PSHE teachers can testify!

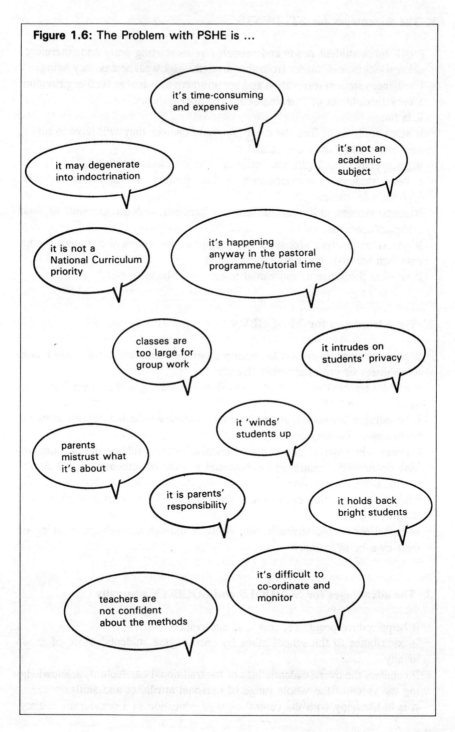

Figure 1.6: The Problem with PSHE is ...

33

1. The advantages for STUDENTS

· PSHE takes student needs and concerns as its starting point and, therefore, acknowledges and works from the strengths and weaknesses they bring.
· It enhances student motivation and commitment to learn, as well as providing a very flexible set of learning skills and approaches.
· It is fun.
· It helps students to face the most important choices they will have to make, now and when they leave school.
· It gives students a legitimate stake in their own assessment.
· It helps students gain confidence in their powers of oral communication, especially in groups.
· It acknowledges individual differences between students, as well as their common concerns.
· It generates positive and supportive relationships within the student group, based on sharing, co-operation and trust.
· It reduces the sense of individual failure and blame.

2. The advantages for TEACHERS

· It permits teachers to act as resource persons and facilitators rather than transmitters of pre-established 'facts'.
· It enables teachers and students to work in partnership and to learn from each other.
· It encourages teamwork among teachers, offering valuable opportunities for professional learning and support.
· It lessens the barriers between subjects and between school and the surrounding community, enlarging the potential sources of information and skills.
· It capitalises on the diversity of individual strengths and skills within the student group, giving each student the chance to make worthwhile contributions.
· It capitalises on the strengths and skills of individual teachers, working on their own or in teams.

3. The advantages for SCHOOLS and SOCIETY generally

· It helps reduce prejudice, fear and intolerance.
· It contributes to the school ethos by encouraging students' sense of group loyalty.
· It counters the over-academic bias of the traditional curriculum, acknowledging the value of the whole range of personal attributes and skills.
· It is in harmony with the central aims of education in a democratic society.

34

· It provides opportunities for debate on important issues and gives students and teachers an opportunity to feel that their views are known within the school system.
· It encourages close and sympathetic links with the local community.
· It counters the constraints of specialisation by encouraging students to 'learn how to learn'.

We hope you will experience more of the advantages of PSHE for yourself and that, in the pages which follow, we shall be able to convince you of its importance within the curriculum.

CONCLUSION

In this chapter we have outlined some of the justifications for PSHE, referring particularly to educational aims. The issues involved are particularly complex, so it is not surprising if teachers continue to ask: what is PSHE? Whether it is viewed as a cross-curricular theme; a principle of selection and co-ordination; a range of contents; a particular methodology, or any combination of these, the place of PSHE is inextricably bound up with other, highly contentious, aspects of English education. These include the debates about:

· Liberal versus vocational and technical education
· The desirability of a 'national', 'core', or 'entitlement' curriculum
· Teacher and/or school and/or LEA autonomy
· The relative importance of academic knowledge, personal knowledge and affective knowledge
· Forms of assessment and accreditation
· Mixed-ability teaching
· Parent and/or governor powers
· Equal opportunities, particularly in terms of race, class and gender
· The integration of students with special needs
· Competition versus collaboration
· Discipline/rewards and sanctions, such as those of corporal punishment
· The role of schools as socialising agencies
· The status of pastoral systems in the welfare network
· Health 'crises' such as AIDS, drug addiction, child abuse and the role of schools in combating/preventing them
· Unemployment/training schemes/further and higher education

We do not intend to engage directly in any of these debates, except as they crop up in the course of more practical concerns. At this point we will simply offer a working definition of PSHE:

PSHE integrates students' personal and social learning and empowers them to reach their full health potential. It develops the knowledge, attitudes and skills necessary for effective participation in society.

In the next chapter we examine some of the chief features of contemporary society and ask what likely futures there are for schooling — and for PSHE in particular.

FURTHER READING

Broadfoot, P. (ed.) (1986) *Profiles and records of achievement: a review of issues and practice*, Holt, Rinehart and Winston, London

Brockington, D. *et al.* (1985) *The 14–18 curriculum: integrating CPVE, YTS*, TVEI, Youth Education Service, Bristol

David, K. (1983) *Personal and social education in secondary schools*, Longman for Schools Council, London

David, K. and Williams, T. (eds) (1987) *Health education in schools*, 2nd edn, Harper and Row, London

ILEA (1984) *Improving secondary schools*: Report of the Committee on the Curriculum and Organisation of Secondary Schools, chaired by Dr D.H. Hargreaves, ILEA, London

Lawton, D. (1981) *An introduction to teaching and learning*, Hodder and Stoughton, London

Lee, R. (1980) *Beyond coping: some approaches to social education*, FEU/Longman, London

Lee, V. and Zeldin, D. (eds.) (1982) *Planning in the curriculum*, Hodder and Stoughton for the Open University, London

Pring, R. (1984) *Personal and social education in the curriculum*, Hodder and Stoughton, London

Seedhouse, D. (1986) *Health: the foundations for achievement*, John Wiley, London

2

The Social Condition

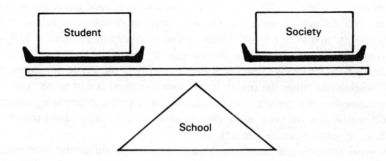

The main task of this chapter, moving on to the second stage of Lawton's cultural analysis, is to outline the chief features of contemporary British society, including current policies on education and training. Lawton distinguishes eight aspects of human society, which he terms 'cultural invariants'. While these may differ in detail from one society to the next, they are to be found universally. The eight invariants are as follows:

the social system
the economic system
the communication system
the rationality system
the technology system
the morality system
the belief system
the aesthetic system

We shall look at what characterises these systems in present-day society and ask how they relate to the goals of Personal, Social and Health Education. This leads into a consideration of some alternative models and approaches to PSHE in Chapter 3.

Before going any further, it will be helpful to use each of the cultural invariants as a step-by-step focus for some reflections on the process of curriculum planning. Consider in the case of your own school, for example, how subjects are changing in response to the contemporary economic, technology, morality and other systems. Or, turning things around, how the curriculum is challenging current realities in the social, economic, communications and other systems.

EDUCATION AND SOCIETY

To avoid an over-simplistic view, we first need to examine the relationship between education and society. In functionalist models (dominant in sociological theory until the late 1960s), this relationship was seen very much in terms of service. Accordingly, schools were held to 'perform functions on behalf of the wider society' and to 'serve social needs'. The simplicity of this kind of analysis has considerable attractions. It is still uncritically embraced by many who have urgent agendas for change (the Black Paper authors in the 1970s, for example). The consequence (since the reality is far more complex) is that far too much is often claimed — or expected — from schools: for instance, in preparing students for the world of work (as if more Physics or more Life Skills could transform the facts of youth unemployment!).

A good example of how functionalist theory simplifies the relationship between education and society can be found in what Ron Best *et al.* (1980) term the 'conventional wisdom' of pastoral care. This account claims that pastoral structures in secondary schools were created 'both to manage the tensions and alleviate the anomic effects of rapid industrialization and urbanization, and to maximize society's utilization of human talent'. With hindsight, this kind of argument can be seen to be both limited and naïve. As Best suggests, as well as being a response to pressures from society at large (inner-city decay; family breakdown; multi-cultural communities; the collapse of traditional religious and moral codes, and so on), the evolution of pastoral structures in the 1970s was chiefly a response to the needs of schools. These included the provision of a 'workable division into teams for sports', the administration of the register, dinner money and notices, and the solution to the problem of how to create a stratified career structure in newly merged grammar and modern schools.

The truth about the history and rationale for pastoral care need not concern us here. There are probably different truths for different schools. What the example does usefully point out is the very complex web of institutional and individual factors which together produce given patterns of schooling. In defining their aims schools are at best a mirror for society, reflecting demands which come from the outside world and, only if they are very bold, setting more idealistic standards for their students. What is more, even at their most responsive, schools only accommodate in terms of the best diagnoses of need available at a particular time. These are not always accurate and there is often considerable delay in applying them. The succession of policies directed towards securing greater equality of educational opportunity within the English educational system is a clear illustration of this mismatch. Thus, in spite of 40 years of free and universal secondary education and a variety of strategies aimed at ending privilege and discrimination, the relative chances for students from different social backgrounds are still virtually the same as they were in the first half of the century (Halsey *et al.*, 1980).

The complex reasons behind these inequalities remind us, as Basil Bernstein pointed out in a seminal article in 1970, that 'Education cannot compensate for society'. However, this does not necessarily mean that there is nothing schools can do on behalf of their students to respond to pressures and changes in the wider society. Indeed, one of the most encouraging aspects of the by now considerable volume of research on school effectiveness is the finding that 'Schools do matter' (Reynolds, 1985). Not only is there strong evidence to suggest that schools 'produce' different amounts of truancy and disaffection but also that some schools are much more effective than others at producing positive academic results and at responding positively to current social needs (Rutter *et al.*, 1979; Reid *et al.*, 1987).

No one pretends that making such a response is easy. The constraints, especially in a time of teacher action and financial restriction, are all too familiar. Opposition from local councillors; lack of parental support; antagonism in the local press; too little time and money for planning and staff development; too few resources; conflicts within the staff — all these, and others, are eloquently described, for example, in John Watts's (1977) account of the early years of Countesthorpe College in Leicestershire in the 1970s and in Colin Fletcher's (1983) study of the Sutton Centre in Nottinghamshire some years later. In the 1980s there have been retrenchments but it is the successes of these and countless other less well publicised schools of which we need to remind ourselves because they demonstrate quite emphatically that change in the taken-for-granted structures of schooling is possible.

EDUCATION AND SCHOOLING

If schools are not to have an impossible role in coping with current social demands, as well as acknowledging the gap between policy and practice, they also need to remember the gap between education and schooling. Simply to state the fact that there is a difference is perhaps to make the point. However, in the past this relationship has produced a whole range of myths, including the notions that:

· education only happens in schools
· education lasts only until you leave school

- · some people are always teachers, others are always learners
- · being educated means knowing many facts
- · being clever means passing exams
- · 'experts' and those in authority always know best (Hopson and Scally, 1981)

And there is still a widespread tendency, particularly among policy makers and employers, to assume that formal institutions, like schools, colleges and universities, are the only true sites of learning. This is patently not so. Consider your own education: probably many of the items of learning which you value most (being able to drive a car, being a parent, enjoying good wine, growing vegetables, playing squash, running a youth club) were not acquired at school — or not in formal lessons. In fact, most of what you value may have little to do with school knowledge and skills at all. That is because education is a much wider process than schooling. Potentially, it engages us throughout our lives — both formally and informally. The agencies that help are large in number and varied in form: family; church; trade unions; television and radio; leisure pursuits; films and books; records and tapes; extramural classes; counselling agencies; occupational training groups; travel and so on.

Schooling is only part — if a very crucial part — of this total process. At a minimum schools have the task of providing a foundation in the basic skills of numeracy and communication and an introduction to the various worlds of formal learning and experience. Their other important responsibility, which connects directly to the role of PSHE, involves aspects of students' socialisation. But it is important to remind ourselves that the time schools have is relatively short. What is more, unless students are fully motivated and engaged by teachers in their studies they may make poor use of what is on offer — especially if the skills and knowledge they do learn at school are difficult to transfer to everyday situations.

So schooling cannot substitute for the potential of lifelong education any more than schools can be made directly to serve society's needs. In fact, the three are intimately related, all part of what Silver (1980) terms 'the social condition':

The expectations of radical groups, disadvantages, the actualities of urban life — these are not 'factors' which impinge on education, they are not a context. They are part of that social condition which is integral to education, which is education.

Moving on from these preliminaries about education, schooling and society, we can now examine the current social condition in Britain. For the sake of convenience, we shall have to speak of various elements in this condition as if they were separable from each other and from what goes on in schools. But Silver's point is important and should be borne in mind.

THE CURRENT SOCIAL CONDITION

A large number of texts analyse trends in contemporary Western society and describe possible scenarios for the future. They range from challenging polemics like Alvin Toffler's *Future Shock* (1970) and *The Third Wave* (1980) to more weighty sociological studies like Daniel Bell's celebrated work, *The Coming of Post-industrial Society* (1973). But the main features of this society are already clear. They have been summarised by Naisbitt (1984) in terms of what he calls ten 'megatrends'. These he describes as the shifts from:

industrial society to information society
forced technology to high tech/high touch
national economy to world economy
short term to long term
centralisation to decentralisation
institutional help to self-help
representative democracy to participatory democracy
hierarchies to networking
north to south
either/or to multiple choice

Another feature of today's society is its appetite for self-analysis. Has there ever been a society in which so many hours of media analysis have been devoted to contemporary trends and 'problems'? The list in Figure 2.1 is a reminder of some of these — important and relatively minor — in no particular sequence. It is a list which could easily be used with students as the basis for class discussions in PSHE. Which trends do they feel will affect them most? Which do they think matter most for the future of world peace? Which trends are likely to have the greatest impact on women's/men's lives? Which do they feel able to influence and which are 'inescapable'? How would you respond to such questions?

Eight aspects of current society were highlighted by the authors of the Australian core curriculum (Horton and Raggatt, 1982):

· increased demands for basic and essential skills, for example, in communication, human relationships, economic management and working life
· the multi-cultural composition and interests of our population
· our growing regional and broader international roles and interests
· the disturbance effect of rapid scientific and technological change
· changing patterns of employment and the emergence of structural youth unemployment
· more open, flexible and varied ways of life or life-styles
· the impact of powerful new and interacting forces in our culture such as television, the leisure industry and 'pop' culture, which affect children's tastes, values and interests.

Figure 2.1: Key Features of the Current Social Condition

change

technological innovation

rampant consumerism

better living standards

cuts and controls

multi-culturalism

frequent job changes

shorter working lives

early retirement

urban disintegration

more home ownership

choice — and over-choice

'the mighty micro'

commercial exploitation

higher expectations

unemployment

social and geographical mobility

shorter working hours

planned demotion

the 'black', 'grey' and 'mauve' economies

collapse of public transport systems

credit cards

Inequalities: north/south

rich/poor

black/white

waged/unwaged

young/old

Third World/industrialised West

healthy/handicapped

men/women

new 'family' patterns:

  contraception

  abortion

  divorce/separation

  single parents

  gay parents

  remarriage/serial marriage

  communal households

  surrogate motherhood

law and order issues:

  violence

  rape

  mugging

  vandalism

  uprisings

  racial confrontations

  football hooliganism

  terrorism

Ideological divides: East/West

Protestant/Catholic

Arab/Jew

socialist/capitalist

nuclear/non-nuclear

high tech/low tech

collapse of the welfare state

disappearance of international frontiers

alienation

bureaucracy

hijacks

domination of world trade by multi-national corporations

health foods and fads

adolescent fashions

Greenpeace

test-tube babies

bikes

supermarkets

labour-saving devices

job creation schemes

redeployment

three-party politics

cultural pluralism

trial by television

poverty

decline of traditional religions

worldwide economic inter-dependence

secrecy

instant communications

wider travel and leisure opportunities

telephone shopping

convenience foods

jogging

pop

genetic engineering

AIDS

windmills

hypermarkets

job sharing

redundancy

regional regeneration

'new' religions

the occult and mysticism

Band Aid

self-help

In a moment we will look at the implications of these trends for PSHE. However, there is one feature of contemporary social life which merits particular attention: the development of government policies for education and training over the past ten years.

CURRENT EDUCATIONAL POLICIES

You can perhaps generate your own catalogue of developments here. Figure 2.2 is a list produced by a group of teacher trainers. How many of these are you familiar with and what is their likely impact going to be on you as a teacher? These innovations in educational policy have the following main features, many of which we shall be discussing more fully in subsequent chapters.

Figure 2.2: Key Developments in Current Educational Policy

the core curriculum	partnership:	PSE
special needs	with parents	recurrent education
equal opportunities	with industry	distance learning
parental choice		open learning
autonomous learning	effectiveness	open tech
process learning	accountability	community schools
process skills	appraisal	'better schools'
graded assessment	information skills	networks
APU	unit credits	criterion-based
CPVE	negotiation	assessment
TVEI	computer-based	life skills
GCSE	learning	guidance
profiles	modules	skills of transfer
records of achievement	team building	active tutorial work
CATE	staff development	curriculum 5–16 and 14–19
GRIDS	time and boundary	technology
INSET	management	CDT
TRIST	SLS	progression
GRIST	LAPP	

1. Increasing involvement by the government (via the Manpower Services Commission and the Department of Industry as well as the Department of Education and Science) in areas of planning, decision making and control that were previously the responsibility of teachers and LEAs. There are two issues here: the presence of government agencies in territory formerly reserved for professionals and the shift in view (from welfare to economic instrumentalism) about what purposes education should serve in society.

2. An emphasis on the notion of accountability and on banking models of management and administration. This involves, for example, 'formula-led' funding (a process whereby budgets are allocated according to fixed ratios,

regardless of special needs and circumstances) and the devolution of financial responsibility to individual 'cost centres' — again regardless of local differences.

3. The attempt to define a national core curriculum for all students from 5 to 16 and from 16 to 19.

4. A concern with certification and standards — for teachers as well as students. This has led, for example, to the setting up of the Council for the Accreditation of Teachers (CATE) to oversee teacher training, the proliferation, for students, of pre-vocational and other forms of award at 16 plus, as well as a wide range of graded assessments for the earlier years of schooling.

5. The systematic development of pre-vocational training for 14 to 19 year olds (outlined in more detail below).

6. A concern to respond to the potential divisions but also the potential richness of life in a multi-cultural, multi-faith society; for example, by tackling inherent racism in the curriculum and by requiring schools to produce policies which will promote equal opportunities for both sexes — at a personal, institutional and curriculum level.

7. A determination to extend the possibilities of parental choice and partnership: for example, through changes in governance; the endowment of City Colleges; schemes to enable schools to opt out of local authority control; the encouragement of parental fund-raising and voucher schemes.

These policy emphases have found their way into the curriculum through a concern with 'preparing students for life in the modern world'. The rhetoric is progressive but the stance adopted towards that world is generally conservative. Consider this statement, for example, at the beginning of the document, *Curriculum 11–16* (DES, 1977a):

> It is very unlikely that the mass of citizens in general or that parents and local education authorities in particular, would countenance a curriculum for violent change, still less that they would be willing to pay for it. For the purposes of curriculum planning we need to have in mind the virtuous citizen, probably living as part of a family, in a largely urban, technology-based industrial society, with minority cultures, working in general towards a social harmony which can accommodate change and differences.

The authors of the HMI Report, *Curriculum 11–16, Towards a Statement of Entitlement* (1983a), appraising the LEA response to the original 11–16 document, reasserted the need for schools to 'relate the needs of individuals to the demands of society and to the worlds of work and unemployment'. Considering where and how this should occur, they raised a number of very pertinent questions:

> How do we help children to understand sexual relationships and their implications?

Do we prepare children well enough for more leisure and less work as unemployment becomes more structural and less cyclical?

How do we prepare them to understand the social and political impact of unemployment?

To what extent do we try to help them understand the ethical problems raised by new technologies which can, for example, create nuclear weapons and make possible surgical transplants?

Do we give pupils an understanding that they are living through a third industrial revolution which may lead to personal and social disturbance?

When pupils can legally marry at 16, and vote at 18, what should the curriculum do to help pupils with these matters of fundamental importance to adult life?

The implicit expectation is still, apparently, that schools will be able to do something to 'help'; but help whom — and in the interests of what values for society? Since, as PSHE educators, we are so closely involved in tackling questions and issues like the ones above (even if we also accept the impossibility of solving them single-handedly), we must be clear about our priorities. Do we wish to help those least able to help themselves, the socially and educationally underprivileged, for example? If so, how — and in the interests of what future lifestyle? Or do we want to enable all students to develop skills of critical social analysis on the basis of which they can make their own decisions about the future?

PRE-VOCATIONAL INITIATIVES

One of the most contentious features of current educational policy arises from the emphasis on pre-vocational training for 14 to 19 year olds. Wallace (1985) lists the main initiatives taken by 1985:

- · Youth Training Scheme (YTS), for those who have left school at the age of 16.
- · Certificate of Pre-Vocational Education (CPVE), a public examination for 17 year olds. This has developed from the long-standing idea of a one-year course in general education and has now been made into a specifically pre-vocational offering.
- · Promotion of micro-computer applications and training for them by the first appointment of a Minister for Information Technology, the establishment of ITECs (Information Technology Centres), the Micro-electronics in Education Programme (MEP), and the Department of Trade and Industry schemes to subsidise the acquisition of micros and allied equipment by schools.
- · British Schools Technology Programme, organised by the DTI in consultation with the MSC and the DES to promote technology as a school subject.

- Open Tech Programmes which aim to provide opportunities for adults to retrain and acquire skills at technician and supervisory levels.
- The Technical and Vocational Education Initiative (TVEI) announced by Margaret Thatcher in November 1982 to secure 'new institutional arrangements' for 14 to 18 year olds, in partnership with the local authorities (and with massive extra funding from the MSC). The courses, for both sexes, were to combine general education, including the students' personal and social development, with technical and vocational training.

These initiatives to reduce the gap between schools and work have been paralleled by a whole range of School/Industry projects and work-experience schemes (including Project Trident, Education for Capability and so on), whose impetus has come from within educational circles. But however much the smaller schemes offer in terms of worthwhile educational opportunities, their limited financial resources put them at a severe disadvantage compared to government-funded projects like TVEI. In fact, the government-backed schemes have met with considerable suspicion in some quarters (see Dale, 1985). It is suggested, for example, that there is a quite deliberate streaming element between the 'high tech' (TVEI) and 'low tech' (YTS and CPVE) schemes — not to mention the very limited or 'no tech' possibilities open to many girls and blacks.

What is more many of these developments are about 'skills for skills' sake', with little appreciation of the need for relevant knowledge and understanding if skills are to be put into practice effectively in real life. Even more worryingly, the new vocationalism and its particular style of pedagogy may have the effect of persuading students who are unsuccessful at getting jobs at the end of their courses that, since they were responsible for their own learning, they are to blame; the implication being that they negotiated the 'wrong' learning objectives or made 'inadequate' use of the resources provided for them. As Stronach (1984) points out, this is an insidious shift of responsibility when, simultaneously, other government policies are actually reducing opportunities for young school leavers: a classic 'Catch 22'.

We shall return to a discussion of pre-vocational training in later chapters, for it impinges on PSHE in quite substantial ways — through links with both careers education and social and life skills. However, as Quicke (1985) warns, while observing government guidelines and constraints, teachers attempting to work out new programmes for PSHE will need to steer a careful course between the kinds of dangers inherent in the new vocationalism (outlined above) and those of the equally unwelcoming shores of 'pragmatic pastoralism' (described in Chapter 3). As we shall argue, PSHE can play a much more challenging and worthwhile role for students than either of these.

RESPONDING TO CURRENT REALITIES

It is time now to return to the wider realities of contemporary life, to ask what are the key developments to which schools generally and PSHE teachers in particular must respond. We also need to consider the most likely scenarios for future society. The following sections will discuss these two questions and outline some implications for the curriculum.

Changes in the structure of employment and in the meaning of work are perhaps the major area of concern for most of us, given the fact that work can no longer be defined in the traditional terms of a lifetime's career of paid employment. How is your school, for example, responding to Handy's predictions outlined in Figure 2.3?

Figure 2.3: A New Agenda for Work

---

1. More people than at present not working for an organisation.
    what will they be doing?
    how will they be organised?
2. Shorter working lives for many people.
    what will they do?
    how will they be paid?
3. Fewer mammoth bureaucracies, more federal organisations and more tiny businesses.
    how will they be managed?
    to whom will they be accountable?
4. More requirements for specialists and professionals in organisations.
    how will they be trained and retrained?
    what will the rest of us do?
5. More importance given to the informal, uncounted economy of the home and the community.
    will work in the home be real work?
    how will it be recognised and rewarded?
6. A manufacturing sector that is smaller in terms of people but larger in terms of output.
    what will it be making?
    how will it be fed with new ideas, skills and finance?
7. A smaller earning population and a bigger dependent population.
    how will wealth be distributed?
    what taxation will be appropriate?
8. A greatly increased demand for education.
    for what?
    by whom?
    at what age?
    how will it be paid for?
9. New forms of social organisation to complement the employment organisation.
    what will they be?
    will the family be one of them?
    will they be political?

Source: Adapted from Handy (1985)

And what response is appropriate to the teenage concerns highlighted in the collage in Figure 2.4 made up from some typical magazines? Do they suggest a particular responsibility for teachers of PSHE?

These two examples highlight a number of features of post-industrial society which raise urgent considerations for the curriculum. But work patterns are not all that has changed in Britain in the last 25 years. As the comments in the collage suggest, there have been equally significant changes in people's social and moral values. These are partly a function of changing demographic trends — themselves a cause and a consequence of higher nutritional standards, changing patterns of birth control, and developments in medicine and health care. How, for instance, is your school taking account of the set of changes, summarised in a leaflet over-viewing a TACADE course in 'Skills for Adolescence'?

- Changes in family structure. The traditional family with two parents who have never been divorced and a mother whose primary role is home-making and child-rearing has been joined by other forms of family grouping. What is known is that some children from every kind of family structure do not have the kind of nurturing and support within the home that they need, and parents are often too busy dealing with stresses in their own lives to provide it.
- Changes in the extended family structure. At one time children had a range of family members to learn and draw immediate support from ... Social changes have drastically altered the nature of the supportive circle surrounding many children ...
- Drug and alcohol abuse. For most adolescents today, experimenting with alcohol and other drugs has become a predictable rite of passage. The average age of first use of alcohol and drugs among young people has declined steadily in the last decade and has now reached down to early adolescence. In recent years studies have indicated that about one-third of secondary-age children smoke, some quite heavily; almost all have tasted alcohol with around 50 per cent drinking more or less regularly, and perhaps 15–19 per cent having taken or still taking illegal drugs ...
- Other problems of youth ... These include juvenile delinquency, adolescent pregnancy, truancy and suicide. Many of these problems, including drug use, are interrelated. All of them can be found at alarmingly high levels among youth throughout our society, regardless of social class, ethnicity or geographical location.

Underlying the developments we have considered so far are three central facts:

- the rapid, and accelerating, pace of social *change*
- wide, and widening, *inequalities*
- a bewildering, and growing, *range of choices* — especially in leisure, consumption and life-styles

Figure 2.4: Collage

(Acknowledgements to Suke Ryder)

These are of crucial significance to teachers of PSHE. Even without other arguments, they provide a powerful justification for the kind of learning objectives outlined in Chapter 1: flexibility, respect for others, teamwork, decision-making skills, self-confidence and the ability to weigh evidence rationally in the light of both personal and social needs, for example. (See further Thacker *et al.*, 1987.)

But while the challenges are real and urgent, it is important that, in attempting to find appropriate responses, schools do not overlook the views and wishes of parents. In such a dramatically changing world and threatened by a quite bewildering variety of changes in their children's schooling, it is crucial that parents' anxieties are recognised and their questions responded to. If they are not, and if innovations are imposed without prior consultation, it is likely that parents will withdraw their support and choose more traditional schools.

Perhaps it is important, in this connection, to remind ourselves how cautious parental feelings tend to be. For example, asked what their priority was for improvements in schools to meet current social conditions, 27 per cent of parents in 1984 chose 'more training and preparation for jobs', followed by 'stricter discipline' (19 per cent) and 'more emphasis on developing skills and interests' (13 per cent). Items such as 'better buildings', 'better pay for teachers', 'involvement on governing bodies' and 'emphasis on basic skills' all achieved a very low priority (Central Statistical Office, 1985). This is hardly a surprising outcome (even if it does appear highly instrumental) since given a choice of just one item probably most people, thinking long term, would rate job skills as a priority. These are certainly highly valued by those in the least favoured social groups in society for whom a relevant education and 'good' qualifications still hold out the main promise of advancement. What this suggests, as we shall argue in more detail in Chapter 7, is that parents (and, where appropriate, students) should be involved directly or through their representatives on governing bodies in any planning for curriculum change — especially where the changes are in areas involving sensitive personal and social values.

GOALS FOR THE FUTURE

Consideration of the various pressures, possibilities and constraints which make up the current social condition suggests a number of ideals for what Handy (1985) calls 'educating for tomorrow'. First, more people will need more education, but not of the conventional kind. Rather, the call will be for flexibility — for a greater variety of types of learning and for a chance to undertake it at different points in life. Second, because of this diversity, there will be a need for a greater variety of assessment models and wider criteria of 'success'. As Handy remarks: 'Capability, creativity and community are at least as important as culture and comprehension.' Third, we shall need a much more flexible attitude to where learning takes place. Given distance learning technologies and learning networks, this could just as easily be in the home or the local community as in a formal educational establishment. Such arrangements, in turn, will mean more flexibility about credit transfers and course accreditation. For example, there could easily be a measure of student transfer between consortia of schools or, at a different level, between universities, colleges and local work and community centres.

Changes like these will not happen overnight. Indeed, there are currently signs of countervailing pressures, to maintain centralised control. However, one development does seem fairly certain: the establishment of some form of core curriculum. We considered the aims of the entitlement curriculum in the Introduction (p. 3). These were accompanied in the HMI report by a list of skills:

communication skills	organisational and study skills
numerical skills	physical and practical skills
observational and visual skills	social skills
imaginative skills	problem-solving and creative skills

and by a list of attitudes which, it is suggested, pupils should be encouraged to form:

adaptability	tolerance
commitment	empathy
co-operation	consideration for others
reliability	curiosity
self-confidence	honesty
self-discipline	integrity
perseverance	

We would argue that it is a major task for PSHE to find and develop opportunities for the growth of such skills and attitudes. They must also find expression in the hidden curriculum and in the wider life of schools and their surrounding communities.

FUTURES

The development of effective PSHE programmes depends on appropriate school structures which are agreed by everyone concerned: teachers, parents, students and governors. However, there are considerable tensions and conflicts in this area — witness the difficulties faced by the Humanities Curriculum Project in introducing its Race pack; the controversy over Peace and Development Studies in the mid-1980s, and the very sensitive issues raised by the role schools should play in sex and drug education following the 1986 Education Act. In some schools, a move to more accommodating arrangements (team teaching; block timetables; integrated course planning; programmed time for staff development and effective parental liaison, for example) will require a radical shift. This will undoubtedly create tensions, given the highly controversial and politicised nature of the debates concerned — especially in the climate of a national curriculum.

But what choices are there? What alternative futures exist for our society? Gershuny (1983) suggests two possible 'ideal types' of post-industrial future:

1. The Hyper-Expansionist (HE) Future

This takes the form of a high technology, affluent, service society. It is a knowledge-based society with accelerating growth in the aerospace industry, telecommunications, computing and genetic engineering. Manufacturing industry as we know it will have disappeared — the micro-processor having had its effect. The growing points of the service sector will be universities, consultancies and research institutes producing the know-how for super-growth. To succeed in this society a high level of scientific and technological expertise will be needed as well as entrepreneurial and competitive qualities.

2. The Sane, Humane, Ecological (SHE) Future

In this scenario the new technology is welcomed as a means of eliminating the old heavy, boring and repetitive manufacturing jobs and of creating new jobs which will be labour-intensive rather than capital-intensive. High-tech techniques and inventions will be applied to small-scale workshops in order to create an appropriate human-scale technology. Jobs will be de-institutionalised; they will take place in the home or local community rather than in the factory/office/city. Workers will use the techniques of IT (information technology), on a networking model, to which everyone will have access, rather than on a hierarchical, passing-on-of-information model. A high rate of economic growth will be neither possible nor seen as a necessity. To participate successfully in the SHE society the skills of co-operation and community living will be needed, as well as such qualities as self-reliance, initiative and caring.

To see what these two forms of society imply in terms of schooling, you (or your students) might be interested in Exercise 2.1.

There is no way of knowing how accurate these scenarios are likely to prove. However, alternatives closely resembling them are currently in stark contention in debates about schooling. At a party political level, centrally and locally, proponents of one or the other alternative argue for different distributions of scarce financial resources; for example, for INSET, for particular forms of assessment or for different patterns of schooling for 14 to 19 year olds.

Exercise 2.1: What Kind of Future?

Instructions: Examine the systems outlined below and decide:
1. which of them is closest to the school you presently work in?
2. which is closest to your preferred style of schooling?
3. how might PSHE best be integrated in the curriculum in your preferred model?

The hyper-expansionist educational system	The sane, humane, ecological educational system
Aim	
To create an elite 10 per cent of the population capable of exploiting the new technology for maximum growth. The winnowing out of the wheat from the chaff is the prime function of the secondary school.	To create a more equal society in which everyone is involved in realising the potential of the new technology for making full use of people's abilities and skills.
Access to technology	
The knowledge, essential new languages and skills are confined to the few — the elite. For the rest, low-level 'hands on' skills are required. Access to computerised data would be restricted.	An understanding of the scientific principles underlying the new technology, an appreciation of the uses to which it might be put and participation in decisions regarding its use are extended to all. Everyone would have access through computer networks to local and national databases.
Systems of schooling	
Under centralised control, a segregated or differentiated schooling system is established.	A decentralised system of all-ability community-based schools along the lines of Henry Morris's Cambridgeshire village colleges or Leicestershire's community colleges is established.
Type of curriculum	
A hierarchical, or differentiated curriculum which emphasises cognitive skills, scientific knowledge and academic excellence is developed. This involves definitions of knowledge as 'high status' and 'low status'.	A common curriculum which all children follow is developed. The core would be in commuity studies and the expressive arts. Knowledge is no longer seen in terms of subject disciplines but is holistic and person-centred.
Rewards	
Rewards are seen in terms of wealth and status and are centrally distributed.	Rewards would be negotiated in terms of community use value and personal satisfaction.

They are also hotly debated by different groups within the teaching profession. Generally PSHE teachers find themselves happiest working within the SHE scenario — for reasons which should be clear from what was argued in Chapter 1. But this should not mean neglecting excellence and high standards in our work — a real danger, as the APU team looking at PSE discovered. Even without competitive teaching strategies, it is important that PSHE teachers should stress the need for personal goal-setting and should demand ambitious standards of performance from students. Equally it is important that a 'soft' area of the curriculum, like PSHE, should establish clear criteria for what counts as valid subject 'content' and that this is seen to embrace the highest regard for rationality and critical judgement. We will examine these requirements more fully in Chapters 5 and 6. Meanwhile we need to conclude our review of present social trends.

CONCLUSION

One fact about the current social condition compared to 25 years ago is inescapable, as Hopson and Scally (1981) point out:

> Schools are different now, society is different, values are different, knowledge is different, communication is different, roles are different, families are different, life-styles are different, and above all the future is different. One may lament or applaud the facts, but to deny them is futile or perilous.

All of these differences pose challenges for schooling and, because they are so intimately bound up with people's sense of security as well as their ability to lead truly healthy lives, they impose a particular responsibility on teachers of PSHE. But, as we shall argue in the next chapter, this does not absolve others of their responsibilities in the area. On the contrary, the needs created by the current social condition and the informal learning which they bring with them to school suggest that concern for students' personal and social development must permeate the entire curriculum. How, for example, is your school — with or without the benefit of planned PSHE — facing up to these questions? How can education ...

1. strengthen family units?
2. become more responsible for the social, ethical and moral development of children and adolescents?
3. increase contact between people of different age groups?
4. make better use of television as a learning tool?
5. utilise computers as learning tools?

6. prepare learners who can anticipate change and cultivate needed flexibility?
7. prepare learners who are tolerant and can accept reasonable alternatives?
8. avoid oppressive atmospheres in educational institutions?
9. help learners develop outlets to channel personal pressures?
10. prepare students for productivity in general but with an emphasis on independent living?
11. enable citizens to make effective use of leisure time?
12. prepare individuals for lifelong learning?
13. make citizens aware and aggressive in the areas of environment and energy?
14. prepare citizens for possible new life-styles?
15. prepare citizens to live in an age based on computers and communications technology?
16. enable citizens to deal with the moral and ethical issues surrounding the increased use of computers and information technology?
17. help citizens avoid a computer-managed society and move towards a society marked by participatory democracy where humanity controls destiny?
18. help learners develop and clarify their own beliefs and values? (Saylor *et al.*, 1981)

In the next chapter we look at four different models of PSHE and see what they offer as a base for discharging this kind of responsibility.

FURTHER READING

Bates, I. *et al.* (1984) *Schooling for the dole? The new vocationalism*, Macmillan, London

Dale, R. (ed.) (1985) *Education, training and employment: towards a new vocationalism?* Pergamon for Open University, Oxford

Davies, B. (1986) *Threatening youth: towards a national youth policy*, Open University Press, Milton Keynes

Department of Education and Science/Welsh Office (1983) *Curriculum 11–16: towards a statement of entitlement, curriculum reappraisal in action*, HMSO, London

Fletcher, C. *et al.* (1985) *Schools on trial: the trials of democratic comprehensives*, Open University Press, Milton Keynes

Galton, M. and Moon, B. (eds) (1983) *Changing schools ... changing curriculum*, Harper and Row, London

Harber, L. *et al.* (eds) (1984) *Alternative educational futures*, Holt, Rinehart and Winston, London

Hargreaves, D. (1982) *The challenge for the comprehensive school*, Routledge and Kegan Paul, London

Hopson, B. and Scally, M. (1981) *Lifeskills teaching*, McGraw-Hill, Maidenhead

Meighan, R. (1981) *A sociology of educating*, Holt, Rinehart and Winston, London

Moon, B. (ed.) (1987) *Modular curriculum: remaking the mould*, Harper and Row, London

Ryder, J. and Silver, H. (1985) *Modern English society*, 3rd edn, Methuen, London

Slaughter, R. (1987) *Futures, tools and techniques*, Department of Educational Research, University of Lancaster

Watts, A.G. (1983) *Education, unemployment and the future*, Open University Press, Milton Keynes

3

Models of PSHE and the Pastoral Curriculum

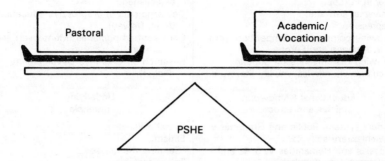

In this chapter we present our 'selections from culture' in the form of four approaches to Personal, Social and Health Education. These alternative models emerge from a consideration of the philosophical and sociological questions raised in the last two chapters. They also take into account historical movements in ideas about society, about the conditions of learning and about the purposes of education. What we shall be describing are necessarily 'ideal' selections, in Lawton's sense. For, given the conditions of everyday classroom life, it is hard to operate with a single approach. Nor can the different models exist in isolation from current notions about the curriculum. Among these, ideas and practice in relation to the pastoral work of the school will have a major impact on the role of PSHE.

Our concern, then, is to relate ideas and ideals and to explore the resulting conflicts and contradictions which arise in planning the curriculum. We begin by outlining the various strands which have contributed to the present uncertain status of PSHE in schools. In the process we shall be able to witness the emergence of related activities, like guidance and counselling, and of revamped subject areas like the humanities, health and moral education. We shall also be able to identify the often contradictory sources from which they have all sprung.

First, a word of caution is required. As Julienne Ford *et al.* (1982) confess in their account of provisions for maladjusted and disruptive pupils:

Figure 3.1: A Historical Overview of Curriculum Developments re PSHE

1870–1944

Social, economic and political context

'Two nations'
Urbanisation. Industrialisation.
Empire. Colonialism. Bureaucracy.
'Self help'. Voluntary welfare. 'The sanctity of the family'.
Class conflict: strikes, unionisation, syndicalism.
Early social welfare legislation.
War in Europe.
Universal suffrage.
Depression.
Growing commercial competition from N. America and Europe.
Growing US influence on popular culture via movies, music, literature.

Significant developments in research and allied professions

1907 Creation of school medical service.
Psychometrics (Burt, Binet).
1913 Burt appointed first Child Psychologist by LCC.
Child Psychotherapy develops (M. Klein, A. Freud).
1921 Child Guidance clinics established.
Developments in progressive education (Neill, Dewey).
Child-centred primaries (Montessori and Macmillan).
Research on Cognitive Development (Piaget).

Educational framework: policies and structures

A dual system: Public and Grammar v. Elementary schools.
Classics and Humanities v. 3 Rs and 'Payment by Results'.
1902 Act creates Scholarship ladder.
1918 Fisher Act raises leaving age to 14 and extends 'free' and 'special' places at Grammar schools.
1922 Tawney advocates the Common Secondary School.
Henry Morris starts Cambridgeshire County Colleges as Community Schools.
1926 Hadow Report acknowledges 'adolescence' as a special stage.
1938 Spens and 1943 Norwood Reports prefigure tripartitism.
Progressive primaries.

Underlying rationale

Social efficiency.
Elitism.
'Gentling the masses'.
Talent matching.
Social justice.
Entitlement.
Democracy.
Valuing of individual needs.
Talent matching.
Child-centred learning.

Figure 3.1 contd.

1944–1964

Social, economic and political context

Austerity. Rationing. Post-war reconstruction. Planning.
Welfare State created on principles of social insurance.
Politics of consensus.
Cold war. The Bomb. Suez.
Collapse of Empire.
Beginning of mass culture.
Extension of car ownership and rising living standards.
Full employment.
Higher levels of social and geographical mobility.
Decline of traditional heavy industries, mining and dock labour.
New Towns and light industries.
Sputnik and the space race.
Inroads into traditional moral/religious views: Profumo, *Lady Chatterley, Look Back in Anger*.
The Beatles.
Accumulating evidence of social deprivation and disadvantage.

Significant developments in research and allied professions

1948 Consolidation of Youth Employment Service.
1955 World Education Year Book on *Guidance and Counselling in Schools*.
From USA, non-directive counselling (Rogers).
Sociological critiques of selection (Glass, Halsey, Floud et al.).
Concern re 'wastage of talent' (Early Leaving Report, Crowther, Newsom, Robbins).
Separate teacher unions and separate routes to qualification for primary sec.mod and grammar schools.
1963 Nat Assn for Mental Health holds conference on 'Counselling Services in Schools'.
1964 Careers Research and Advisory Centre (CRAC) set up.

Educational framework: policies and structures

1944 Act creates free, universal secondary education according to 'age, aptitude and ability' up to 15.
Some authorities choose to set up comprehensive or community schools.
Selection based on rapidly discredited 11+ test.
1951 GCE replaces the Matriculation for top 25 per cent ability.
Continuation of trad. Grammar school curriculum, practical emphasis in sec.mods.
Prefect and house systems modelled on public school ideal.
Pastoral Care/PSE piecemeal or non-existent.
RE and a daily religious service compulsory.
Preponderance of single-sex schools and sex-stereotyped curriculum
1965 CSE examination introduced for middle 40 per cent ability.

Underlying rationale

Economic efficiency.
Social justice.
Entitlement.
Equal opportunities (access).
Equal valuing.
Talent matching.
Elitism.
Certification.
Utilitarianism.
Social control, training for leadership/followership.
'Gentling the masses'.
Normative needs.
Economic efficiency, promotion of talent.

Figure 3.1 contd.

1965–1975

Social, economic and political context

Successive waves of Commonwealth immigrants.

Collapse of post-war consensus and of traditional relationships of authority and power.

'Adolescence' as a way of life and as a commercial concept: mods, rockers, hippies, flower people.

Growth of homosexual, black and women's rights movements.

Decline of traditional sexual standards (the Pill).

The 'permissive society'.

'Swinging London'.

Student protest, 1968.

Accelerating pace of social change especially in consumer choice.

Inner-city decay.

Family and community dislocation.

High levels of marriage breakdown.

Growth of leisure industries: foreign travel, hi-fi, eating out.

Celebration of individuality.

Significant developments in research and allied professions

1965 first counselling courses open at Keele and Reading.

1965 establishment of Vocational Guidance Research Unit at Leeds (to become CCDU in 1976).

1969 National Association of Careers Teachers set up.

1969 Hamblin starts Counselling courses at Swansea.

1971 Standing Committee for the Advancement of Counselling set up.

1973 *British Journal of Guidance and Counselling* begins. Two HMI created.

The de-schoolers (Holt, Goodman, Friere).

Black Paper backlash (1969–77).

1974 Marland publishes *Pastoral Care*.

1975 Nat Inst Careers Education and Counselling (NICEC) set up.

The 'new sociology of education' offers critique of curriculum.

Research on moral development and ego-strength (Kohlberg, Loevinger).

1975 APU set up.

Educational framework: policies and structures

Circular 10/65 leads to comprehensive reorganisation countrywide.

Amalgamations, split-site working etc. create pressure for pastoral systems to facilitate admin, liaison, control.

1965 first school counsellor in post.

First wave of curriculum developments (initially in high status areas like Nuffield Science, then embracing Social Ed (1968) and Moral Ed (1972), Humanities (1970), Political Ed (1974), Careers (1976–9) and Health Ed (1977).

1967 Plowden Report on *Educational Priority Areas* leads to development of Compensatory Education

Pioneering Community Schools set up (Countesthorpe, Sidney Stringer, the Sutton Centre etc.).

1973 School Leaving Age raised to 16.

The 'logic of comprehensive schooling' leads to mixed-ability teaching, mode 3 CSE examinations and the development of structures to aid academic and vocational guidance.

Mid-1970s crisis of staff morale/high teacher turnover.

High levels of disruption and truancy.

Creation of on- and off-site centres.

Underlying rationale

Social justice.

Equal opportunities (access).

Social control.

Normative needs.

Economic efficiency.

Knowledge-centred initiation.

Emancipation? Control?

Deficit/Compensation.

Socialisation.

Social engineering.

Equal valuing.

Equal opportunities (curriculum and outcomes).

'Relevance'.

Figure 3.1 contd.

Post 1976

Social, economic and political context	Significant developments in research and allied professions
Economic crisis begins to bite.	1977 White Paper on *Health Education in schools*.
Growing levels of youth and adult unemployment.	1980 Best *et al*. publish critique of 'conventional wisdom' of P. Care.
Britain increasingly susceptible to shifts in European and world economy.	1978 Lifeskills Associates set up.
Intensification of inner-city decay.	1978 Warnock Report on *Special Educational Needs*.
North-south divide.	School effectiveness studies published (Rutter, Reynolds).
Collapse of manufacturing sector.	1979 *Active Tutorial Work* scheme published.
Growth of service industries.	1980 FEU publishes *Developing Social and Life Skills*.
Development of information technologies, satellite communications, etc.	Schools Council Health Education Projects 5–13 (1977), 13–18 (1981).
Successive crises of social legitimacy and social reproduction fed by youth and black resistance (Brixton, Tottenham, the miners' strike, Wapping, etc.)	1980 Schools Council HEC and NICEC begin discussions on PSE.
High levels of family breakdown.	1981 APU document on *Personal and Social Education*.
Football hooliganism leads to successive waves of moral panic.	1983 Nat Assocn for Pastoral Care in Education set up, plus journal.
Massive increase in population of over-75 year olds.	Anti-racist/anti-sexist policies.
Collapse of Welfare State in the face of demographic changes, high levels of needs and Thatcherite policies of individual responsibility.	Growth of assessment-led projects e.g. APU, Graded Assessment, Profiles, Records of Achievement.
Health crises: AIDS, child abuse.	Psychological research re locus of control, personal constructs, learned helplessness.
	Sociological research re the impact of the 'new vocationalism', the micro-politics of schooling etc.

Figure 3.1 contd.

Post 1976

Educational framework: policies and structures	Underlying rationale
Callaghan's Ruskin speech heralds the 'Great Debate' and the re-politicisation of education.	'Social improvement'. Normative needs. Economic efficiency.
New emphasis on accountability, cuts, contraction and centralised control.	Instrumentalism. Social control.
Second wave of curriculum developments focuses on assessment.	Social engineering? Socialisation. Entitlement.
1980 DES/HMI announce that 'Personal and social development is a charge upon the curriculum'.	Training. Centralisation. Equal opportunities (outcomes).
1981 MSC funds the New Training Initiative leading to Youth Training Scheme.	Talent matching. Centralisation. Accountability.
1982 Schools Council abolished.	Individual responsibility.
1983 White Paper sets tighter controls on selection, deployment and training of teachers.	Normative controls.
1983 MSC sets up TVEI to create more vocationally relevant curriculum.	
1984–7 Teacher Action.	
1986 GCSE replaces GCE 'O' levels and CSE.	
1982 Lower Attaining Pupils Project.	
Proliferation of new pre-vocational qualifications and of new records of achievement, profiling schemes etc.	
1987 Decisions re INSET funding pass to LEAs under DES supervision.	
Parental contributions/parental choice.	
Greater powers to governors, especially re Sex and Health Education.	
1987 announcement of a National Curriculum 5–16 and attainment targets at 7, 11, 14 and 16	

The relationship between historical development and present circumstances is one which from time to time tempts philosophers, historians and fellow-travellers into the most profound insights. Since they are usually disagreeing with someone else's previously profound insight it is often difficult for those who are not specialists in the field to know whom to follow.

And they warn:

The prevailing point of view at a given moment on a given topic is the result of many complex processes, not all of which have even the slightest connection with the truth of the matter.

THE HISTORY OF CURRICULUM DEVELOPMENTS RELATED TO PSHE

The outline of developments in Figure 3.1 is offered in the hope that it will illuminate, as well as in the knowledge that it is a very personal selection. It shows both the broad sweep of social and educational changes since the start of this century and more specific shifts in emphasis in the organisation of the curriculum as it relates to PSHE. (More detailed accounts of the historical context are suggested in the further reading at the end of this chapter.)

As this summary reveals, the different theories which have influenced curriculum developments over the last century derive from a number of fields and represent different levels and forms of analysis. These span childhood socialisation and strategies for learning and the culture and organisation of schools. But while in some instances these different perspectives have been mutually reinforcing, as in the marriage between some theories of adolescent development, non-directive counselling and group dynamics, which gave rise to active tutorial work, in others they have been in tension, if not outright contradiction, as in the case of recent accounts of educational achievement and its determinants (see Meighan, 1981). This is because researchers and theorists, like teachers, embrace different values and ideals.

THE IDEOLOGICAL CONNECTION

The connections between teachers' ideologies and learners' experiences are set out in Figure 3.2, which is adapted from an Open University model (1983).

We find it disturbing that, in spite of occasional outbursts against 'extremism' or 'indoctrination', the links between B and C and between D and E are still scarcely acknowledged in political debates about education. An important part of our PSHE rationale is to make these connections more explicit. Different ideologies, though sometimes obscured, can be traced in almost any curriculum document, defining different versions of teacher-pupil relationship, different views of assessment and different learning goals. They are also evident, indeed highlighted, in the four models of PSHE which we shall elaborate shortly.

Our historical analysis (pp. 58–62) has indicated the most significant ideological influences on the curriculum. Three main types of influence can be discerned, which are shown in Figure 3.3, together with their areas of overlap. It is important to note that proponents of each ideology share a view of education as being 'worthwhile' and a means of 'social improvement'. However, this is perhaps the limit of their commonality! The discrepancies between the different perspectives are obvious — and scarely surprising — given the tensions already present in schools and society. There are also powerful pragmatic grounds for variation, including the influence of local and regional pressures, of financial considerations and of the micro-politics of school organisations (Ball, 1987).

Figure 3.2: The Ideological Connection

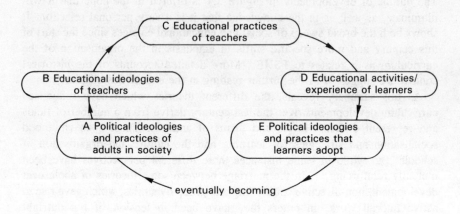

Figure 3.3: Three Educational Ideologies

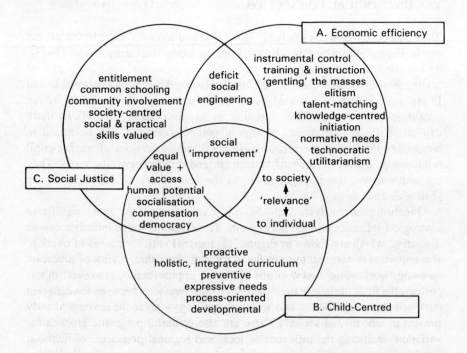

We now turn to the particular case of PSHE and the tensions between educational ideology and classroom practice which it throws up.

MODELS OF PERSONAL, SOCIAL AND HEALTH EDUCATION

The different approaches to PSHE contained in Figure 3.4 are each distinguishable within current practice. Before looking at them in detail, however, we need to explain our choice of terms: pastoral, educational, radical and medical. PASTORAL is a well-established term in schools (although often used to mean different things) which now has welfare rather than theological connotations. We use it here because most existing pastoral programmes have sufficient common ground to constitute a distinct approach. Our use of the word EDUCATIONAL does not imply that other models are not! However, much current educational parlance emphasises the kinds of processes, skills and knowledge which are exemplified in this approach. RADICAL does not necessarily mean revolutionary but this model is avowedly political and to the extent that it fosters opportunities for change and collective action could be considered extreme. The term MEDICAL was originally used by Vuori and Ripela (1981) but has subsequently appeared in several analyses of Health Education (see Tones (1986) and Beattie (1984)). It implies a didactic approach based on validation of 'facts' and 'expert' knowledge. Although the labels we have chosen are similar to those used elsewhere in the book to describe wider political ideologies, please note that the way they are used in this model should not be taken to imply any direct connection to other education, political or health care systems.

The respective advantages and disadvantages of the different models are compared in Figure 3.5.

Clearly a diagrammatic representation must miss out a good deal of detail and we are aware of the risk of caricaturing the different approaches. However, by setting the four models alongside each other, with their respective strengths and weaknesses, it is possible to make some comparisons which are far from superficial. Note, for instance, the different modes of assessment and pedagogy each implies. A more detailed understanding of what the different models embrace can be gained by consulting some of the packages listed in Appendix 4.

As with all of the models used in this book, we hope that this clarification of the four approaches to PSHE will enable teachers to reflect helpfully on their own practice. We are particularly concerned, for instance, with the frequent mismatch which can exist between aims, methods and assessment. Surely it cannot be good educational practice to use instructional films to try to foster self-esteem and creativity and then hope to assess this by means of a group project (an approach we have certainly seen)! Not that we are advocating the adoption of one 'pure' model. As we shall indicate in a moment, teachers often find themselves using a mixed approach.

Figure 3.4: Four Models of PSHE

	A. PASTORAL/ INDIVIDUAL	B. EDUCA- TIONAL/ RATIONAL	C. RADICAL/ POLITICAL	D. MEDICAL/ TRADITIONAL
UNDERLYING PRINCIPLE	Autonomy	Choice	Change	Orthodoxy
AIMS	To foster self-esteem and self-empowerment To develop effective inter-personal relationships	To provide access to knowledge and resources To promote understanding To foster development of reasoning	To encourage respect for self and others To develop strategies for group problem solving and for critical social analysis	To promote conformity to social norms To initiate 'worthwhile', 'objective' knowledge
TEACHER ROLE	Teacher as 'facilitator' promoting self-awareness	Teacher as 'arbitrator' exemplifying rational decision making	Teacher as 'energiser' negotiating boundaries	Teacher as 'expert' controlling the transmis-sion of knowledge
METHODS	Providing group settings: 1.To permit self-disclosure and reflection 2.To encourage constructive feedback	Discussing information: 1.To integrate personal understanding 2....as a basis for developing decision-making skills (including analysis & synthesis)	Analysing social situa-tions and issues: 1.To recog-nise power relationships and know-ledge control 2.To develop action research skills	Providing information: 1.To raise awareness 2.To reinforce pre-determined 'approved' behaviours
	via: Role play simulations Trust and communica-tion exercises/ games	via: Investigations Trigger films Role play Debates Checklists	via: Media studies Community programmes Group discussions Surveys	via: Films Lectures Posters Worksheets Texts

Figure 3.4: contd.

	A. PASTORAL/ INDIVIDUAL	B. EDUCA- TIONAL/ RATIONAL	C. RADICAL/ POLITICAL	D. MEDICAL/ TRADITIONAL
STUDENT ROLE	a) Active, interactive within pre- determined 'safe' frame- works b) Individuals' behaviour and learning processes become the content c) Engagement virtually inescapable	a) Involved, scope for individual contributions b) Individuals/ groups may negotiate some content c) Active participation encouraged but engage- ment variable	a) Active, collaborative and divergent b) Individuals/ groups likely to negotiate content and process c) Engagement depends on individual motivation and commit- ment to shared projects	a) Passive, conforming b) Individuals assimilate fixed content c) Engage- ment optional
EVALUATION/ ASSESSMENT OF STUDENT	Mainly individual formative, criterion- referenced, based on personal development. Participative, main emphasis on behavioural outcomes/ prescribed competencies. Some self- assessment (private or shared)	Individual, formative and criterion- referenced based on evidence of reasoning. A range of achievements is valued in relation to individual progress. Applied knowledge valued as well as 'pure'.	Mainly group- based (responsibility shared), formative and summative. Criteria for success generated by the group itself. Assessment visible and public.	Individual, summative and norm- referenced, based on recall of facts. Quantitative with in-built pass/fail criteria. Greater emphasis on cognitive than on behavioural outcomes.
	e.g. Ongoing reviews and individual feedback Attitude questionnaires	e.g. Profiles Self- assessment Creative writing	e.g. Action research Projects Diaries	e.g. Written exams and tests

Figure 3.5: Advantages and Disadvantages of PSHE Models

MODEL	ADVANTAGES	DISADVANTAGES
PASTORAL/INDIVIDUAL	— Based on concrete personal experience — Values the student — Maximises student participation and collaborative learning — By valuing the development of self-esteem and group support, can enhance motivation and enjoyment of learning process	— Requires appropriate space and time slots — May isolate skill learning from real life contexts — May be over-intrusive and involve students in too much risk-taking — 'Failure' is public and can be painful — May ignore cultural variations in stressing 'we know what's best for you'
EDUCATIONAL/ RATIONAL	— Wide variety of methods increases likelihood of student involvement — Values student contributions — Encourages students to select and apply knowledge and understanding — Skills learnt are transferable and valued by wider society	— Heuristic methods may lead to frustration at teacher's abdication of 'expert' role — Can be time-consuming — Teachers need training and support — Possible conflicts with hidden curriculum — Problems of moral relativism and teacher neutrality
RADICAL/POLITICAL	— Students connect with real and relevant-to-them issues and take responsibility for their own learning — Encourages development of skills for adult life — Reduces barriers between school and community — Mobilises a wide range of individual contributions and group support — Adequately debriefed, failure can be turned to advantage	— Practical difficulties in setting up suitable learning opportunities — Time-consuming and requires long-term planning — Politically contentious — Effective group work requires careful support and sensitivity to individual needs — Because learning outcomes are variable and hard to specify, they are hard to assess — Lends itself to manipulation
MEDICAL/TRADITIONAL	— Efficient transmission of knowledge — Efficient use of expertise — Aims easily communicated and monitored — Methods 'safe' — Can work successfully with large groups and in inflexible spaces	— May induce dependency — or rebellion and withdrawal — Overemphasises established orthodoxies — Ignores individual differences in motivation, readiness to learn, etc. — Potentially failure- and blame-inducing — Fails to capitalise on sources of support for learning within the group

THE PERM MODEL

We ourselves have found the following PERMutation idea a useful application of our summary table. A PERM diagram can be drawn in a variety of contexts as a 'rough and ready reckoner' of approaches to PSHE. For example, we have used it to assess exercises and teaching packs, as in Chapter 6 and in Appendix 4. And while we concede that any one individual's PERM model may differ from the next person's, the resulting comparisons can be illuminating. Another possible use is to 'do a PERM' on some specific elements of one's own teaching — as planned and as performed! Is there a difference? Where and why? How could one move one's actual approach closer to the preferred PERM model? Clarity about aims is essential to effective classroom practice. The PERM model helps by providing an instant means of checking these.

Here is what we mean by a PERM diagram:

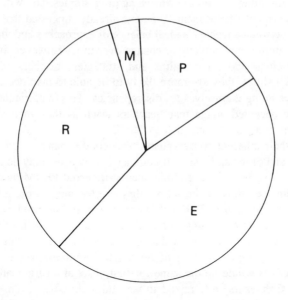

The different segments of the pie-chart labelled, respectively, P, E, R and M represent the approximate proportions of the whole approach which can be characterised as either Pastoral, Educational, Radical or Medical. Thus, the diagram above describes our preferred model of PSHE — and the one informing our approach in this book. The examples overleaf were produced by groups of PGCE students, when invited to 'PERM' Active Tutorial Work and Life Skills materials. You might like to compare the diagrams with your own assessments of these well-known packages.

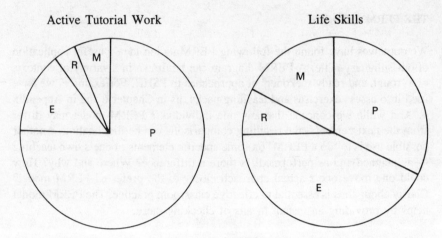

In reflecting on your own PERM models for these packages, or those appropriate to any other resources or teaching programmes, you will notice that PERM models are not PERManent. We have already suggested that there may be differences between a teacher's ideal balance of approaches and the way they actually teach. Both are also likely to change over time. However, if, by being more self-conscious about their aims and strategies, teachers can identify reasons for such shifts, they are more likely to be able to take decisions about reducing (or resigning themselves to) discrepancies. This is particularly important, given the accepted adage that 'teachers teach as they themselves were taught' — even in a 'new' area such as PSHE.

In spite of their inherent conservatism, teachers do change — in terms both of their values and of the skills at their command. However, they do not operate as free agents. This means that an individual's preferred PERM model may be at variance with the ethos of the school they are teaching in or, indeed, with current views on education. But such external constraints need not alter the overall balance of their teaching perspectives. What they will affect is their choice of strategies within a particular approach, since the preferred PERM model governs teaching irrespective of the immediate context. For example, our aims and objectives would be the same for first years at a rural Catholic girls' school as for fifth years in a mixed urban comprehensive, even though the planned teaching strategies were totally different. Thus, in the instances suggested, a group project on the popularity of school meals and an evaluation of the local 'Meals on Wheels' service, respectively, would each be considered radical.

LOCATING PSHE IN THE CURRICULUM

Necessary as it is to have a clearer picture of alternative approaches to PSHE, undoubtedly the biggest problem facing the future status of work concerning students' personal and social development is not what models it should embrace but where, and in what form, to find space for it at all.

The relationship between PSHE and more traditional subject areas is taken up in Chapter 5. In the next sections we shall consider two other areas of potential overlap: that between PSHE and the pastoral work of the school and between PSHE and the para-curriculum. The ground which is contested here includes everything in Figure 3.6 which is not part of the 'pure' subject curriculum. Note that in our schema the 'academic' curriculum embraces 'pure' subjects as well as pre-vocational education and that the 'para-curriculum' is an umbrella term which includes the hidden curriculum (or ethos) of the school as well as its extra-curricular activities.

THE PASTORAL-ACADEMIC CONTINUUM

Writers from different professional backgrounds have offered different perspectives on the balance between vocational, academic and pastoral tasks in schools. This theme has also been an important one for contributors to the newly established NAPCE journal, *Pastoral Care in Education*. However, with notable exceptions, the arguments for one set of arrangements or another have tended to be more pragmatic than principled.

Pastoral care structures in their modern form arose in response to pressures generated by the creation of comprehensive schooling in the late 1960s and the raising of the school leaving age in 1972. Their justification was in terms of supporting increasingly diverse and urgent student needs and of facilitating communication, both within schools and with parents and other professionals outside. In practice, however, pastoral work was more often a matter of systemising procedures for discipline and control and of coping with student (and even staff) crises, than of promoting the goals of positive mental health. At that time most student-centred work tended to be exported to the newly created cadres of school social workers, education welfare officers, psychologists and counsellors. The consequence, perhaps accidental more than intended, was that pastoral care became mainly identified with a 'fire brigade' or 'zoo-keeping' approach. Non-academic classes were coaxed into co-operation through more 'relevant' teaching strategies, while the hard core of disaffected students was dispatched to a variety of off- and on-site units (euphemistically known as 'sanctuaries', 'sin-bins' or 'learning and support centres') where their difficulties could be 'cooled out' or 'remediated'.

Only slowly was the possibility seriously acknowledged that schools themselves might be contributing to students' difficulties and disaffection. Once this realisation dawned and in the face of mounting concern about standards of educational achievement, pastoral care structures began to accommodate a more explicitly tutorial function. Perhaps the most influential figure in this phase was the psychologist, Douglas Hamblin of Swansea University, whose many

71

Figure 3.6: PSHE and the School

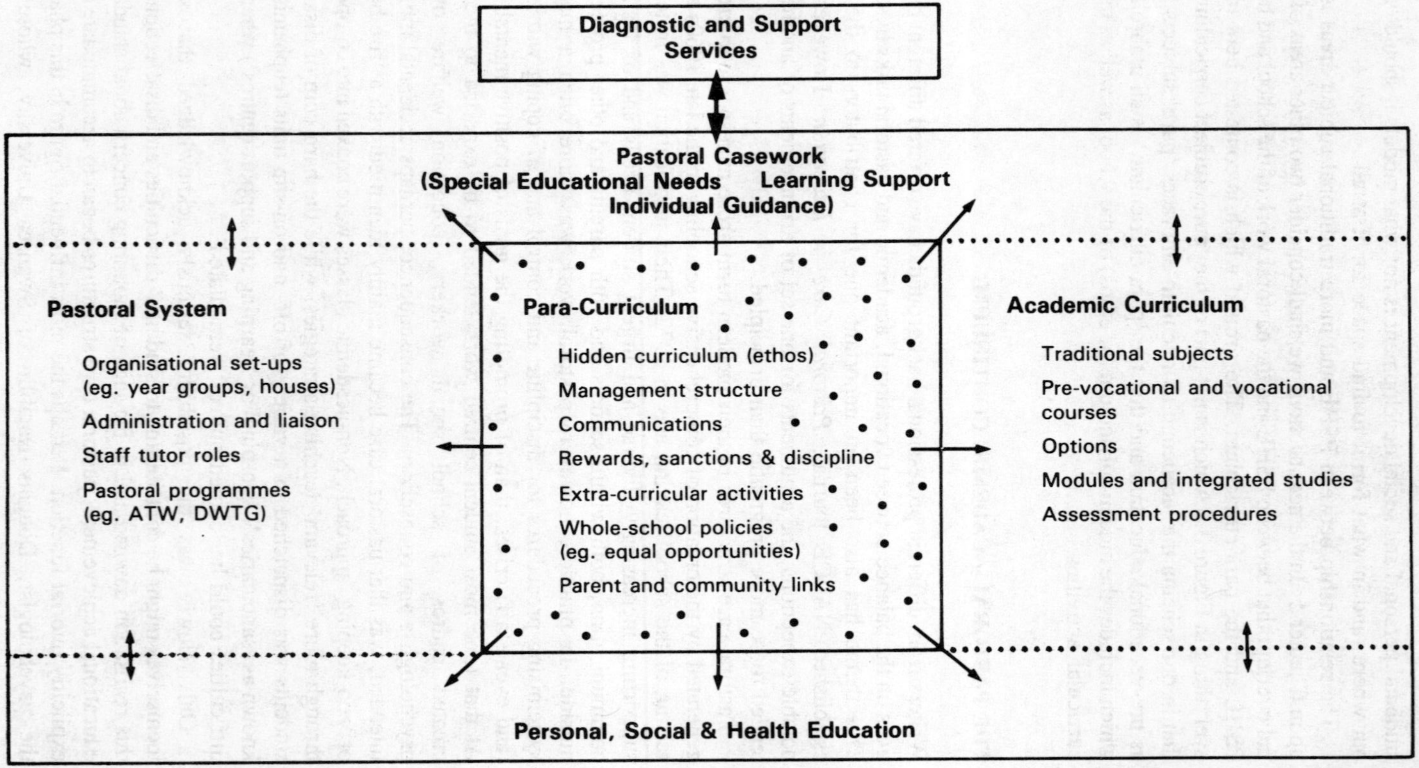

Diagnostic and Support Services

Pastoral Casework Learning Support
(Special Educational Needs
Individual Guidance)

Pastoral System

Organisational set-ups
(eg. year groups, houses)

Administration and liaison

Staff tutor roles

Pastoral programmes
(eg. ATW, DWTG)

Para-Curriculum

Hidden curriculum (ethos)

Management structure

Communications

Rewards, sanctions & discipline

Extra-curricular activities

Whole-school policies
(eg. equal opportunities)

Parent and community links

Academic Curriculum

Traditional subjects

Pre-vocational and vocational
courses

Options

Modules and integrated studies

Assessment procedures

Personal, Social & Health Education

publications and courses in the management of pastoral care were, for a long time, the only source of practical support for pastoral staff. Hamblin's chief contribution (1978 and 1984) was to popularise the notion that pastoral care should be centred on students' developmental needs. This meant anticipating the transitions that are an inevitable part of secondary schooling (primary-secondary transfer, option choices, examination entry and so on) and, using a variety of structured materials (checklists, self-assessment schedules, questionnaires, sentence-completion exercises etc.) to prepare students to meet these 'critical incidents' purposively. Hamblin himself hoped that this process would transcend the pastoral-academic divide in schools. But, for many years, the prophylactic role which he advocated was only taken up half-heartedly, the argument frequently being advanced that 'We do it already' or 'It's the job of subject teachers'. Where pastoral work was initiated successfully, as for example in Arthur Rowe's school in Hull, it depended crucially on the goodwill and commitment of the whole community of teachers (Rowe, 1971).

By the end of the 1970s fully worked-out tutorial schemes became available, overlapping and extending Hamblin's work by the addition of substantial group work programmes. These included the Active Tutorial Work scheme (ATW) developed by Jill Baldwin and Harry Wells with teachers in Lancashire, and Leslie Button's pioneering Developmental Group Work programmes, taken up, amongst others, by the ILEA. But in spite of highly professional in-service courses to complement such developments and the enthusiastic welcome they received from some authorities, implementation by the mid-1980s was still piecemeal and haphazard (Bolam and Medlock, 1985).

A parallel and, from the point of view of uptake, more successful set of initiatives was introduced into schools to combat the crisis of growing youth unemployment. Social and life-skills training, school-industry projects, work on employers' premises, and a variety of pre-vocational training courses for 14 to 19 year olds were all part of this package, as we saw in the previous chapter. However, not all observers of the so-called 'new vocationalism' were sanguine about what they saw as the thinly disguised exploitation of young workers and the divorce between techniques and values in their training. Few, at any event, wished to stake a claim for this kind of work within the pastoral sphere. These developments, which have in common a notion of 'preparing young people for adulthood', are discussed in Chapter 9.

Schools organised themselves in different ways to provide a particular diet of tutorial and pre-vocational offerings. But in most (for practical as well as political reasons — including the allocation of scale posts and responsibilities and the vagaries of budgeting and resource allocation), there was a virtually complete separation between academic and pastoral concerns. More recently, following the upheaval caused by the arrival of the DES and the MSC in the forefront of curriculum debates, there has been a move on the part of those formerly involved with pastoral 'care' and active tutorial work to claim a place in the school timetable for work in the so-called 'pastoral curriculum'. This move, signified most publicly by the initiation of the National Association for Pastoral Care in Education (NAPCE) in 1983, is entirely laudable in its attempt to raise the status and professionalism of practitioners in the field. It also reflects a valid concern to avoid splitting the 'care' and 'control' elements of educational guidance. Unfortunately, thinking about what constitutes the 'pastoral' as opposed to an 'academic' or 'subject' curriculum has been somewhat muddled. In some quarters this has led to the mistaken belief that, while the former is solely about 'process', the academic curriculum is exclusively concerned with 'content'.

The issue for us is where PSHE stands in relation to these pastoral and vocational developments. Clearly there is no one right answer. In fact, given the importance of leadership for effective work in the pastoral field, there are likely to be as many different detailed answers as there are schools operating developed pastoral systems. There are also likely to be differences depending on whether the school in question is a community college, with a mini-school approach; a school with a full- or part-modular curriculum; or a more traditional kind of organisation.

The view we take about the location of PSHE is based on a particular view of society and schooling which we have already outlined. However, in what follows, although we may appear to be advocating a particular 'right place' for PSHE, this is only in order to clarify the distinctions in purpose between what we take to be the different elements along the pastoral-academic continuum. These range from pastoral casework at one extreme, through the pastoral curriculum, PSHE and vocational training, to 'pure' academic work. We are fully aware that in individual schools labels may be used differently, so it might be the case that PSHE could be found in Biology, in English or in PE, just as easily as in a child development course or community service programme. Our point is that it is important to be clear about intentions and about the principles underlying work in different parts of the curriculum. It is also necessary to be conscious of the potential contradictions (and genuine differences) between the underlying values of pastoral, vocational and academic work.

PASTORAL CASEWORK

Pastoral casework involves responding to individual students' needs for support and guidance. These needs may be disciplinary, emotional or behavioural and they may arise from material hardship, from ethnic or cultural differences, from physical handicaps or from learning difficulties (or, frequently, from a mixture of all of these). In most schools front-line responsibility for pastoral casework, as for the more routine aspects of pastoral administration on which it depends, is carried by the registration tutor. It is her job, by observing and getting to know students on a day-to-day basis, to anticipate difficulties, respond to referrals from colleagues, initiate any counselling or remediation procedures and communicate with parents. More 'serious' pastoral matters are dealt with by senior staff, who, in addition, are responsible for liaison with out-of-school welfare agencies.

Given the Warnock Committee's widely accepted estimate (DES, 1978b) that, at some point in their school career, one child in five will exhibit a difficulty requiring special support, pastoral casework is clearly vital. Indeed, it is the very heart of what we understand by the pastoral task of the school. However, given the individual emphasis of pastoral casework (which is perfectly proper in terms of its own objectives), we do not believe that it should be confused with PSHE (or vice versa). Through the process of individual guidance and support, it may happen that students are helped towards a healthier personal adjustment. *En route*, they may also gain insight into themselves and into their social relationships. The danger is that they are likely to learn more about normative roles and adjustments than they do about creativity and critical judgement. They may also miss the opportunity to learn about the value of collaborative experiences. What is worse, they may be subject to the process that Williamson (1980) has termed 'pastoralisation', or find that the pastoral system acts as a labelling agency, 'officially confirming deviant identity' (Guthrie, 1979). For as Armstrong (1985), like several other commentators, has noted:

what the pastoral system is actually doing as contrasted with what its intentions are, may be just to socialise the children into the particular educational and institutional regime of the school and/or to compensate those children who are unable readily to fit in with that regime for themselves.

THE PARA-CURRICULUM

We will interrupt our discussion of PSHE and the pastoral-academic continuum here to consider its relationship with the para-curriculum. As we saw in Figure 3.6, the para-curriculum underpins every aspect of school life. It embraces the management and disciplinary structures, the hidden curriculum or ethos of the school, its programme of extra-curricular activities, its links with the community and so on.

The significant thing to point out here is the way relationships in both the pastoral and the academic curriculum contribute to (and are reflections of) the para-curriculum. Anne Jones (1984), one of the two counsellors appointed to Mayfield School in Putney in 1965 and later head of a community school in outer London, explains the relationship in this way:

In teaching we often fail to realize how many 'non-verbal' messages our institution will convey to its users. Nor do we always realize to what extent our users may be sensitive to contradictions between our stated objectives and what actually happens. For example, a school may claim to like and

75

respect its pupils, to value them, to wish to encourage their full development. Yet the organization of the school may spell out mistrust, the curriculum may stifle any active learning or any real growth and development in the individual, the relationship between staff and pupils may be based on fear or indifference, rather than love or commitment. We trust you; but we can't allow you to do anything for yourself in case you get it wrong. We want to prepare you for an adult role; in the mean time you must do as we say when we say it. We welcome parents; but only by appointment and preferably at our command.

Other features of school organisation, for example, the use of assemblies and school councils; attitudes to homework and lateness; the range and vitality of extra-curricular activities and community links; the value placed on the school's physical environment (public spaces, fabric and decorations, toilets and outdoor recreation facilities); the use of relevant community languages; anti-racist and anti-sexist policies and opportunities for genuine parental involvement, are also important (Hoyle, 1986). Positive discipline (Watkins and Wagner, 1987), is another crucial feature which, for some, is synonymous with effective pastoral care (Clemett and Pearce, 1986). In our view, even at their most sensitive, the pastoral qualities of the para-curriculum are not a substitute for a formal programme of learning activities to support students' personal and social development; a point reinforced by David (1983):

> The complexities of a changing society make it essential that schools attempt to develop all the inner resources of students, emotional as well as intellectual. This development cannot be achieved in an *ad hoc* manner, or by dependence on the ethos of the school alone. It requires constructive thinking and planning, and properly structured programmes.

Such programmes might be expected to exist within the so-called 'pastoral curriculum'. However, there is little consensus about what the pastoral curriculum actually contains.

THE PASTORAL CURRICULUM

We have already outlined some typical features of the pastoral system: discipline and sanctions, organisational set-ups like year and house groups, routine administration and liaison tasks and links with parents. Here we shall move on to a consideration of the so-called 'pastoral curriculum'. Marland who first coined the term in 1980, six years after the publication of his influential book, *Pastoral Care*, conceives the pastoral curriculum in an eclectic sense:

> My argument is that the individual 'personal, educational and vocational guidance' of a school's pastoral work has to be prepared for by a

'pastoral curriculum' which is devised to teach the underlying facts, concepts, attitudes and skills required by the individual for personal and social development, and also for any individual guidance. This whole-school pastoral curriculum is then divided amongst subject and pastoral teams. That which is reserved for the latter is called the 'pastoral' and within that is the scheme of work for tutors in their group sessions, and this is the 'tutorial programme'. (in Lang and Marland, 1985)

What this definition fails to make clear is how that which belongs specifically to the pastoral curriculum is to be distinguished from that belonging to other areas. Here Elliott tries to be more helpful. Replying to McLaughlin in a debate on 'The idea of a pastoral curriculum' (reprinted in the *Cambridge Journal of Education* (1982), he suggests that the pastoral curriculum ties up with the idea of a liberal education:

It seems to me that helping pupils to clarify the values imposed by the social situations they typically confront, or are likely to confront in the future, and helping them to explore the implications of alternative options with respect to the ways of life involved, ought to have priority in planning the liberal education.

However, this only moves the problem to a different place. We are now left trying to define what we mean by a liberal education — a task unresolved in spite of several centuries of debate.

For us, a safer conception of the pastoral curriculum is one which sticks to Hamblin's skills emphasis and ties it to 'preparing pupils for the various "decisions and adjustments facing them in their lives"' (McLaughlin, 1982), although many would no doubt feel this is again either too vague or too restrictive. McLaughlin himself certainly prefers a less instrumental view and, while admitting that 'there is no one clear usage of the term "pastoral curriculum"', argues that it in fact belongs within Personal and Social Education. Here we come full circle in the discussion. Whatever we conclude (and clearly there is no agreed position still), it is evident that — wherever the boundaries lie — given the focus of the pastoral curriculum on aspects of adolescents' personal and social development, this is an area of work whose aims and pedagogy are bound to overlap very closely with those of PSHE.

Consider this list of pastoral aims (Davies, 1986), which very clearly illustrates the overlap:

· to assist the individual to enrich his or her personal life,
· to help prepare the young person for educational choice,
· to offer guidance or counselling to bring about autonomous action,
· to support the subject teaching,

· to assist the individual to develop his or her own life-style, and to respect that of others,
· to maintain an orderly atmosphere in which all this is possible.

To clarify your understanding of the relationship between the pastoral curriculum and PSHE, you might try to distinguish the extent of agreement between pastoral and PSHE aims in your own school. Our own hesitation about wishing PSHE to be seen as part of the pastoral curriculum arises from several considerations. Before elaborating these, however, we should like to acknowledge the really valuable impact made on schools by schemes such as ATW and DWTG — both on the pastoral curriculum and on approaches to teaching generally. Our first reservation has to do with the use of the prefix 'pastoral'. This carries a number of connotations, both in image and in reality. One of these relates to the fact that in most schools the identity and status of pastoral work is distinctly secondary. Compared to academic and even vocational departments, time and training are minimal, and tutors are given little guidance in their tasks: a matter to which HMI have frequently drawn attention, as O'Sullivan points out (1987). Reviewing a random selection of 28 HMI reports on schools visited during 1982 and 1983, he found their opinion was that:

The pastoral period is a blank beginning to the school day for the majority of pupils, who merely fill the time with incidental talk or reading.

and:

An agreed policy is needed to provide suitable content which might make a direct contribution to the personal and social development of the pupils.

Another index of the marginal status accorded pastoral work in most schools is the fact that appointments rarely specify pastoral qualifications. What is more, if redeployment issues arise, subject qualifications are again the prime determinant of who moves. This means that generally, even where staff do contribute to worthwhile pastoral/tutorial programmes, there is a notorious difficulty of guaranteeing adequate training, timetable space and resources. What is more, in the short term, there appears to be little prospect of this situation improving. According to a survey conducted by Jeanette Raymond in 1982 (see Figure 3.7), most tutors find that their tutorial time is dominated by administrative tasks.

A more serious difficulty for work within the pastoral curriculum is that here, more starkly than elsewhere perhaps, we meet the existence of tensions such as those outlined in the last chapter. In particular there is a contradiction between the generally conservative and regulative concerns of pastoral staff and the demands placed upon them by a pedagogy which focuses on active learning. Thus, messages conveyed by teachers in their tutoring role risk being compromised by the normative, control-oriented values of their managerial

Figure 3.7: Functions Carried Out by Form Tutors

Actual Rank	Functions	Ideal Rank
1	Administrative duties	13 =
2	Act as a source of discipline	12
3	Develop close relationships with pupils	5
4	Provide individual counselling for pupils	1
5	Develop positive attitudes towards school	6
6	Help pupils develop problem-solving skills	2
7	Give out school notices	13 =
8	Develop good study habits in pupils	9
9	Develop independence and maturity in pupils	7 =
10	Foster good peer relationships among students	10 =
11	Ensure no serious problems arise in the future by ensuring good coping strategies	3
12	Develop coping strategies that can be used outside the school environment	4
13	Develop a thorough understanding of the school as an institution	10 =
14	Develop self-awareness among pupils	7 =

Source: adapted from Raymond, 1982

position. This is especially likely given the lack of academic rigour in some tutorial programmes. As John Quicke (1985) observes, describing a section on trade unions from ATW book 5:

> it is not just 'skills' which are being taught. The pupil will learn that knowledge about trade unions is on a par with preparing a curriculum vitae, constructing an interview checklist, form filling and other career guidance activities which constitute the rest of the term's work. He or she will also learn that 'political awareness' is a skill which described thus does not therefore involve a great deal of reflection or thought and by implication is not something which is connected with the fundamentals of his or her existence. The whole effect is to dilute the topic and keep discussion on a personal level.

There are perhaps two problems here: (i) the generally weak intellectual nature of the materials and (ii) the inflexible way in which they are sometimes used. This was a feature commented upon by the organiser of the Birmingham Young Volunteers Project (Sames in Brown *et al.*, 1986). Sames writes that, in spite of some very real excitement when staff came across active tutorial work, 'the books, as they appeared to be widely used, gave pupils very little control over what they wanted to learn'. Given other pressures on their time and a general lack of confidence, it is not surprising that tutors should use the ATW books rather rigidly. However, a 'we know what's best for you' approach, which ignores students' needs and interests by presuming a fixed route through each term's course, is anathema to the goals of PSHE.

79

A third difficulty about work within the pastoral curriculum arises from another feature of the ATW approach: its potential for being personally intrusive and emotionally damaging, particularly in the hands of untrained practitioners. For example, consider the extent to which 'success' in ATW work is bound up with self-disclosure and energetic participation in a whole variety of 'trust' and 'sharing' activities. What does it mean not to succeed in a trust walk or not to wish to contribute to a class discussion? Why, if you are a black student, should you have to trust everybody? Or, if you are handicapped, have to disclose your feelings of embarrassment or loss? There are clearly difficulties here for some groups of students as well as for individuals who are withdrawn, isolated, shy or linguistically inept. A related difficulty is the tendency for pastoral issues to become over-personalised. Thus, the focus on finding individual meanings and examining individual social situations can lead to students feeling that all of their life has to be analysed in these terms. Such an approach ignores the influence of wider political and economic realities, and risks leaving students with the feeling that they are to blame if aspects of their experience diverge from the 'norm'. As one observer comments:

I think it possible that some of our pupils' lives — and problems — are difficult, if not impossible, to cope with, and that it would be inappropriate to imply that we 'blame the victim', or to suggest that the child alone can affect his/her social situation. (Fiehn, 1986)

There may be some interesting parallels to note here for the emerging profiling movement. In common with many ATW activities, formative profiling potentially offers exciting opportunities for students to learn about themselves and to determine new learning objectives. However, they require handling with the utmost sensitivity and in full awareness of the politicial messages they can convey. The chief danger is of teachers adopting — either consciously or unconsciously — normative expectations about what students should be doing or feeling and of overemphasising the value of consensus solutions. PSHE is explicitly not aimed at these goals, as Bernard Davies (1979) insists:

PSE is not about adjustment to the status quo. It is more about understanding the nature of the status quo and alternative views about social action in relation to the existing order. There is a critical thrust to education which is absent from the socialization approach of much pastoral work.

There are a variety of problems, then, in identifying PSHE too closely with a pastoral label; none of which deny the importance of individual pastoral casework or of suitably structured tutorial work which prepares students to meet the critical incidents which Hamblin and others have identified. Part of the problem is perhaps semantic, as one writer has commented:

It is almost quaint that a term used to describe the often hectic and usually critical work of the head of year or house in an urban secondary school derives from the work of a clergyman, has the ideology of a shepherd and the visual imagery of an idealized rural scene. (Cooper, 1984)

However, the fact is that labels matter and usually only exist where they have some legitimacy. That the pastoral label has stuck must be because it has recognisable currency. From the point of view of PSHE — or any activity which is about academic as well as personal learning — this is a real source of difficulty because the welfare connotations of pastoral work are in direct opposition to those of a liberal education. Jones articulates some of what he terms the static dimensions of pastoral welfare:

1. Welfare reinforces the perception of a child as being weak or vulnerable
2. Welfare creates a relationship of dependency
3. Welfare is associated with the distribution of largesse
4. Welfare is only for a small group of children
5. Welfare tends to be a crisis response
6. Welfare is not preventive
(in Ribbins, 1985)

Such orientations do not belong in the territory of PSHE as we have described it. But, as Jones concedes, welfare can have a dynamic and preventive aspect. In curriculum terms, this implies flexibility and negotiable learning objectives, which, as we shall see in Chapter 6, are precisely what characterise teaching in PSHE. One key to the distinction between pastoral concerns and PSHE, then, lies in this active orientation.

LOCATING PSHE ALONG THE PASTORAL-ACADEMIC CONTINUUM

Where PSHE is located depends critically on the way it (and pastoral matters) are interpreted in a particular school and what its intentions are. As we have seen, pastoral and tutorial work tend to be conceived in a managerial or welfare sense. They thus have specific connotations for students (and parents) and specific boundaries. On the whole, although we would concede some areas of overlap, we do not believe that PSHE and work in the pastoral curriculum possess the same orientation or necessarily share identical values.

There is an argument which says that PSHE requires a pastoral location because it is best taught by tutors. However, this case sometimes appears to be made more in terms of the needs of the pastoral system than in those of PSHE. Watkins (1985), for example, argues that:

If schools develop PSE in a relatively narrow way ... without engaging pastoral heads of section, a consequence is likely to be that the role of Head of Year/House will remain subject to the forces which distort and marginalise it into a demand-led, event-led crisis management.

This may be a valid point but surely it is not a reason for restraining efforts to develop PSHE more effectively. In any case, it does presuppose — as, for present purposes, we have done — the traditional curriculum set-up. In future, if an increasing number of schools switch to various forms of modular or unit-based curricula and negotiable learning packages, the whole notion of the pastoral-academic split will need rethinking. The advantage of more integrated curricula, amongst other things, is that the rather spurious content/process divide which at present separates academic and pastoral work in many people's minds should evaporate. This would mean that the frequently mentioned difficulty of work in the pastoral curriculum lacking intellectual rigour is less likely to exist. It should also mean that method and content are both clearly focused on realistic, short-term goals and not, as so frequently happens at present, separated. That, at any rate, is the hope. The reality, under some form of National Curriculum, may be disappointingly different.

CONCLUSION

Returning to the reality that most teachers know, we will finally set out our thoughts about the location of PSHE. Because Figure 3.8 does this in the form of a continuum, it is perhaps easier to see the way in which pastoral, vocational and academic activities interpenetrate. It also emphasises the importance of the para-curriculum.

As well as pointing to the overlap between pastoral, vocational and academic concerns, Figure 3.8 illustrates the divergence in their underlying goals. It is this fundamental difference in orientation which makes us uneasy about too close an identity between PSHE and the pastoral system. The concepts, content and methodologies of PSHE are examined more fully in Chapters 5 and 6. For the moment all we would wish to emphasise is the importance of PSHE not being confused with the compensatory and control-oriented values of the pastoral system (included in many so-called pastoral curricula). Our view is that, whatever model or PERM of PSHE teachers adopt, it merits a rigorous, analytical approach and a separate place in the curriculum. To achieve this, teachers themselves need to be rigorous and analytic about the purposes and assumptions underlying their work.

Figure 3.9 illustrates the results of an exercise designed to help uncover the deeper implications of a particular piece of work: a group rock exercise. You might like to go through a similar process for some of the activities which you use. Starting with a blank sheet of paper on which there are two concentric

Figure 3.8: The Pastoral-Academic Continuum

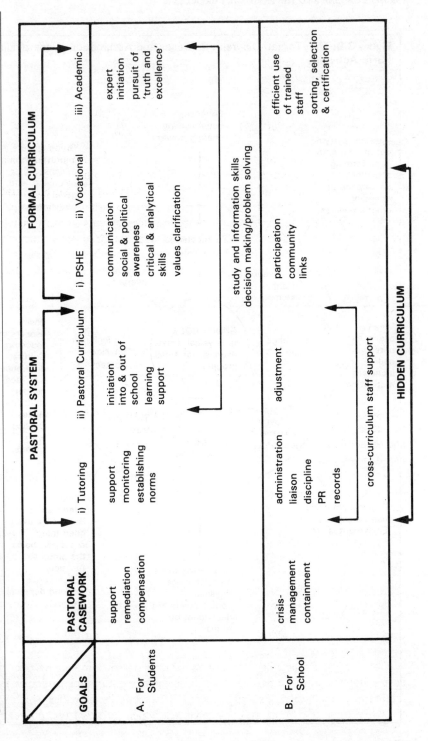

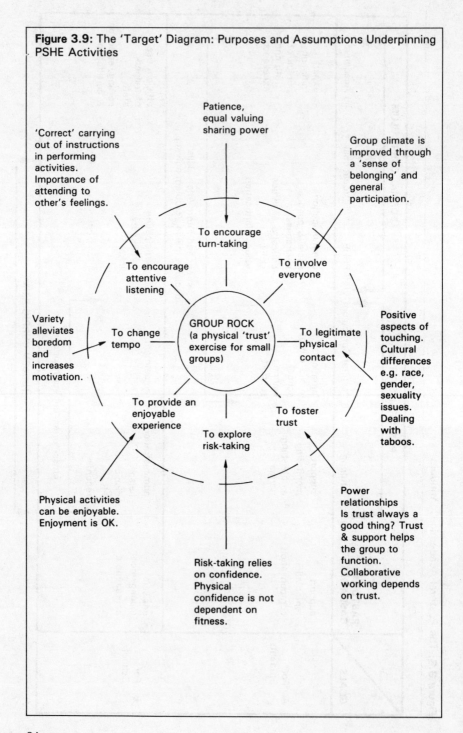

Figure 3.9: The 'Target' Diagram: Purposes and Assumptions Underpinning PSHE Activities

Patience, equal valuing sharing power

'Correct' carrying out of instructions in performing activities. Importance of attending to other's feelings.

Group climate is improved through a 'sense of belonging' and general participation.

To encourage turn-taking

To encourage attentive listening

To involve everyone

Variety alleviates boredom and increases motivation.

To change tempo

GROUP ROCK (a physical 'trust' exercise for small groups)

To legitimate physical contact

Positive aspects of touching. Cultural differences e.g. race, gender, sexuality issues. Dealing with taboos.

To provide an enjoyable experience

To foster trust

To explore risk-taking

Physical activities can be enjoyable. Enjoyment is OK.

Power relationships Is trust always a good thing? Trust & support helps the group to function. Collaborative working depends on trust.

Risk-taking relies on confidence. Physical confidence is not dependent on fitness.

circles, write in the inner circle the name of the particular activity: for example, group discussion, blind walk, group sculpt, decision-making simulation. Inside the outer circle, write the purposes of the activity. Finally, around the outside, jot down some notes on the implied underlying values/assumptions of the exercise. As Figure 3.9 demonstrates, this can be a very revealing process. It is also a great help in designing relevant teaching strategies.

Another aspect of working out appropriate strategies for PSHE involves taking account of students' cognitive and social/emotional needs. This is the subject of Chapter 4.

FURTHER READING

Bell, P. and Best, R. (1986) *Supportive education: an integrated response to pastoral care and special needs*, Blackwell, Oxford

Best, R. *et al.* (eds) (1980) *Perspectives on pastoral care*, Heinemann Educational, London

Bolam, R. and Medlock, P. (1985) *Active tutorial work: training and dissemination — an evaluation*, Blackwell for the Health Education Council, Oxford

Brown, C. *et al.* (1986) *Social education: principles and practice*, Falmer, Lewes

Draper, P. (1980) 'Three types of health education', *British Medical Journal*, 16.8.80, pp. 493–5

Hamblin, D. (1986) *A pastoral programme*, Blackwell, Oxford

Jenks, J. (1984) *The role of health education in the integration of personal and social education in the secondary school*, unpublished paper for ILEA, 10.4.84

Lang, P. and Marland, M. (eds) (1985) *New directions in pastoral care*, Falmer, Lewes

McNiff, J. (1985) *Personal and social education: a teacher's handbook*, CRAC/Hobsons Press, Cambridge

Quicke, J. (1985) 'Charting a course for personal and social education', *Pastoral care in education*, vol. 3, no. 2, pp. 91–9

Ribbins, P. (ed.) (1985) *Schooling and welfare*, Blackwell, Oxford

Williams, T. (1986) 'School health education 15 years on', *Health Education Journal*, vol. 45, no. 1, pp. 3–7

4

The Needs of Adolescents

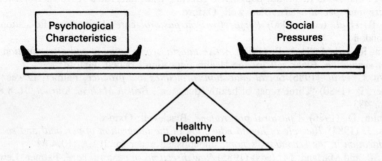

In this chapter we turn to the fourth stage of Lawton's cultural analysis model: psychological questions about adolescents and their learning. Our main concern is the connection between perceptions of students' needs and practice in PSHE. As well as the basic question: 'What are the needs of students?' there are important corollaries:

who determines these needs?
how are they decided?
are they problematic?
whose responsibility is it to address them, and how?

Following these questions is that of the particular role of PSHE. The chapter draws on an array of theoretical literature relating to young people but focuses, wherever possible, on its practical implications. The words adolescents and adolescence are used throughout, in spite of the fact that interpretations differ. Our usage simply denotes a period of transition between childhood and adulthood, commonly associated with the years of secondary schooling. Sections of the chapter will examine the arguments for different kinds of demarcation for this period and the identification of its distinguishing features.

FINDING OUT ABOUT ADOLESCENT NEEDS

Before discussing the phenomenon of adolescence, the purpose of this chapter needs to be re-emphasised: the determination of students' needs. The most obvious means of finding these out is to ask students themselves. This is not as simple, or as trite, as it sounds. The method of asking: using interviews, questionnaires, postal surveys, and the size of the sample approached influence the results enormously (which, for instance, is more reliable — a single, in-depth interview or a thousand anonymous replies to a closed question?). Teachers should be mindful of such potential sources of distortion in their own information-gathering but also when considering the conclusions of other researchers, including those cited here. The appropriateness of research methodology may depend on the predilections, skills, circumstances or source of funding of the researcher, as well as its 'fit' with a particular theoretical paradigm. Within PSHE, for example, there is a trend away from large-scale surveys to less generalisable but more probing methods, such as case studies. Choice of method can also affect the way results are interpreted: for instance, over the question of responsibility for meeting student needs.

Perhaps the best course is to be cautious about prescriptive conclusions and to look for areas of similarity from different sources of data. Working with your own classes, you could use the findings of large-scale surveys, such as HMSO (1983), a Young Guardian feature in the Guardian (7.1.87), Allen (1987), as a trigger for discussion and then compare the results with those arising from more personal and open-ended techniques. It is clearly useful to be aware of general patterns and tendencies but, ultimately, we have to deal with individual students and their unique concerns and experiences.

Another, often undervalued, source of information about the needs and concerns of young people is ourselves. We were all adolescents once! Many teachers have found it helpful to recall some of their own thoughts and feelings during this period. The structured fantasy exercise (p. 88) helps focus such recollections. It may also help you to reflect on any connections between the way you felt about yourself as an adolescent and the way you perceive and relate to adolescents now, and your reasons for choosing to work with them as a teacher. The intention is not to transpose your personal memories on to the concerns of today's young people but to reflect more deeply on the unique quality of your individual recollections in order to empathise more accurately with the adolescents you teach.

IS ADOLESCENCE A DISTINCT STAGE IN LIFE?

Evidence for the existence of adolescence as a distinguishable period derives from several sources: history, literature, the media, empirical research and theory. As the authors of the Latey Committee pointed out reporting the arguments for a change in the voting age in 1967, youth, as opposed to

Exercise 4.1: Being an Adolescent

Instructions:
This exercise is ideally one for use in a group. However, it can be attempted in part even on your own.

1. Individually:
Think back to when you were a 15 year old. Imagine yourself sitting at a desk in a particular fourth-year lesson. Try to recreate as much of the experience as possible: the arrangement of furniture; the writing on the blackboard; any decoration on the walls; the quality of the lighting; views from the windows; noises; smells; the other students around you; a particular teacher; the lesson you were involved in, and how you felt about it all. What were your chief interests and preoccupations? How did you feel about yourself and about your classmates? Write down ten adjectives (more if they occur to you) describing the kind of person you were then. (5 mins)

2. In pairs:
i) Compare your lists and discuss why you chose the particular kinds of adjectives you did. Are these words you would have chosen yourself at the time or are they words other people used to describe you? Are they words that you are using from the perspective of how you see yourself now? (10 mins)
ii) Group the adjectives according to the area of life they concern (e.g. emotional, intellectual, family, social, sexual) and rank them in terms of their importance to you then. Consider which you would rate positively and which you felt more negatively about. (10 mins)

3. Whole group:
Compare the range of preoccupations and concerns reported and compare their importance in different people's lives. What are the similarities and differences based on? If you had to repeat the exercise on behalf of students you teach in the fourth year now, how different do you think the second list would be from your own? Why? What are the implications of all this, if any, for you as a teacher, and as a teacher of PSHE in particular? (10 mins)

childhood, has been castigated throughout history. Contemporary writing is in much the same vein. But is adolescence, in fact, merely a social construction?

Conger and Petersen (1984) contend that the 'era of adolescence' began at the turn of the century when increased industrialisation and educational provision greatly extended the time young people spent with their peers. As Aries (1962) points out, such segregation is not only relatively recent, it is a facet of particular social mores which are not shared in all cultures, even within British society. This points to a deficit in existing research: is adolescence perceived in similar ways by different ethnic groups and, if not, what account do teachers take of the differences? Whether adolescence exists cross-culturally or not, it is the case that in the post-war years the period of dependency has increased as a consequence of such factors as the extended length of formal schooling, the earlier onset of puberty and higher living standards. Anomalies in legislation to do with assumptions of formal maturity — voting, age of sexual consent, driving and drinking ages and so on — are enough to cause confusion as to the legal rights and responsibilities of adulthood. This is exacerbated by increased commercial pressures exhorting young people to conform to particular life-styles — in terms of fashion, make-up, music, movies, magazines and television programmes. In some ways teenagers have more options open to them than ever and yet the complexity of our rites of passage are a source of confusion and conflict.

The first theoretical approach to the study of adolescence came from Hall in 1904 (Conger and Petersen, 1984). Despite the subsequent discrediting of many of his conclusions, his writings were widely accepted, as, for example, by the authors of the Hadow Report (1926). This, for the first time, focused on the education of adolescents as a distinct and separate phase. More recently, Coleman (1980) has criticised the view of adolescence as a 'special' phenomenon because of the lack of empirical evidence. He prefers to describe it as a transitional, dynamic process between childhood and maturity, claiming that this interpretation is supported by the findings of the markedly increased amount of research about young people conducted since the 1960s. This shift in perspective is probably not unconnected with the research methodologies employed. Thus, the recent use of large-scale surveys as opposed to individual studies is more likely to emphasise the diversity of adolescents and their development than their shared characteristics.

A different approach to the question of whether adolescence exists is to consider whether young people's needs are any different from anyone else's. Kelmer-Pringle (1980), after analysing the National Children's Bureau Study, suggests:

There are four basic emotional needs which have to be met from the very beginning of life to enable a child to grow from helpless infancy to mature adulthood. These are: the need for love and security; for new experiences; for praise and recognition; and for responsibility. Their relative importance changes ... during the different stages of growth as do the ways in which they are met.

Maslow (1968), from a psychological perspective, proposed a hierarchy of needs, summarised as follows:

Physiological	— food, water, sleep, touch sensations, etc.
Safety	— anticipation of danger, avoiding pain or harm, seeking protection, etc.
Love and belonging	— loving others, being approved of, group membership, adopting roles, etc.

| Esteem | — responding, being appreciated and applauded, need for hierarchies and stability, etc. |
| Self-actualisation | — consistency, standards, conscience, respecting own and others' identities, confidence in self, creativity, responsibility, allowing peak experiences, empowerment of self and others, etc. |

Given the respective aims of 'mature adulthood' and 'self-actualisation', there are similarities between these lists which could be translated into a core of needs to be addressed by schools. Is this, though, primarily a task for teachers, given the heterogeneity of students and the likelihood that some students will never fully achieve such aims? Would young people themselves recognise or express such needs? Winnicott (1971) argues that, while young people should be given the space to express themselves, the real needs of adolescents should not be confounded with assertions about whay they think they need. How can teachers decide? Here again we would advocate balance. Teachers can and do negotiate with students on the basis of shared respect for different perspectives, balancing wider social and educational priorities against individual needs and concerns. Indeed, this type of negotiation is a feature of the sort of PSHE practice which we value.

The remainder of this chapter focuses on features of adolescence to help elucidate the contribution PSHE can make to meeting students' needs. Whether adolescence is clearly demarcated has not been resolved. However, Coleman's notion of adolescence as a transition phase (similar to but different in detail from other passages of life) is useful in terms of its implications for PSHE, so we shall continue from this basis.

Exercise 4.2, the Salmon Line, which derives from personal construct theory, can be used by both adults and young people to clarify their perceptions of adolescent needs. Note that, although the exercise assumes progressive developmental gains, it is possible (even likely) that some adolescents, at some stages, will actually regress in their behaviour. It is the overall developmental pattern which matters for the exercise.

THEORETICAL PERSPECTIVES ON ADOLESCENCE

There have been two distinct theoretical perspectives on adolescence which, although complementary, give rise to different interpretations of adolescent needs and, hence, to different views of who is responsible for 'successful' emergence into adulthood.

Exercise 4.2: Determining Adolescent Needs: the Salmon Line

Childhood _____ Adulthood
    1   2   3   4   5   6   7

Instructions:

1. Thinking about a group of students you know well, place three sets of initials at 1 on the line above; three sets of initials at 7; one set of initials at 4.

2. List your criteria for locating pupils at these points on the chart below:
   Point 1 criteria   *Point 4 criteria*   *Point 7 criteria*

3. Identify those achievements/developmental tasks pupils would need to accomplish in moving from 1 to 4 and 4 to 7.
   Achievements for 1 to 4 shift   *Achievements for 4 to 7 shift*

4. Where are you on this scale? What else do you need to accomplish?

Acknowledgements to Dr P. Salmon

1. The Biological Perspective

The biological or psychoanalytic perspective highlights adolescent features which are a result of physiological and concomitant psychological changes. Early proponents of this view, such as Gessell (1956), stressed the genetic determinism of adolescent behaviour. More recent investigators, such as Erikson (1968), accept environmental influences as being important too. Overall, the biological perspective has a number of characteristics. First, the effects of puberty, in terms of adjustment to physical and hormonal changes, are emphasised. Second, it is suggested that the physically mature adolescent experiences changes in his relationships with parents and friends which lead to increased vulnerability and confusion. There may be feelings of loss concerning the previous parent-dependent relationship and ambivalence over the independence associated with increased reliance on peers. Such contradictory emotions can cause fluctuations and inconsistencies in mood. Accordingly, erratic or non-conforming adolescent behaviours can be seen either as inadequate psychological defence mechanisms or, more positively, as coping strategies to deal with inner conflict. Finally, adolescence is seen as a time of identity crisis when young people must resolve fundamental issues about their unique personalities, this process of self-analysis being a necessary step to maturity.

Most advocates of the biological view of adolescence have been psychotherapists working in clinic or hospital settings; for example, Freud (1937) and Blos (1962). This may account for the emphasis on concepts like *'Sturm und Drang'* (storm and stress). Another problem, pinpointed by Beckett (1986) is the virtually exclusive emphasis of this kind of research on boys and their experiences. The result has been, until recently (see Eichenbaum and Orbach, 1983 and 1985), an inadequate portrayal of adolescent development for both genders, but particularly for young women — and for members of minority cultural and ethnic groups.

2. The Cultural Perspective

The cultural, or sociological, perspective emphasises external factors as the prime determinants of adolescent behaviour. This approach has been supported by anthropological studies of cultures, such as those described by Mead (1928), Benedict (1934) and Bettelheim (1969), in which the experience of adolescence is very different from that in the United States or Britain. Working from the premise that behaviour at adolescence, as at every other stage of life, is culturally determined, the key notions which these theorists adopt are those of 'socialisation' and social 'roles'. They suggest that individuals absorb the values and beliefs of the society in the process of growing up, in both family and community settings, adapting behaviour according to others' expectations of what is 'normal' in given roles (e.g. being a son, a school pupil, a brother, a British-born child of Muslim parents and so on). For an individual, the effectiveness of the socialisation process is indicated by the ease with which such roles can be assumed without conflict or internal disonnance. During childhood, roles are ascribed by 'significant others' like parents and teachers, but throughout adolescence, young people begin to reject and select roles according to their own predilections as well as in response to social pressures. For some, there may be conflict, for instance, between parental norms and expectations and those of the peer group and its culture. It is also likely that some roles will need to be adjusted or changed in emphasis; for example, when the 'local cricketing hero' becomes the 'diligent student' to meet increased study demands. As Elder (1968) points out, given our rapidly changing society, adolescents have a mulitiplicity of roles to juggle with and repeated choices and adjustments to make.

Although the two theoretical perspectives on adolescence which we have outlined are similar in describing adolescence as a time of stress, they have different implications for the assessment of adolescent needs and related teaching strategies.

IMPLICATIONS OF THE BIOLOGICAL AND PSYCHOLOGICAL PERSPECTIVES ON ADOLESCENCE

The *psychoanalytic approach* focuses on individual behaviour and extrapolates from this to general norms. Supporting evidence comes from case studies, often of 'non-conforming' adolescents. Needs are seen as universal and relatively predictable according to age and stage of development. Personalities are not immutable but personal development takes place largely as a result of individual motivation and effort. Ideally, an adult emerges with a strong sense of who he is and what he wants to do (identity formation).

On this view, the appropriate teaching strategy is to address adolescent needs by fostering personal coping skills to deal with internal conflict. Adolescents should therefore be encouraged (through personal education?) to recognise sources of tension and to take responsibility for resolving any personal problems. Parents and teachers have a responsibility to clarify the physiological and psychological nature of disturbances, to encourage 'normal' behaviour (using punishment and rewards) to help young people develop feasible coping strategies and to foster feelings of significance and self-esteem. Specific health education would help adolescents gain insight into the motivations for their own health-related behaviour.

The *cultural approach* interprets adolescents' needs in terms of social pressures. Crises or confusions are seen, not so much as inevitable facets of growing up, but as a result of societal changes. Gender, race, class and sexuality are highly significant issues as are particular national and community concerns, such as education and training, unemployment and nuclear war. Young people's 'problems' are directly related to wider controversies and conflicting values in society.

The appropriate educational response on this view might be for students to examine (through social education?) the structures of society and to develop a critical awareness of their own socialisation, perhaps comparing it with that in other cultures. Parents and teachers have a responsibility to monitor their own practice in terms of role expectations and the socialising of adolescents, to clarify codes of practice, to help young people develop adaptive skills and to foster feelings of collaborative power leading to self-esteem. A health education programme would eschew the 'victim-blaming' approach and encourage adolescents to weigh up the strengths of different influences on their health-related behaviour.

THE BALANCED APPROACH WITHIN PSHE

As we have shown, both theories of adolescence offer insights into how young people's needs might be met. A balanced view, acknowledging both biological and cultural perspectives, sees adolescence as a 'psycho-social phenomenon' (Wall, 1977) and emphasises the interdependence of psychological and social influences. As Lewin (1951) makes clear, behaviour is a function of the inter-relationship between an individual and his environment. For instance, is the assumed preoccupation of adolescents with their own image a manifestation of anxieties over pubertal changes, a feature of role ambiguity, a direct result of media pressure or a physiological artefact derived from adults' assumptions and envies? As Rosenberg (1965) shows it is probably all four, and more.

Within PSHE each of these considerations is relevant and needs to be addressed. Putting it simply, psychological and sociological perspectives on adolescent needs can be viewed as poles of a continuum with personal and social education providing a complementary rationale for meeting them. Personal education, focusing on individual reflective psychology can help students understand 'what makes them tick' and, perhaps, foster their self-esteem. Social education, by examining relationships between groupings of people can increase understanding of 'their place in the world' and, perhaps, foster self-respect. (For a fuller discussion of the differences between self-esteem and self-respect, see Sachs, 1982).

In the past ten years, health education has encompassed both personal and social dimensions and has been the vehicle, through its content and methods, by which their contributions have been kept in balance. For example, it has taken account of individual motivations and social influences, using teaching strategies such as personal reflection and community-based action research. A further unique element of the health education contribution has been with regard to peer group influences. These have usually been viewed as 'problematic', with several health education programmes exploring strategies for 'saying no' to friends, for example. However, more recently, work such as that of Dorn and Nortoft (1982) has recognised the value of adolescents' sub-cultural affiliations and has encouraged recognition of group norms. This is of paramount importance when considering the PSHE needs of young people in relation to gender, class and race. Roles, expectations, developmental stages, cultural norms of behaviour and health are all likely to vary widely in any mixed class of adolescents. Increase in self-esteem is unlikely if such differences are dismissed or ignored. On the other hand, there may be some common features of adolescent experience which also need to be recognised. These are examined in the next section.

COMMON FEATURES OF ADOLESCENCE

The physical features of adolescent development associated with increased maturity and puberty: adult bone structure and dentition, reproductive functioning, secondary sexual characteristics and so on, are undoubtedly 'real'. But while all adolescents go through these changes they do so at different rates and at different chronological ages. The integration of children with special educational needs requires particular sensitivity in this respect. To ignore students' individuality, and the considerable variations in maturity within the same class group, is clearly to deny the source of very different student needs. These particular differences will not be discussed further in this book (see Tanner, 1962) since our concern is more with the psycho-social features of adolescence. Following Coleman (1980), we will consider the validity of three main concepts: 'storm and stress', the 'generation gap' and the 'identity crisis', and their implications for PSHE.

The prevailing view of adolescence for most of this century has been that of a period of 'Sturm und Drang'. Both the psychoanalytic and the sociological perspective already outlined accept as inevitable the turmoil and strain which young people apparently undergo. However, recent large-scale studies of teenagers have shown remarkably little evidence of unrest. Rutter et al.'s (1976) longitudinal study followed the development of 10- to 11-year-old children for five years and included evidence from parents and teachers. Although the findings revealed evidence of self-doubt and heightened awareness of problems, there was no evidence that psychiatric problems were of higher incidence or higher prevalence during this period. As Rutter himself asserts:

> Although the period of adolescence has provided a constant source of fascination to adults, psychiatric and psychological writings on the topic are characterised more by confident assertion than by the presence of well-based knowledge.

Where there was evidence of adolescent disturbance in Rutter's study, for

95

instance in the South London sample compared to the Isle of Wight group, this could be explained in socio-economic terms rather than as a result of age-related stress. So there still appears to be a discrepancy between established theory concerning storm and stress and the findings of empirical research.

The '*generation gap*', an expression which gained widespread currency in the 1960s, has a similarly long history but little corroborative evidence. Indeed, studies in the USA, by the Offers (1975) and Bandura (1972) show that, although differences of opinion with parents may increase during the teen years, there was insufficient evidence of a state of alienation. In this country, while Coleman (1974) found that the numbers of young people reporting conflict with their parents did increase during adolescence, relationships, on the whole, remained warm, cordial, supportive and loyal.

The third concept, that of '*identity crisis*', has been explored by Erikson (1968) and others. Identity crises are perceived as including various components: problems with intimacy, problems with future planning, problems with decisions and priorities, problems with self-image. These areas do seem to be of concern to young people but there is a big distinction between a 'concern' and a 'problem' or 'crisis'. Questionnaires and interviews with teenagers (Coleman, 1974 and Rosenberg, 1965) show that approximately one-quarter of teenagers have a low self-image but this is hardly sufficient justification for the assumed inevitability of an 'identity crisis'. (Might not one-quarter of adults have an equally low self-image?) Interestingly, Lewin (1939) also accepted a view of adolescent crisis which he attributed to the 'marginalising' of young people in society. He explained adolescent 'problems' as a feature of transition between the privileged positions of childhood and adulthood. The extent of the 'problem' of adolescence, if there is one, thus remains unclear.

Coleman (1980), who is critical of the lack of empirical research in the field, presents a theory of adolescence based on his own studies. Put simply, this 'focal theory' suggests that adolescents cope by dealing with one concern at a time.

They spread the process of adaptation over a span of years, attempting to resolve first one issue, and then the next. Different problems, different relationship issues come into focus and are tackled at different stages, so that the stresses resulting from the need to adapt to new modes of behaviour are rarely concentrated all at one time. It follows from this that it is precisely in those who, for whatever reason, do have more than one issue to cope with at a time that problems are most likely to occur. Thus, as an example, where puberty and the growth spurt occur at the normal time individuals are able to adjust to these changes before other pressures, such as those from parents and teachers, are brought to bear. For the late maturer, however, pressures are more likely to occur simultaneously, inevitably requiring adjustments over a much wider area.

That there are particular problems associated with the teen years is not in question (just as there are, for other reasons, associated with the mid-thirties, the mid-fifties and the post-retirement years!). However, the overemphasis on the 'problems' of adolescence has mirrored a lack of recognition of young people's adaptive resources and coping strategies. This book does not deal with the severe problems and disturbances which individual adolescents may undergo. Although teachers clearly need skills to help such youngsters, at the very least in recognising signs of serious disturbance and being familiar with referral procedures, these are pastoral concerns in the first instance and, ultimately, the province of specialists.

If it is accepted that adolescent problems are mostly less severe than theory has suggested, then PSHE may be able to escape its 'trouble-shooting' label. We believe that young people have important concerns which can be explicitly addressed without posing them as 'problems'. For example, students can be helped to understand and deal with family tensions but not from the premise that they are necessarily deeply estranged from their parents and siblings. This shift permits PSHE to take on a more constructive focus, aknowledging the power of young people to live their lives to the full. A consequence of the shift is the need for specific methods to be used in teaching PSHE, as we shall see in Chapter 6.

In this section, various commonly held features of adolescence have been noted. Given the relatively small amount of empirical evidence to substantiate these views it is worth asking why the 'problem-centred' view of adolescence still carries so much credence. The media analysis exercise on p. 98 provides useful triggers for such a discussion.

THE TASKS OF ADOLESCENCE

One approach which can be used to determine adolescent needs is to stipulate the 'tasks' deemed necessary for the attainment of adulthood. However, as we indicated earlier, formal recognition of adulthood is confused by a plethora of contradictory rules and regulations which differ from one society to the next. Maturity, which carries more judgemental connotations, is not so age- or society-specific. It is generally used to describe someone who is a non-dependent, self-governing person. If we assume that the desirable end-point of adolescence is adulthood, then young people's principal needs are those related to the tasks of maturing. Such tasks may be based on philosophical, psychological or sociological inquiry but lists that have been compiled have several features in common.

Havighurst (1972) listed eight 'developmental tasks of adolescents' which have formed the basis of much further work:

1. Achieving new and mature relations with age mates of both sexes
2. Achieving a masculine or feminine role

Exercise 4.3: Portrayal of Adolescents in the Media

This simple exercise is best carried out with small groups (of adults or students).

1. Provide a selection of newspapers and/or magazines — the more variety the better.

2. Skim through the material and cut out all references/articles about adolescents.

3. Make a collage depicting a theme(s) relating to how young people are portrayed; for example: gender stereotypes, fashions, leisure interests, popular culture, idealism.

4. Ensuing discussion might focus on:
   · the general tenor of references to young people
   · words most commonly used about adolescents
   · the 'hidden messages' contained within the imagery
   · the particular themes related to young people
   · comparisons between different source material
   · implications for teaching and PSHE
   and so on.

This type of exercise can also be used to analyse the portrayal of adolescents in television programmes, listing the characteristics, behaviour and concerns of young characters.

---

3. Accepting one's physique and using the body effectively
4. Achieving emotional independence of parents and other adults
5. Preparing for marriage, for long-term relationships and for family life
6. Preparing for an economic career
7. Acquiring a set of values and an ethical system as a guide to behaviour — developing an ideology
8. Desiring and achieving socially responsible behaviour

Although these goals may be central to adolescent development and relevant to PSHE, there are problems in translating them into curriculum guidelines. The list begs the question, for example, of who determines 'socially responsible' behaviour and what the prime components of a 'masculine' or 'feminine' role are. Even if these tasks are generally accepted as being desirable, how should progress towards such goals be evaluated — and by whom?

Wall (1977) suggested a different angle when he formulated the general goals of adolescence in modern Western societies as follows:

1. To define a new concept of physical self — acquire a much modified body image

2. To develop a sexual self — to come to terms with their own sexuality
3. To find a vocational self — to develop some satisfaction in work and prepare for economic independence
4. To find a social self — a clear and differentiated series of roles in the smaller and larger groups of adult society into which they are moving
5. To find a philosophic self —a set of ideas, ideals, principles and interpretations of life itself which are some sort of guide to action in difficult circumstances

Development within each of these area, Wall argues, is directly related to the openness and complexity of any society. Discrepancies exist within (and between) individuals regarding their rate of development in a particular area. Teachers may wish to decide which of the above goals do, or should, feature most strongly within PSHE. Is there an assumed hierarchy?

In his discussion of the pastoral curriculum, Watkins (1985) produced a list similar to Wall's focusing on the learner's learning about him/herself. Wilson (1979) also took the concept of 'self' as the basis for charting development. He suggests that the self has three components:

1. self-awareness
2. self-evaluation $\Big\}$ related to an individual's judgement of his worth
3. sense of personal power — describing an individual's assessment of his power and effectiveness in influencing the world

In his development from birth, a child goes through four stages: bodily self, psychological self, schizoid self and adolescent self, each of which is subdivided on the basis of the three components above. Wilson advocates a 'moratorium' enabling adolescents to experiment with identities and suspend, evade or delay problems of self-definition, but asserts that 'the problem is called life, and demands consistent revision of the individual's self-concept'.

The emphasis on 'self' in the three schemes above raises again the dilemma of personal versus social education. However, there is no reason why learning about oneself should be at the expense of learning about others. Teachers may need to reinterpret the tasks and needs of adolescents in a social context if they are to strike a healthy balance. In this way, self-knowledge can develop hand-in-hand with understanding others (both in an inter-personal and in a political sense). This is the essence of PSHE.

The significance of particular tasks for healthy adolescent development is justified not only by philosophical and psychological inquiry but also by empirical evidence, such as that deriving from longitudinal studies of mental health and surveys of young people's concerns. Kohlberg *et al.* (1971) discovered that the best predictors of all forms of adult maladjustment were poor peer relationships in young adolescents and anti-social behaviour in older teenagers (both indicative of poor ego development and inability to perform adolescent tasks). Lindsay (1983), however, asserts that, while it is normal in our society for adolescents to have problems as they change from child to adult, serious disturbances can be traced back to stress in early childhood.

Having surveyed 235 older adolescents in secondary schools and 36 in employment, Hopson and Hough (1976) concluded:

> From these data, it is quite clear that these young people had considerable difficulties in relating to parents and teachers, in asserting themselves to achieve their goals, and in relating to the opposite sex and people in authority. They had inaccurate and damaging ideas on the degree to which they could change themselves or their life situation.

The similarity between these concerns and the tasks of adolescents already cited is clear but such conclusions appear to ignore the influence of economics, culture, politics, race, gender and sexuality. Whose responsibility is it if these influences go unrecognised and, as a consequence, tasks are not fully accomplished?

Before returning to questions of responsibility, the particular social context within which young people are functioning is worth remembering. Chapter 2 highlighted some examples of rapid social transformation. As well as adapting to specific developments like these, we are all having to cope with change as an everyday phenomenon. As Toffler (1970) warned, there are psychological dangers attendant on this accelerated pace of universal social change. Perhaps the existing schema of assumed adolescent needs is by now seriously askew. Hopson and Scally (1981), for example, argue strongly that teachers should help young people develop skills to cope with change, uncertainty and diversification. In an unstable, volatile society is the route to fulfilment via insularity and security or diversification and *laissez-faire*? For the present, we delegate the task of solving such questions to the psychologists and sociologists.

However, other problems over responsibility remain. First, priorities regarding adolescent needs will depend on standpoint. Thus, a philosopher might interpret maturity as autonomy, a psychologist might emphasise the development of self-esteem, while a sociologist might be more concerned about adolescents fitting in with society or achieving legal voting age. Parents, teachers and young people themselves work towards a combination of goals, including practical considerations such as getting a job or social security payment.

There may be broad agreement (at least in different sub-cultural groups) about the needs of young people and even about the general aims of education but clearly there is little consensus about how they should be met. For example, there may be agreement that young people 'need to come to terms with their own sexuality' but how are they to do this? Parents, teachers, governors, politicians and young people themselves are likely to have very different and contradictory views: experimentation, conformity to given sexual codes, serendipity or consistency with a particular ideology are all possibilities!

Alongside the issues of *how* is the question of *who* should decide? Do schools have any responsibility to meet the needs of adolescents in the sexual sphere, for example, or are their responsibilities confined to vocational skills? Obviously, as writers of this book, our answer to the first question is 'Yes'. But who is accountable to whom? Parents can, and do, criticise teachers for not improving children's numeracy. Should they also blame schools if adolescents seem to have low self-esteem? Conversely, should teachers be openly critical of parental standards of upbringing? At a time when teachers are being made more and more accountable for their actions, they need to be cautious about assuming cardinal responsibility for meeting all the needs of adolescents.

There is one area of adolescent development which is accepted within the province of the school: learning. We therefore now turn to the major theories of cognitive development.

ADOLESCENTS' LEARNING

Education implies learning and learning implies change. None of this takes place in a vacuum and our main concern, as teachers, is to increase our understanding of the process of learning in order to help young people realise their potential — whatever their stage of development. The most influential contributor to the field of child and adolescent psychology, particularly in terms of cognitive development, was Piaget. He claimed that there are stages of intellectual development, following biological laws and characterised by a certain potential for growth, which depend for their realisation on favourable environmental conditions (including adequate opportunities for exploration, talk and play). Flavell (1962) gives a brief summary of Piaget's developmental stages as follows:

1. period of sensory-motor intelligence (0–2 years) 6 major stages
2. period of preparation for and organisation of concrete operations (2–11 years)
   i) pre-operational representations (2–7 years) 3 stages
   ii) concrete operations (7–11 years)
3. period of formal operations (11–15 years)

The characteristics of these periods and the theories which underlie them are very complex but, put simply, they describe a process of reasoning from 'taking things at face value' to 'exploring relationships between tangible entities' to 'recognising relationships involving unseen events' to 'abstract conceptualisation'. Approximately 20 per cent of adults do not attain the period of 'formal operations'. Piaget (1971) himself stressed that these 'characteristic age ranges' are based on averages and that there is considerable variation both between children and within a child's individual development. He also emphasised the

101

significance of environmental influences and suggested that children may learn more from peers than from their assigned teachers!

Peel (1971) studied another aspect of cognitive development: the nature of adolescent judgement. By assessing responses to a number of 'problematic' scenarios, he classified judgement on three levels:

1. where the reasoning is inadequate and based on irrelevant information
2. where the individual's judgement is adequate but highly specific
3. where reasoning goes beyond the specific content and considers a range of possibilities

He showed that the most marked change, the shift to level 3, took place between 13 and 15 years and suggested that school curricula should closely reflect such evidence of development.

Bruner (1966) has also made important contributions to learning theories. He categorises intellectual development in terms of 'levels of knowing':

1. enactive (doing)
2. iconic (representing)
3. symbolic (describing)

Bruner suggests that the role of experience is more important than motivation or cognitive growth and claims that almost limitless learning is possible if the presentation of content to an individual 'matches' his level of knowing. These ideas led to the notion of a 'spiral curriculum', revisiting themes through successive stages of schooling in the appropriate representational mode.

As well as theories of cognitive development, which are essential for planning effective teaching strategies, theories of moral development are particularly relevant for PSHE practitioners. Kohlberg's (1984) research, which complements Piagetian theory, has been most influential in this field. Using 'justice' as his yardstick, Kohlberg suggests that there are six levels of moral development. These can be classified in three stages as follows:

Level I: Preconventional
    Stage 1: Heteronomous morality — sticking to rules backed by reward and punishment. Obedience for its own sake.
    Stage 2: Individualism, instrumental purpose and exchange — following rules if in one's own interest. Right is what is fair or an equal exchange, deal, agreement.

Level II: Conventional
    Stage 3: Mutual interpersonal expectations, relationships and interpersonal conformity — living up to what is expected by people close to you. Keeping mutual relationships such as trust, loyalty, respect and gratitude.

Stage 4: Social system and conscience — fulfilling duties to which you have agreed. Contributing to the society, group or institution.

Level III: Post-conventional (or principled)

Stage 5: Social contract or utility and individual rights — being aware of moral relativism and that a social contract is based on this pluralist acceptance. Some non-relative values, e.g. right to 'life', are upheld.

Stage 6: Universal ethical principles — following self-chosen ethical principles of universal justice: equality of human rights and respect for the dignity of human beings as individuals.

Kohlberg points out that it is difficult to match these stages chronologically and that it is possible for adults to regress to a lower level when confronted with a particular problem. He stresses, however, that each level is a prerequisite for the development of further moral reasoning and that children will only 'make sense' of problems and develop if issues are presented to them according to their particular stage, or the immediately subsequent one. Moral reasoning implies purposeful, rational judgement rather than conformity although the relationship between moral practice and reasoning has yet to be fully explored within cognitive developmental theory.

A different aspect of adolescent development which can affect both cognitive and moral reasoning is that of 'egocentrism'. Elkind (1967) extended this Piagetian notion by arguing that two particular manifestations of egocentrism, the 'imaginary audience' and the 'personal fable', may help explain the cognitive behaviour of some adolescents. Although a young person who has reached 'formal operations' can conjecture as to others' feelings, his own all-consuming self-awareness may be transposed on to others in such a way that differences between them are obscured. The 'imaginary audience' is an extension of the adolescent's own preoccupations and he constructs a 'personal fable' to justify feelings of uniqueness. Hence the potential for empathetic understanding is clouded by self-obsession.

The ability to appreciate the perspectives of others has been investigated by Selman (1976), whose stages of 'social perspective-taking' parallel Kohlberg's sequence of moral development. (See Figure 4.1 below.) The main significance of Selman's work is its connecting role between moral reasoning and the social settings within which moral behaviour is enacted. Individuals develop in, and through, social situations so an ability to acknowledge the perspectives of others will probably lead to more stimulating social encounters and, hence, to personal development. Social and political education, like PSHE, clearly depend on this kind of perspective-taking ability.

Figure 4.1: Summary of Developmental 'Profiles'

Approx. Age (years)	Piaget (cognitive devt.)	Kohlberg (moral devt.)	Selman (soc.perspect-ive-taking)	Skills and Attributes
4	intuitive, takes at face value	oriented to rewards, avoids punishment, obedience	egocentric, doesn't see others' perspectives	1. self-esteem and self-awareness 2. literacy 3. numeracy
7	heteronomous (rule-following morality, logical, though concretely based thinking, ability to connect tangible entities	oriented to instrumental values, fairness oriented to mutual inter-personal expectations, reciprocity	'concrete individualistic perspective', acknowledge-ment of conflicting viewpoints, awareness of shared feelings and interests	4. concrete logical thinking 5. initiative-taking 6. work/adult-hood 7. delay of gratification 8. response to social order
10	an increasing ability for abstract thought/specu-lation, a tendency to 'reconstruct' events cognitively, increased ability to 'think	oriented to a wider society perspective, including agreed duties oriented to individual rights, moral relativism, social contract	acceptance of different view-points, follows system of roles and rules, 'prior to society perspective', awareness of validity of others' views'	and self-respect 9. formal logical thought 10. social skills 11. vocational speculation 12. moral reasoning 13. sexual identity 14. greater
16	beyond the present', capacity to relate abstract conceptions to reality, autonomous morality	oriented to universal principles of justice e.g. equality of human rights	greater impar-tiality of judge-ment, mutual role-taking and agreed rules, recognition of the 'generalised other'	independence 15. emotional autonomy 16. hypothesis-ing 17. ego ident-ification 18. increasing sense of reality 19. moral autonomy

Source: adapted from Pring, 1984, and McGuiness, 1982

OBSTACLES TO LEARNING

Figure 4.1 summarises some of the main developmental profiles which we have reviewed and identifies the corresponding skills which indicate 'progress'. For most young people, these processes are not necessarily smooth and linear. Any development can be hindered, either on its own or in conjunction with developments in other areas. Thus, Seligman's (1975) studies of 'learned helplessness' offer fascinating examples of the kinds of 'blocks' which thwart progress, while Dweck's (1986) research on girls' academic self-evaluation shows that demonstrable success is largely irrelevant to their progress. Many bright young women continue to perceive themselves as less able and, consequently, give up their studies. Frequently, however, there is a positive connection between self-esteem and academic achievement. A popular, sociable student, for example, tends to be less anxious and better able to concentrate on work when necessary (Coopersmith, 1967; Leviton, 1975; Coleman, 1974).

A useful concept which provides further insight into the relationship between self-evaluation and learning readiness is that of 'locus of control'. This term, coined by Rotter (1966) and developed by Phares (1976), describes individuals' assessments of their own power over their lives. Those with an internal locus of control see themselves as powerful, in control and responsible for their own progression whereas those with an external locus see themselves as being at the mercy of exigent forces, having little choice and being unable to alter their circumstances or attitudes significantly. In educational terms, the more 'powerful' students will be less anxious about their own ability to learn and, presumably, will be more confident in different learning situations. There is a strong correlation between an internal locus of control and our desired PSHE outcomes for students (Chapter 1) and the learning skills we perceive as belonging to PSHE (Chapter 5).

These studies point to a major responsibility for teachers being the removal or reduction of obstacles such as anxiety and low self-evaluation so that adolescents can learn according to their own developmental pattern. One thing is clear: learning ability does not depend solely on cognitive development. Although different patterns can usefully be identified, our holistic viewpoint encourages us to acknowledge the interrelatedness of all aspects of development. For too long teachers have concentrated on intellect, ignoring the effects of students' feelings and emotions.

Another word of caution that may need to be stressed concerns the assumption that 'the more development, the better'. There are two issues here. One is the choice of criteria against which 'progress' is measured. Beckett (1986), for instance, asks why, according to Kohlberg, 'universal justice' indicates a higher order of morality than 'caring for others'. Second, we need to ask whether the end-point of development should always be given priority. So much of our thinking about adolescents is based on a concern that they should become adults; it would be a shame if this lessened our acceptance of them, as they are, as young people.

Within PSHE, teachers have an explicit responsibility *vis-à-vis* students' social and moral development. The onus is not on schools alone, however. Young people learn and develop far more outside of school than they do inside. None the less, our principal role is to help them learn and, for that, we need to take account of all the factors influencing their development.

105

CONCLUSION

In this chapter we have outlined some of the theories pertaining to adolescent development and students' needs. In so doing we have assumed that reflection on theoretical perspectives can help teachers make sense of their own practice. But there are no right, or complete, answers.

Familiarity with theory is not the only tool we would advocate. We have already referred to various deficiencies in the existing body of research, including the general lack of empirical evidence and the paucity of attention to girls' needs and the concerns of different ethnic groups. There is no substitute, in fact, for teachers' own observations. Numerous opportunities exist for gaining information about students (either formally or informally):

- · ask them
- · watch them
- · ask their parents
- · ask others in the community
- · watch television programmes for young people
- · read case studies
- · analyse statistics
- · consult whatever theories seem relevant
- · read a range of teenage magazines

The whole list probably sounds daunting but teachers do much of it spontaneously. We are simply suggesting that these are important activities and worth spending time on in quite a self-conscious way.

Finally, a comment about the relationship between needs and education: as teachers we clearly have a responsibility to meet any student needs which affect learning — and within PSHE the focus of learning is, necessarily, broad. However, teachers are not psychotherapists or social workers and cannot assume total or sole responsibility for the healthy development of their students. Both personal and professional boundaries exist and need to be respected. Having said that, teachers can, and do, play an important role in meeting students' needs and it is our hope that the development of PSHE will enhance that task.

FURTHER READING

Coleman, J.C. (1979) *The school years*, Methuen, London
—— (1980) *The nature of adolescence*, Methuen, London
Erikson, E. (1968) *Identity: youth and crisis*, Faber and Faber, London
Gilligan, C. (1982) *In a different voice: psychological theory and women's development*, Harvard University Press, Cambridge, Mass.
Likona, T. (ed.) (1976) *Moral development and behavior*, Holt, Rinehart and Winston, New York

Loevinger, J. (1976) *Ego development*, Jossey-Bass, San Francisco

Nielsen, L. (1987) *Adolescent psychology: a contemporary view*, Holt, Rinehart and Winston, New York

Peters, R.S. (1981) *Moral development and moral education*, Allen and Unwin, London

Piaget, J. (1971) *Science of education and the psychology of the child* (trans. D. Coltmer), Longman, London

Pring, R. (1984) *Personal and social education in the curriculum*, Hodder and Stoughton, London

Wall, W.D. (1977) *Constructive education for adolescents*, Harrap, London

5

PSHE and the Curriculum

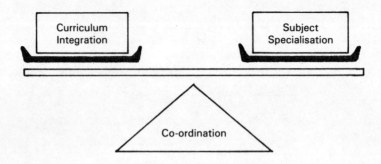

Cameo

It is a Wednesday afternoon at the beginning of December. Under the watchful eye of Dr Potts, Form 3M at Loamshire High are mounting a display of their work. In a few days parents and other visitors are expected at the school for the annual carol concert and senior school drama festival and, along with the rest of the third year, 3M have been allocated a whole wall space to decorate.

The decision about what 3M should display has been left to the students. Their brief, in common with that for all the other forms, is to agree on a theme or topic that they would like the rest of the school to share. Once the decision-making process has been set in motion, using a checklist exercise, Dr Potts simply acts as a referee. Two topics emerge as possibilities for the display: a survey of local retail outlets, done in geography, and some work on sexuality that had been part of the English course. Eventually, the latter is chosen — chiefly because the students feel, 'we want our parents to realise how grown up we can be about this'.

The form decide that everybody's writing should be displayed. This takes the form of poems on the theme: 'what it means to be a woman or a man'. Neatly re-copied, to take account of the teacher's corrections, these are mounted on coloured sheets with bold, eye-catching headings designed by Eddie Fox, the form artist, and some assistants. Other students collect a variety of magazine illustrations and photographs (bringing many of them in from home), which are sorted and used to complement particular pieces of writing. When all the layout and pasting-up is done, Eddie, with enthusiastic help from his friends, works out how to get everything in the best array and organises each group to pin up their posters.

This chapter, which takes us to the fifth stage in Lawton's cultural analysis, explores some of the issues raised by planning for PSHE in the curriculum. Which of the activities described in the cameo above, for instance, 'belong' to PSHE? Does the cameo actually depict a PSHE lesson or an activity containing some PSHE elements? Before proceeding, we need to be clear about the use of the word 'curriculum'.

WHAT IS THE CURRICULUM?

Musgrave (1979) defines the curriculum as 'those learning experiences that are purposively organised by such formal educational agents as schools'. This ignores the para-curriculum but reflects the focus in this chapter, which is on planned PSHE. It also raises the question of who does the planning and organisation — and for what purposes. Individual teachers undoubtedly hold different views about the quality, the relevance and even the significance of schooling. However, as a staff, they are likely to be effective if they share ideas about the aims and general organisation of the curriculum.

What, then, are the aims of schooling? We looked at one set of aims in the Introduction (p. 2). Another set, which can be found in the ILEA report (1984b), is as follows:

The curriculum of schools tries to do four main things. It tries to give young people an idea of what we know about the universe and that part of it called the Earth, which we inhabit; of how we find out about it and, to some extent, control it. It tries to develop in each young person a sense of his or her own identity, and of what part to play in adult life; to develop a sensitivity in and an understanding of individual personal relationships, of relationships between groups of people and between nations. It attempts to foster in them the ability to communicate what they know and what they feel, by talking and listening, by writing and reading words and mathematical symbols; by illustrating and looking, by taking part, sometimes as performers, sometimes as appreciative audience, in art, dance, drama and music. And, hardest of all, it attempts to deal with the fact that people in all societies have tried to recognise ultimate values and to grapple with the meaning of life.

This broad range of aims encompasses many of our goals for PSHE, but it does not solve the problem of translating ideals into practice. In terms of school curricula, this involves clarifying the different potential components of PSHE and finding a meaningful way to sequence them.

Some current curricular offerings are the result of historical accident. But there have, in fact, been yardsticks to guide curriculum planners, such as the 'forms of knowledge' proposed by Phenix (1964), Hirst and Peters (1970) and Whitfield (1971). These classifications have concentrated on the academic curriculum, with an emphasis on cognition and initiation into predetermined knowledge areas; 'learning about' rather than 'learning how to'. Significantly, they have not always succeeded in informing what happens in the classroom.

The 'entitlement curriculum' proposed by the DES (1983a) incorporated eight 'areas of experience' which were considered as fundamental to the education of young people:

aesthetic/creative
ethical
linguistic
mathematical
physical
scientific
social/political
spiritual

But although these different areas of experience can be recognised within existing school subjects, even the most cursory analysis indicates that they are not weighted equally in traditional curricula or, indeed, in the proposed national curriculum.

One reason, historically, for the different weighting given to different areas is the emphasis curriculum planners have placed on the transmission of fixed bodies of knowledge at the expense of developing wider attitudes, understanding and practical skills. For an area like PSHE to succeed, therefore, means breaking the mould. However, as far as skills and attitudes are concerned, those addressed in science and mathematics lessons may be just as pertinent to students' healthy personal and social development as to their scientific understanding. So there is no neat correspondence between 'areas of knowledge' and curriculum locations. As Bruner (1966) observes, a curriculum is a thing in balance. It cannot first be developed for content, then for method and then for some other feature. These are all simultaneously in tension.

Recently schools have begun to look for ways of recognising the interdependence of knowledge, attitudes and skills in students' learning. Some institutions have established mini-schools (see Watts, 1977), others have reduced subject boundaries by establishing faculties of related disciplines and introducing integrated courses (cf. Warwick, 1987). The 'Hargreaves Report', ILEA (1984a), was also indicative of this trend in emphasising previously neglected aspects of student achievement. It recommends that motivation and commitment (achievement aspect IV), personal and social skills (III), application and practical skills (II) should be regarded as equally important as knowledge recall (I), and that all of these aspects of achievement should be reflected in school curricula. Clearly, such shifts carry important implications for the organisation of PSHE.

THE LOCATION OF PSHE IN THE CURRICULUM

We have no wish to be credited with, or even accused of, pioneering PSHE as some strange new beast within schools. For some, it may seem a many-headed monster but it is not merely 'this month's flavour', nor has its emergence been spontaneous. PSHE is already present, both explicitly and implicitly, in different aspects of the mainstream curriculum. From the point of view of subject contributions, the ILEA list of 16 PSE areas (see p. 15) indicates the wide range of potential locations. And as we saw in Exercise 0.1, the aims of PSHE are inseparable from those of education as a whole and, hence, are addressed in all aspects of the curriculum.

Acknowledging the eclectic and all-embracing nature of PSHE is one thing; establishing practical locations for teaching it another. Figure 5.1 shows the most common forms of PSHE organisation and summarises some their advantages and disadvantages. Obviously, the major constraint on any school wishing to further PSHE work is the existing curriculum. Each school is different and it is often in this particular area that its uniqueness is most evident — perhaps because PSHE is so inextricably bound to underlying aims. You may find it useful to consider the implications of different locations for your own school, using a scheme similar to the one in Figure 5.1.

Our preferred location is a 'mixed model', i.e. number 5, with PSHE visible as a distinct subject as well as being integrated throughout the curriculum. This is because we see PSHE as being necessarily a cross-curricular activity and because we believe it contains some elements which merit its being accorded the status of a subject in its own right.

CO-ORDINATION

There are many apparently tangential issues which need to be resolved in co-ordinating PSHE in the curriculum. First, it is important to take account of the general educational climate and wider trends in schooling. Unless this happens, any new initiatives risk being piecemeal. Exercise 5.1 is a useful reminder of current developments. What are their implications for your school? Who will they affect most — and how?

A second issue is the relationship between PSHE and the pastoral curriculum. We have already discussed their respective goals in Chapter 3. But there are practical implications concerning curriculum co-ordination. All schools have tutorial/assembly/pastoral time which can be juggled with to accommodate a planned pastoral or PSHE programme. Many schools also adopt a pastoral system which allows year, or house, meetings to take place, thus providing a forum for tutors and middle management to share ideas about PSHE and perhaps to undertake some 'in-house' training. This solution to the location of PSHE has the advantage of not threatening the preserves of the academic curriculum.

Figure 5.1: Locations for PSHE

Advantages		Disadvantages
· increased academic rigour; focus on identifiable content; higher status; specific training → greater expertise	**1** a separate subject	· competition with other subjects; contribution to PSHE of other subjects devalued; mystification of PSHE expertise
· commonality of 'caring' aims; existing established programmes and some tutor training; time available	**2** within pastoral system	· low status; lacking in rigour and/or academic focus; confusion with 'control' and 'crisis' aspects of pastoral curriculum
· recognises potential contribution of all subjects and teachers; can enhance all subject teaching; no extra time necessary; increases cohesion of school	**3** integrated across the curriculum	· likelihood of omission/ repetition or poor sequencing; hard to co-ordinate or evaluate; negotiated curricula unlikely
· can be assessed; easy to co-ordinate; no extra time needed; only committed teachers need to be involved; complements existing rationales	**4** within one or two 'appropriate' subjects	· unequal distribution e.g. only for 'less able'; 'hijacked'/diluted by inappropriate rationales
· consonant with belief that PSHE is essential and indigenous; recognises idealistic aims and realism of the curriculum	**5** combination of 1 plus 2, 3 or 4	· hard to establish boundaries; too many vested interests; expensive in teacher time; hard to co-ordinate and monitor
· concentration on academic development less controversy/ contention	**6** no explicit PSHE	· limited development of students' overall potential; likelihood of contradictions re teachers' aims

However, its conceptual difficulties and the potential mismatch of purposes should be apparent.

Another practical issue concerns the status of PSHE. This depends largely on how it is organised. If PSHE is part of the pastoral curriculum it risks being seen merely as a management expedient to secure more effective 'care and control'. If it is integrated within subjects it risks being completely buried. On the other hand, it could become a principal focus, depending on the nature of the subject and the attitude of the teacher. One thing is certain, PSHE will continue to be

Exercise 5.1: Current Educational Developments

Instructions: Consider each of the developments outlined below and jot down a few notes (in the right-hand column) of how they are likely to affect your teaching.

Predominant existing provision	New approaches	Implications
subject syllabuses	integrated courses with learning objectives	
norm referencing, based on standard distribution graphs for grades	criterion referencing, based on record of what students can do	
peripheral social and pastoral education	social and pastoral education integrated with rest of curriculum	
incidental work experience	alternance i.e. work experience linked to learning at school	
standardised learning programmes	individual learning contracts	
study justified by tradition or the demands of higher education	relevant study and training based on student need	
information-based learning	skill-based, experiential learning	

Adapted from Settle and Wise, 1986

a low-status area, irrespective of location, until teachers and students value knowledge of self and others as highly as they do knowledge about things. As we shall see later, evaluation also has a bearing on the status of PSHE. Thus, until it is formally assessed, which arguably can only happen if it is a separate subject, PSHE will never be highly regarded by students.

A fourth set of issues centres on the way decisions are made about the location of PSHE. This is likely to be influenced by existing curriculum structures as well as by the status accorded to PSHE. If there is a traditional staffing structure based on departmental hierarchies, PSHE is unlikely to find much space. However, if a senior member of staff is given responsibility for co-ordinating PSHE across the school there is a much better chance of its gaining effective recognition. The support of senior management will be crucial here, not just tacitly but visibly and permanently. But who are PSHE teachers accountable to? And are fundamental principles of PSHE, such as respect, responsibility and fraternity, reflected in the way decisions about it are made within schools?

Perhaps the critical issue influencing this — and other decisions — is the amount of time allocated to PSHE. Most teachers have a real commitment to their own subject and are understandably concerned if its share of the timetable is reduced. Seeing the possibility of sharing aims (and sharing time) ultimately depends on an individual teacher's views of education and the ideal curriculum balance. As Stevenson (1984) points out:

> It is clear that curriculum balance may be sought among several polarities, between what is to be considered as compulsory and variations from it; between utilitarian and general education; between cognitive and affective and attitudinal elements of the curriculum; between the practical and the theoretical; between the curriculum which is child-centred or centred on knowledge and between specialisation and breadth in studies to be pursued. The weighting given to each of the polarities has varied with the opinions current at any particular time, based on the existing state of knowledge of the educational process.

These continua are not mutually exclusive but each will be significant for curriculum planning. The introduction of a 'new' area such as PSHE is bound to cause anxiety and suspicion unless staff are encouraged to address the implications of these polarities in terms of the overall curriculum.

The selection of PSHE teachers is another practical issue which can be resolved in several ways. Who actually does teach it can be determined using grids (p. 132). Who should teach it is discussed on page 133. Ignoring the question of personalities and personal/professional development, this second question can be seen very much as a question of where PSHE is located in the curriculum. Should all teachers be required to teach PSHE as part of their tutorial role or should involvement be voluntary, or related to interest and subject expertise? If PSHE is organised as a separate subject, how will it be serviced? The issue of status is crucial here again. The important corollary is training. To date few teachers have been specifically trained for PSHE, so how will future recruits be selected — and on what basis? Will schools feel confident enought of their PSHE commitment to advertise for trained PSHE specialists?

THE ELEMENTS OF PSHE IN PRACTICE

We have looked at some practical issues concerning the location of PSHE and outlined our case for making it visible as a distinct subject as well as being co-ordinated across the curriculum. But there is no rule which states that PSHE must be taught in a particular way or in a particular context. Later in this chapter we describe a tool for curriculum development, based on the use of grids or matrices which schools might use to aid thinking about their preferred approach.

First, teachers need to decide what they are looking for — what elements of PSHE can be identified in different areas of the curriculum in order to obtain a valid picture of current practice? This task becomes more manageable if we 'structure' subjects in terms of four components: facts, concepts, skills and attitudes. In reality, all four components are closely interrelated, although different curriculum areas emphasise a different mix. This means that, if PSHE is to be located more prominently, teachers need to consider its 'fit' with existing subjects, not just in terms of content and skills but also in terms of the attitudes they promote.

Although there are ways in which the subject structuring of PSHE differs in emphasis from that of other subjects, PSHE is not new in the sense of introduc-ing hitherto undiscovered facts (like microbiology) or of pioneering unprecedented skills (like micro-electronics). As an amalgamation of many different elements of learning, it has yet to establish its own paradigm. One way of clarifying the parameters of PSHE is to look for evidence of PSHE values and principles in existing subject areas. From this exploration we can tease out any common themes which might contribute to a unified view of PSHE.

First, then, we need to identify the contributions of particular subjects towards the goals of PSHE. Our method is similar to that of Williams and Williams (1980). The specific selection of subject areas which we have examined is not sacrosanct. There are clearly others that might be relevant, such as Religious Education. The profusion of related courses, with non-subject specific titles such as 'Child Development', 'Development Education', 'Urban Studies' and so on, adds to the potential confusion. However, as a starting point, we have singled out six areas: Health Education, Moral Education, Social Education, Political Education, Careers Education and the Pastoral Curriculum. Each of these has aims which, quite legitimately, fall outside PSHE. Yet each has a similar rationale and each is underpinned by an acknowledged, if often contested, school of thought. Rather than present a detailed critical analysis of each area, we simply offer a selection of quotations from relevant curriculum

115

Moral Education

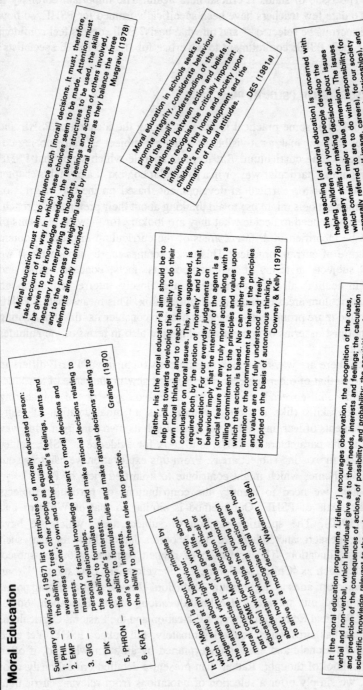

Summary of Wilson's (1967) list of attributes of a morally educated person:

1. PHIL — the ability to treat other people as equals, wants and awareness of one's own and other people's feelings.
2. EMP — awareness of factual knowledge relevant to moral decisions and interests.
3. GIG — mastery of factual knowledge relating to personal relationships.
4. DIK — the ability to formulate rules and make rational decisions relating to other people's interests.
5. PHRON — the ability to formulate rules and make rational decisions into practice.
6. KRAT — one's own interests.
   the ability to put these rules into practice.

Grainger (1970)

Moral education must aim to influence such [moral] decisions. It must, therefore, take account of the way in which these choices seem to be made. Attention must be given to the knowledge needed, the relevant structures seem to be used, the skills necessary for interpreting the thoughts, feelings and actions of others involved, and to the process of weighting used by moral actors as they balance the three elements already mentioned.

Musgrave (1978)

Moral education in schools seeks to promote integrity, considerate behaviour and the pupil's understanding of the relationship between action and belief. It has to recognise the critically important influence of the home and society upon children's moral development and the formation of moral attitudes.

DES (1981a)

The teaching [of moral education] is concerned with helping children and young people develop the necessary skills for making decisions about issues which contain a major value dimension. The issues generally referred to are to do with responsibility for our society and oneself (health, careers), for our society (social mores, citizenship), personal relationships), and for our world (interdependence).

Nottingham & Cross (1981)

Rather, his [the moral educator's] aim should be to help pupils towards developing the ability to do their own moral thinking and to reach their own conclusions on moral issues. This, we suggested, is of 'education'. For our everyday judgements on behaviour imply that the intention of the agent is a crucial feature for any truly moral action along with a willing commitment to the principles and values upon which that action is based. Nor can either the intention or the commitment be there if the principles and values are not fully understood and freely adopted on the basis of autonomous thinking.

Downey & Kelly (1978)

It [the moral education programme 'Lifeline'] encourages observation, the recognition of the cues, verbal and non-verbal, which individuals give as to their needs, interests and feelings; the calculation and prediction of the consequences of actions, of possibility and probability; the acquisition of scientific knowledge relevant to the understanding of consequences, and practice in all forms of creative self-expression including writing. It is much concerned with bringing together any facts, ideas and skills relevant to decisions affecting man. . . .

McPhail, Ungoed-Thomas Chapman (1972)

---

about the principles by
about behaviour, about about right and wrong, and
about behaviour, or that good life and ethical or
which I arrive about or that are about right and
[The 'Moral'] is about or — these are that
Judgements of virtue — how young person
how nature of it — Moral, social, how
to practise. Moral concerns the questions, how
the to concerns (personal, moral issues).
moral PSME) which helps what moral issues).
part of PSME) which helps to recognise a moral decision. Wakeman (1984)
to understand a moral decision.
about, how to at a moral
to arrive at

Wakeman (1984)

Careers Education

Careers education and guidance should help individuals interested in and aware of, in work, individuals:
- to become interested in and aware of, opportunities in education generally;
- to understand themselves in relation to these opportunities in education and in adult life generally;
- to understand their strengths and weaknesses;
- to understand the wider field of opportunities, values, qualifications and interests;
- to make informed, reasoned decisions;
- to make transitions, in particular from school to the next stage.

DES (1983d)

The Secretaries of State endorse the recommendation made in 'Education for 16–19 Year Olds' that careers education and guidance should assess personal strengths and weaknesses; impart knowledge about jobs and qualifications required for them, and the opportunities for post-16 education and training; and develop pupils' skills in taking decisions about these matters.

DES (1981b)

The specific goals of careers education:
1. To encourage individuals to develop and grow in self-understanding.
2. To help youngsters acquire those skills and that knowledge which have particular relevance to living and working in the adult world.
3. To help youngsters acquire a broader understanding of opportunities in education and work.
4. To develop and promote in youngsters a broader understanding of the wider field of adult life, and to help youngsters become aware of their own ambitions and aspirations.
5. To help youngsters in relation to their own ambitions and aspirations.
consider this in relation to their own ambitions and aspirations.
5. To prepare youngsters to make considered choices.

Cleaton & Foster (1981)

These [the aims of careers education] include an understanding of the different OPPORTUNITIES open to young people and the strategies by which they can achieve a match between personal characteristics and what is available; identifying a concept of SELF, in which young people are able to experience, understand and develop understand the pressures, styles, risks and responsibilities of their limitations; the opportunity to experience and skills, knowledge, attitudes and experience which help young people involved in DECISION-MAKING; a recognition of they are to develop the skills involved in changing their environment and taking charge of their own lives.

Elliott & White (1986)

General Objectives in each pupil an realistic awareness of self through comparison
1. To create of self through comparison awareness of social and comparison with other personal people.
   personal analysis and social with other awareness of social and responsibility and
2. To instil an awareness responsibility and involvement to adapt to inevitable an ability in society. to understand the changes pupils to routes (working an ability in society. to understand the
3. To assist world, the role of the working world, the role of the employment, the adult and various differences as well as work and non-working the adult and various environments face up to major occupations face up to major environments as work occupations face up to major
4. To help pupils, social and personal educational, with confidence.

Anzell (1986)

Five aims of careers education:
To enable a pupil to acquire
   – self-awareness skills
   – decision making skills
   – communication of the and understanding
   – world of work and understanding
   – occupational knowledge March (1981)

Objectives in a careers education programme:
Opportunity awareness
Self awareness
Decision making
Transition
Communication (including coping/survival skills)
Study and learning skills
Information skills
Social skills

Rogers (1984)

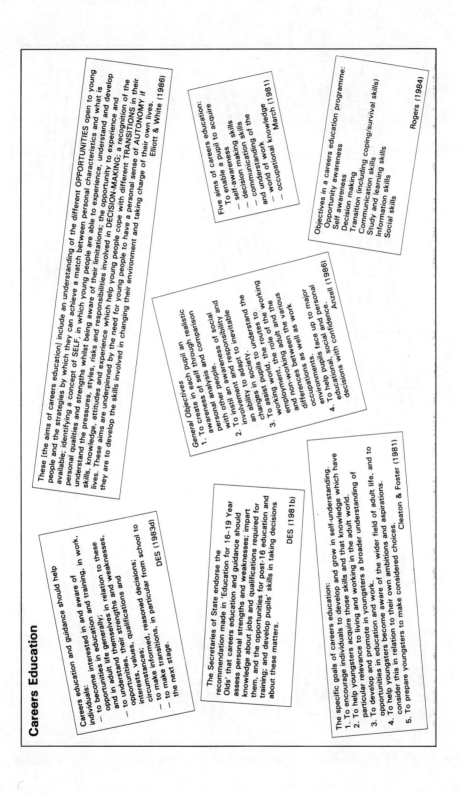

Health Education

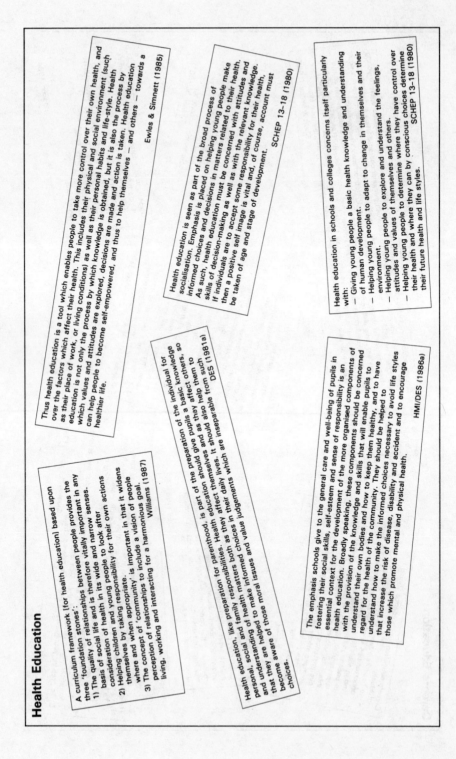

A curriculum framework (for health education) based upon three 'foundation stones':

The quality of relationships between people provides the basis of social life and is therefore vitally important in any consideration of health in its wide and narrow senses.

1) Helping by taking responsibility for their own actions

2) Helping by taking responsibility for themselves when appropriate.

3) The concept of 'community' is important in that it widens themselves and when appropriate.

3) The perception of relationships to include a vision of people where and when appropriate.

The perception of relationships and interacting for a harmonious goal.
living, working and interacting for a harmonious goal.

Williams (1987)

Thus health education is a tool which enables people to take more control over their own health, over the factors which affect their health. This includes their physical and social environment, and as their place of work, or living conditions) as well as their personal habits and life-style. Health education is not only the process by which knowledge is obtained, but it is also the process by which values and attitudes are explored, decisions are made and action is taken. Health education can help people to become self-empowered, and thus to help themselves — and others — towards a healthier life.

Ewles & Simnett (1985)

Health education, like preparation for parenthood, is part of the preparation of the individual for a basic knowledge, personal, social and health matters both as they affect others, so personal, social and health matters both in their daily lives. Health education should give pupils a basic knowledge, and understanding to make informed choices and value judgements which are inseparable from such and they are helped of those moral issues and value judgements which are inseparable from such choices.

DES (1981a)

Health education is seen as part of the broad process of socialisation. Emphasis is placed on helping young people make informed choices and decisions in matters related to their health. As such, health education must be concerned with attitudes and If individuals are to accept some responsibility for their health, then a positive self image is vital and, of course, account must be taken of age and stage of development.

SCHEP 13–18 (1980)

The emphasis schools give to the general care and well-being of pupils in fostering their social skills, self-esteem and sense of responsibility is an essential context for the development of the more organised components of health education. Broadly speaking, these components should be concerned in with the provision of the knowledge and skills that will enable pupils to understand their own bodies and how to keep them healthy, and to have understand how to make the informed choices necessary to avoid life styles that increase the risk of disease, disability and accident and to encourage those which promote mental and physical health.

HMI/DES (1986a)

Health education in schools and colleges concerns itself particularly with:
 — Giving young people a basic health knowledge and understanding of human development.
 — Helping young people to adapt to change in themselves and their environment.
 — Helping young people to explore and understand the feelings,
 — Helping young people to explore where they have control over attitudes and values of themselves where they have control over their health and where they can by conscious choices determine their future health and life styles.

SCHEP 13–18 (1980)

Social Education

Social Education is a process whereby young people are enabled to learn more about themselves, the group of which they are a part, and the society (community) in which they are living. The process fosters the skills which these are designed to enable pupils to develop critical awareness and is confident participation in society possible. BYV (1979)

Social education's prime concern is: any young person's meetings with others, with his capacity in these meetings to accept others and be accepted by them, and (with) the common interests around which these meetings may revolve. Social education is thus concerned with the ideas, thoughts and opinions, the motives and the emotions inherent in such meetings and interests. It is about the interaction of human beings, about their friendships and enmities, about the way these are deepened and extended, and about any individual's consequences. Its product therefore is himself — of his values, attitudes and untapped consciousness of these to others, and of the relevance of understanding of how to form mutually satisfying relationships, and so involves a search by the adult for ways of helping the young person to discover how to contribute to others. It is increased consciousness of as well as take from his association with others.

Davies & Gibson (1967)

The term 'social education' will ... be used to cover all those teaching or informal activities which are planned by curriculum developers, teachers, or other professionals to enhance the development, understanding. professionals to enhance the following: knowledge, in relation to: more of sensitivity, competence, and/or attitudes, and others, and/or
— the self and others, structures and organisation.
— social institutions, structures and organisation.
— and/or
— social issues
Lee (1980)

Overall objectives: of the
a) the stimulation of personal values development and helping pupils clarify them;
and helping pupils clarify them and the provision of the skills
b) the provision for achievement, necessary for achievement, and the including study skills and the ability to plan ahead;
c) the development of belief in the need for inner controls them; opportunity of a wide range
d) the promotion of social of skills necessary from competence, ranging from standpoint-taking to the management of decision-making
e) the learning of decision-making skills. Hamblin (1978)

Four possible overall aims of social education programmes.
1. To help students see the need for political and social change and to develop the relevant action skills.
2. To maximise the life-chances of the individual within society.
3. To initiate students into societal norms related to work, family and citizenship.
4. To encourage informed autonomous choice of social life-style. Lee (1980)

Social education is a process which fosters:
(i) an individual's increased consciousness of herself — her values, attitudes and skills;
(ii) an individual's sense of being part of a group, of the role she plays and can play in the group;
(iii) community awareness.
Brown, Harber & Strivens (1986)

Social education is the conscious attempt to help people to gain for themselves the knowledge, feelings and skills necessary to meet their own and others' developmental needs.
Smith (1981)

Political Education

by political literacy we mean a compound of knowledge, skills and attitudes, to be developed together, each one conditioning the other two. To meet the needs of the vast majority of young people, basic political literacy is to have achieved political literacy is to be predisposed to try to do something about the issue in question in a manner which is at once effective and respectful of the sincerity of other people and what they believe.

Crick & Porter (1978)

Political competence is dependent on education in four categories: content, concepts, attitudes and skills.

Politics is also deeply concerned with *ethical* questions and *moral* problems ...

... It is not the task of political education to recommend particular political opinions, but on the other hand this paper does not claim to be value free. Its values are those of an open society, which accepts diversity of belief, participation, and the rights of individuals to assess evidence and to come to their own conclusions. The aim is to give pupils knowledge and tools for *informed and responsible political participation.*

(authors' emphases) DES (1977a)

In a democratic society — political education does not, and should not, involve the promotion of any one set of political views. Rather, it should provide a coherent and rational framework within which young people can begin to clarify and act on their own views — as well as to appraise the views and actions of others.

ILEA (1983b)

Attitudes are relevant, but the kind of values to be encouraged are rules for civilised procedures, freedom, toleration, fairness, respect for truth and for reasoning, rather than substantive doctrines such as the parties in part

Crick & Porter (1978)

As regards aims, they (political education and social education) jointly share a concern for:
- developing with students conceptual frameworks which they can use to make sense of their experience
- making students more effective participants in social processes
- emphasising certain process aims related to holding discussion and debate on controversial issues, developing an ability to make reasoned arguments and critically to examine evidence and causes of action
- working with students to clarify their own and others' values and principles
- acknowledging the importance of making a tutor's value commitment in relation to the aims explicit to themselves in the first instance (in order to devise coherent programmes) and possibly to students too (if it is appropriate to the pursuit of particular learning objectives)

Butterworth & MacDonald (1983)

It [a course in political education] encourages students to react to and think through situations, to reason, to put forward their own ideas, to challenge and criticise other people's ideas within a framework of tolerance and fairness. It encourages them to compromise, to look for what we have in common rather than for what divides us, to recognise bias and special pleading and to insist on respect for truth and reasoning.

Smith, Southworth & Wilson (1985)

---

a meaningful political education should go beyond mere cognitive understanding and equip young people with the tools to cope effectively with the problems they are likely to meet in their own communities.

Brennan (1981)

Political education is a conscious process of helping people gain for themselves the knowledge, feelings and skills necessary to understand and exercise power in and between societies.

We can see that political education is concerned with questions of personal worth as well as broader social issues ...

... A comprehensive political education entails ideas, values, learning through action and developing motivation through justification.

Smith (1984)

It is the task of political education to help children find their way in modern society; to make things a little more transparent; to provide young people with concepts to order their world; to assist them in their reflection on their own lives, so that they can discover some of the social and political forces which can impede their personal development; to let them discover that many of their problems are typical of their social situation and that they share them with their peers; and to help them to avoid the personalisation of political and social forces and events which is so normal at that age.

Langeveld (1979)

Pastoral Curriculum

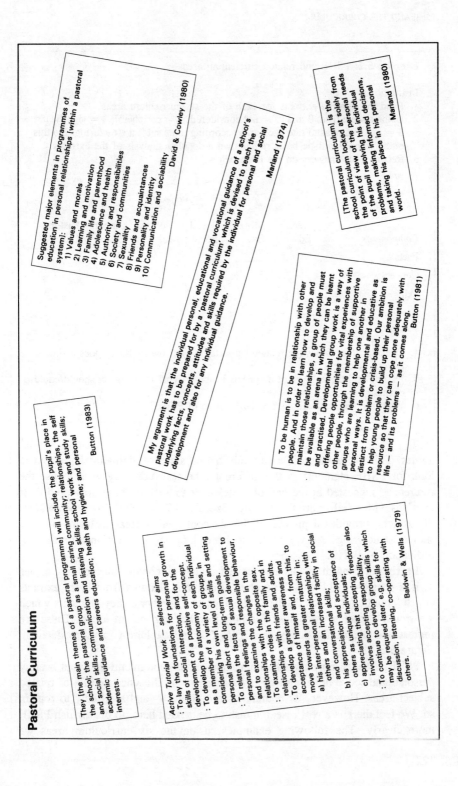

Suggested major elements in programmes in education in personal relationships [within a pastoral system]:

1) Values and morals
2) Learning and motivation
3) Family life and parenthood
4) Adolescence and health
5) Authority and responsibilities
6) Society and communities
7) Sexuality
8) Friends and acquaintances
9) Personality and identity
10) Communication and sociability

David & Cowley (1980)

[The pastoral curriculum] is the solely from school curriculum of the personal needs the point of view of the individual resolving his individual decisions, of the pupil, making informed decisions, problems, making his place in his personal and taking his place in his personal world.

Marland (1980)

They [the main themes of a pastoral programme] will include, the pupil's place in the school; the pastoral group as a small caring community; relationships; the self and social skills; communication and listening skills; school work and study skills; academic guidance and careers education; health and hygiene; and personal interests.

Button (1983)

My argument is that the individual personal, educational and vocational guidance of a school's pastoral work has to be prepared for by a 'pastoral curriculum', which is devised to teach the underlying facts, concepts, attitudes and skills required by the individual for personal and social development and also for any individual guidance.

Marland (1974)

Active Tutorial Work — selected aims

: To lay the foundations for personal growth in and for the skills of social interaction, and for the development of a positive self-concept.

: To develop the autonomy of each individual as a member of a variety of skills and setting considering his own level of skills and goals.

: To relate the facts of sexual development to personal short and long-term development to and to examine the changes in the personal feelings and responsible behaviour, relationships with the opposite sex.

: To examine roles in the family and in relationships with friends and adults.

: To develop a greater awareness and, to acceptance of himself and, from this, to move towards a greater maturity with

a) his inter-personal relationships in social others and conversational skills;

b) his appreciation and acceptance of others as unique individuals;

c) appreciating that accepting freedom also involves accepting responsibility which

: To continue to develop group skills for may be required later, e.g. skills for discussion, listening, co-operating with others.

Baldwin & Wells (1979)

To be human is to be in relationship with other people. And in order to learn how to develop and maintain those relationships, a group of people must be available as an arena in which they can be learnt and practised. Developmental group work is a way of offering people opportunities for vital experiences with other people, through the membership of supportive groups who are learning to help one another in personal ways. It is developmental and educative as distinct from problem or crisis-based. Our ambition is to help young people to build up their personal resource so that they can cope more adequately with life — and its problems — as it comes along.

Button (1981)

Exercise 5.2: PSHE and related curriculum areas

Instructions:
1. Read through the extracts for each of the six curriculum areas.
2. Using a scale from 0 to 3 (0 = not considered; 1 = peripheral; 2 = significant; 3 = main emphasis) rate each area according to its subject structuring. Do this on an impressionistic basis rather than a detailed analysis of the extracts.
3. Record your answers on the table below.

Subjects

Components	Health Ed.	Moral Ed.	Social Ed.	Political Ed.	Careers Ed.	Pastoral Curric.
Facts						
Concepts						
Skills						
Attitudes						

4. Consider these areas (or related subjects) in your own school. Does a similar pattern emerge?
5. Do you feel the balance of emphasis is about right? If not, what should/could change?
6. What are the implications for the location of PSHE?

guides. This presentation is admittedly biased since we deliberately set out to look for PSHE elements in the different schemes. You may wish to use the references suggested at the end of the chapter to analyse these areas and their overlaps with PSHE more thoroughly. Exercise 5.2, which follows the collages of extracts, provides a picture of the six contributing areas in terms of their subject structuring. As we shall see later, this has implications for the co-ordination of PSHE.

Bearing in mind the focus and desired student outcomes, outlined in Chapter 1, it is possible to identify a number of common features from these extracts which 'count', for us, as PSHE. This gives us a number of key elements which we would expect to recognise (or not) in other curriculum areas. These are represented diagrammatically in Figure 5.2 and explained in more detail in Figure 5.3.

PSHE, then, is more than an amorphous set of good intentions about healthy personal and social development and more than an idiosyncratic mix of related subject areas. However, its boundaries are elastic — and are likely to remain so. We feel there is a real research task to be tackled here, to distinguish PSHE more clearly. The following examples, using the six curriculum areas we

Figure 5.2: PSHE Elements in Relation to Selected Curriculum Areas

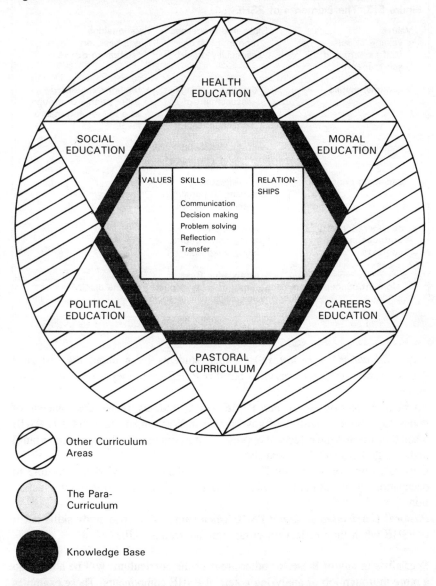

have highlighted, illustrate the sort of distinctions that need to be made. Thus:

Health Education — is not PSHE when students analyse smoking statistics but it *is* PSHE when they weigh up influences on their own smoking behaviour.
Moral Education — is not PSHE when students compare religious practices but it *is* PSHE when they clarify their personal value systems.

Figure 5.3: The Elements of PSHE

Values	Skills and Processes	Relationships
· valuing of self (self-esteem and self-respect)	communication (especially oracy)	· emphasis on self in relation to others
· personal values	decision making (assessment of motivation, influences, consequences)	· relationships between other people or groups at a micro- and macro-level
· social values	problem solving (analysis of strategies)	
· balancing principles	reflection (reasoning, rationality, clarification)	
· consideration of attitudes in given contexts	transfer (making connections, being adaptable)	

Knowledge Base

Content/concepts/knowledge/body of facts derived from the disciplines of philosophy, psychology and sociology

---

Social Education — is not PSHE when students learn about the historical development of the social services but it *is* PSHE when they assess community needs.

Political Education — is not PSHE when students relate the concept of democracy to the processes of government in Western societies but it *is* PSHE when they discuss the effects of oppression at a personal level (e.g. stereotyping) and at a global level (e.g. apartheid).

Careers Education — is not PSHE when students classify jobs according to occupational families but it *is* PSHE when they explore the notion of job satisfaction.

Pastoral Curriculum — is not PSHE when students practise study skills but it *is* PSHE when they reflect on group communication skills.

Specialists in any of these, or other areas of the curriculum, will be able to do a more thorough job of analysing potential PSHE components. These examples are simply intended as a snapshot.

PSHE AND SUBJECT STRUCTURING

The PSHE core which we have just identified can also be related to the four subject components referred to earlier. This breakdown helps us to be even clearer about the parameters of PSHE and its overlaps with other areas.

In terms of *content*, PSHE encompasses factual knowledge and concepts which derive mainly from the disciplines of philosophy, psychology and sociology. Other facts, such as those pertaining to human physiology, may be included but the main focus is on content concerning values and relationships. Putting it simply, knowledge about self is very much the province of PSHE, knowing about others is also integral, but knowing about things is less so. Inevitably, cross-curricular areas, such as PSHE, challenge the customary labelling of facts and concepts as being subject-specific. Are the 'facts of life' biological, sociological or spiritual, for example? It is even tempting to suggest that PSHE has no claim to a particular body of knowledge; indeed, that it can encompass all subject matter if approached in a particular way. Although this view carries weight, some content areas seem especially appropriate for PSHE. The following list is not comprehensive but indicates the range and variety of potential themes:

Physical development
Sexual development
Health; illness; fitness; disease; disability
Mental health and illness
Learning development
Community health and environmental issues
Ecology
Health care and social services
Morals and ethics, values and principles
Sexuality
Leisure
Group dynamics
Prejudice and stereotypes (gender, race, age, class, sexuality)
Power relationships
Social and political organisations and influences
Controversial issues (international relationships, war and peace, drugs, etc.)
Religion
Media
Self-knowledge

These themes, in no particular order, indicate the factual knowledge and fundamental concepts which could be included within PSHE. Inevitably, they also involve attention to related skills and attitudes.

A skill is a capacity or competence which may or may not depend on the possession of related knowledge and concepts. So-called 'lower-order skills', such as writing, are generally improved through practice. 'Higher-order skills' (sometimes called processes), such as interpersonal communication, are more

125

complex. The *PSHE skills* which we have singled out are those most relevant to achieving PSHE goals. Ideally, any skills learnt should be understood and integrated by students so that they form coherent personal attributes and involve felt commitments. For example, it is not very useful to learn to solve problems without understanding their relevance and without caring overmuch about any possible consequences. Let us look briefly at the *PSHE skills* we have focused on.

1. Communication

Within the context of PSHE, the emphasis is on oracy and, particularly, on interpersonal communication. In practice, this involves listening skills, Socratic discussion, summarising, reporting back and an awareness of the benefits and drawbacks of personal disclosure. A particular feature of communication work in PSHE is the encouragement of shared feelings as well as thoughts.

2. Decision making

This involves the assessment of influences affecting healthy decisions and their consequences. In the classroom, it can involve students' actual decision-making behaviour, perhaps using the supportive feedback of peers (e.g. when choosing a research project) or it can be based on simulations such as case studies of social situations (such as a difficulty at home or with members of the opposite sex).

3. Problem solving

Like decision making, this involves an assessment of influences but here the emphasis is on a more active consideration of how to solve problems. The context can be provided by either individual or group problems and both personal and collaborative strategies can be considered. The critical skills concerned are more to do with strategies than with outcomes.

4. Reflection

Within PSHE, we are conscious of the benefits of rational argument. In particular, we are interested in developing students' ability to reflect on their behaviour and the effects it may have on other people. This is because reflection helps to consolidate learning. A few minutes of conversation with a partner to share feelings is the simplest way of encouraging these sorts of skills.

5. Transfer

There are frequent references to 'transferable skills' in current educational reports; the implication being that, with sufficient practice, classroom simulations can enhance real-world skills. Obviously in one sense this is right: if you can talk, you can talk almost anywhere and the more opportunities you have to practise talk, the better you are likely to be at talking spontaneously in social situations. However, we would suggest that practice alone may not guarantee transferability. There are, in fact, particular skills of transfer: translating theory into practice, recognising connections, adaptability, and so on — all of which break down the constraints of being context-bound. The skills of transfer in PSHE involve a recognition that each of us is unique and that every interaction is different but also that there are recognisable patterns in behaviour which can be utilised to plan our lives more effectively. Recognising significant similarities and differences between different situations is an important starting point for transferability.

The fourth element of subject structuring is a concern with attitudes. These, in turn, depend on values. What matters, from the point of view of curriculum planning, is making explicit the connections between values and attitudes. (We have already attempted to exemplify our value base in terms of teacher behaviours, p. 26.) The case of student behaviour can be illustrated by the example of 'autonomy'. Would you wish to foster attitudes such as confidence, self-criticism and courage, for instance? Or are you more concerned with promoting self-direction, initiative-taking, the ability to work independently? Notice that judgements about dispositions depend on interpretation and on circumstances. Thus, 'integrity' could be deemed 'stubbornness' and 'adaptability' can be seen as 'shiftiness'. Listening to students' own interpretations of attitudes can make unfair assessments less likely.

THE CONTENT/PROCESS DEBATE

The content/process divide causes confusion for many teachers, particularly when 'process' is used, inaccurately, to mean 'methods' or 'higher-order skills'. Our view is that there should be far more attention to the 'hows' of teaching and learning, in addition to the 'whats'. We also believe that it is misleading to see a separation between content and process. On the other hand, the assertion that the process *is* the content is not entirely justifiable either. A familiar example is the case of the small discussion group. In the sense that students working in small groups are learning, through experience, about certain forms of communication, this process may constitute the focus, or content, of their learning. However, they are also likely to be learning something about the particular subject under discussion — be it themselves (as is often the case in PSHE) or nutrient values — or whatever. Sometimes the 'whatever' is more important than the interactions or the learning about self and, at such times, small group work is simply an appropriate arrangement for furthering students' understanding of the subject at hand.

Within the context of PSHE, we take 'process' to imply explicit attention to different levels of learning — most notably the relationship between thinking and feeling. Given the complexity of this process, our methodology must be one which allows for different rates of learning, matched to individual students' needs and potential. This, in turn, implies flexible student outcomes so that achievement in PSHE is about the recognition of individual development in relation to different levels of learning, not about standardised test results.

STUDENT ASSESSMENT WITHIN PSHE

An issue which connects very closely to that of who should teach PSHE is the one of assessment. Given the plethora of alternatives currently being dicussed: 'profiles', 'core competencies', 'aspects of achievement', 'graded tests' and so on, it is hard to approach this matter confidently — or with any clear-cut answers. The issue is, in itself, complex so that all we can do here is to raise some questions and offer some tentative suggestions to help clarify the way forward.

Any consideration of assessment must examine first the question of purpose; who, or what, is it for? Is it, for instance, to help students monitor their own progress or is it to encourage parental involvement in their children's education? Is it to establish core standards — a base-line of capabilities for the populace, or is it a necessary yardstick for the pursuit of academic excellence? Is it a practical tool to help employers select suitable candidates for jobs or is it a form of social engineering (however disguised) designed to disqualify sections of the population from demanding further education or employment opportunities? Why do you, as a teacher, assess your students?

It is crucial for teachers to think about questions like these and to be clear about their intentions. One approach is to use a scheme similar to the one suggested by Macintosh and Hale in the Open University text, *Measuring Learning Outcomes* (1981). This distinguishes six kinds of purpose for assessment:

· *Diagnosis*: finding out what is being learned by individuals or groups, particularly in order to determine remedial action.
· *Evaluation*: judging the effectiveness of teaching (materials, strategies, organisation, and so on).
· *Guidance*: helping students to make more relevant, more appropriate decisions, such as in subject choice.
· *Grading*: assigning a 'standard' to individuals, usually according to predetermined, relatively objective criteria.
· *Selection*: providing relevant information about suitability, such as for job applicants.

· *Prediction*: identifying potential so that subsequent education/training is directed and utilised effectively.

Such categories are not clear-cut but they help teachers reflect on the use and usability of a particular piece of assessment. In our view, if there is no clearly understood reason for assessing students then they should not be assessed.

Let us turn now to the case of PSHE. The subject structuring ideas which were described earlier help to identify possibilities in assessing PSHE learning. Their implications are outlined in Figure 5.4.

Figure 5.4: Subject Structuring and Assessment in PSHE

Aspects of learning	Main purposes of assessment	Criteria	PSHE examples
Facts	Grading (predominantly norm-referenced + summative)	Memory (+ some understanding) indicated by reproduction of information	· list major effects of smoking · explain familial relationships, e.g. aunt
Concepts	Diagnosis (criterion-referenced + summative)	Understanding of related notions by application to different contexts (orally or in written form)	· compare features of power in interpersonal relations (within groups and between nations)
Skills	Selection (criterion and norm-referencing + formative)	Capabilities observable by demonstration (often through task analysis)	· summarise a small group discussion in a report-back to a larger group
Attitudes	Guidance (criterion-referencing + formative)	Possession of 'worthwhile' dispositions (through disclosure, by behaviour and reported behaviour)	· complete a 'personal qualities checklist' and select two areas of own behaviour for improvement

As we have already suggested, there is a body of knowledge (facts and concepts) within the field of PSHE which can be comprehended, remembered, applied and, therefore, assessed. The criteria for selecting the particular knowledge to be assessed may be debatable — as might be the appropriate mode of assessment. However, some way of showing retention and comprehension is useful for employers, teachers, parents and students.

The assessment of PSHE skills is more problematic. The key skills we have identified: communication, decision making, problem solving, reflection and transfer, are complex and highly context-dependent. They risk being trivialised by grading schemes which break behaviour down into components. For instance, an example from the City and Guilds (1985) profiling systems handbook classifies progress in one aspect of communication as follows:

· can make sensible replies when spoken to
· can hold conversations and can take messages
· can follow and give simple descriptions and explanations
· can communicate effectively with a range of people in a variety of situations
· can present a logical and effective argument. Can analyse others' arguments.

While these stages admittedly provide a useful yardstick for monitoring student progress, they provide no evidence of motivating factors nor any indication of transferability. Students may decide not to communicate with certain people in certain situations. How can teachers judge the legitimacy of such behaviour? It could be judged a fine example of decision-making skill! Similarly, a student could present a logical and effective (for whom?) argument in one instance but not in another. Which counts and why? Most worrying about such schemes is that they can ignore cultural differences. Overt racism, sexism and classism need careful monitoring here.

The assessment of attitudes is even more open to question. We believe a) that such assessment is difficult and b) that it is unethical to quantify students' dispositions and emotions according to predetermined criteria. Perhaps the best we can hope for is that PSHE teachers, like those in the arts and humanities generally, will use their sensitivity in responding to students' developing views. Expecting students to share attitudes identical with one's own is clearly unrealistic (and undesirable). However, encouraging all students to be able to use reasoned arguments to defend their views is an important goal. Another useful technique in monitoring attainment in this sphere is negotiation. Teachers and students can share their criteria for assessment and both can attempt to represent the views of employers and parents, as seems appropriate. For example, a student group could brainstorm 'desirable' attitudes, say, for pursuing a university course. They might then, with the teacher's help, put these in order or priority and create a checklist against which to assess their own suitability. The same checklist might subsequently be used as a basis for discussion and guidance with the teacher.

Currently, there are many developments in accreditation procedures, all of which are attempting to provide fairer assessment. These were heralded by CSE Mode 3 examinations (now GCSE Mode 3), which are devised by individual schools but ratified externally. Profiling schemes offer a different model of assessment. These entail an explicit commitment to student self-assessment and the process of negotiated learning. Another well-thought-out model is the OCEA Personal Development and Recording Process (the P-component) whereby the student, in consultation with teachers and others, compiles a record reflecting her experiences and achievements both within and beyond the formal curriculum. The P-component, a formative process, is overlaid by the G-component (progress in relation to specific criteria) and the E-component (external examinations). Such schemes attempt to bridge the gap between untransferable subjective comments and over-generalised external criteria in order to provide a meaningful record for transitions from one level or area of education to another. In all of them there is an attempt to find a balance between moral questions and expediency.

Our own view on the issue of student assessment in PSHE is far from settled. Much fuller research and debate is still required. At present, the best approach seems to be via strategies which involve students in monitoring their own performance. However, we are unable to recommend particular techniques for so doing.

Let us now return to the problems of co-ordinating PSHE. The next section offers a tool for identifying existing PSHE practice as a basis for further curriculum co-ordination.

THE USE OF GRIDS

A PSHE curriculum planner needs to know more than what her aims are, she also needs to locate her starting point. Short of sitting in on every lesson and/or interviewing every member of staff and every student about PSHE, she will have to rely on more practical methods of enquiry. One of the most convenient tools is a grid or matrix. There are many variants on the basic grid idea, with progressive degrees of complexity and different foci. As with any tool, there are advantages and disavantages in the application of grids. Some of these are indicated below.

Advantages: quick (if returned!),
             easy to administer and analyse,
             can be collated to give a whole-school picture,
             adaptable — different schools can use them,
             a useful basis for further research e.g. interviews,
             being public and visible, they can raise awareness.

Disadvantages: only a restricted amount/type of information obtained,
             categories open to different interpretations,
             impersonal — feelings about PSHE unlikely to figure,
             risk of significant gaps due to non-completions,
             threatening if seen as a checklist of good practice,
             (is it teacher or subject area which is being researched?).

Figure 5.5: A PSHE/Curriculum Grid

Subject Area		History	Science	English	PE	RE	TVEI etc.
Do you explicitly address these?	Personal and social values	✓	✗	(shaded)	(shaded)	3	1
	Human relationships	✓	✓	(shaded)	(shaded)	3	2
	Communication skills (oracy)	✓	✗	(shaded)		3	0
Do you specifically aim to develop these skills in relation to the above?	Decision-making skills	✓	✓	(shaded)	(shaded)	2	1
	Problem-solving skills	✗	✓	(shaded)		2	0
	Reasoning/ critical/ reflective skills	✓	✗	(shaded)		3	
	Transfer skills	✓	✓	(shaded)	(shaded)	1	2

shading (0–4)   scale (0–3)

Examples of marking: ✓ yes/no ✗

The usefulness of any particular grid will depend on many factors, notably the groundwork and the follow-up. If teachers are clear about its purpose they are more likely to co-operate in completing a matrix. However, grids are only preliminary exercises, not end statements. They work best as a framework for more detailed enquiries. The example in Figure 5.3 relates to our previous discussion of PSHE elements. Teachers can decide which way of marking the grid would be most useful. There are several other curriculum grid models which are also relevant: for example, the HMI *Curriculum 11–16* Areas of Experience Model; the Schools Council *Developing Health Education* grid; and the 'concept' grid developed in connection with the Crick and Porter Political Literacy programme. Each, in a different way, provides an illuminative indication of practice across the school.

WHO SHOULD TEACH PSHE?

While the use of grids offers an overall picture of PSHE practice, further co-ordination will depend partly on this starting point but also on who is available to teach it. In any particular school this is likely to be governed by timetabling constraints. Other factors are also relevant. An emphasis on PSHE as cross-curricular implies that all teachers should share in fostering the healthy personal and social development of students and that any teacher training should take account of this. So far, so good. The corollary is that teachers' contributions to PSHE will vary considerably. One teacher's desire to share her own enthusiasm for her subject might have a highly beneficial effect on her students' overall development while another may be committed to fostering healthy relationships via the para-curriculum: clubs, trips, visits, classroom climate, school parliament and so on. In this PSHE set-up, the most useful training would involve helping teachers to clarify their own perspectives on education, perhaps through the use of PERM models (Chapter 3). PSHE practice would necessarily be diverse and dependent on individual teachers' contributions.

One way for teachers to clarify their preferred role in PSHE *vis-à-vis* subject specialisms is to complete Exercise 5.3. This might be used as a follow-up to a grid analysis.

We believe that, as well as being a function of the whole of schooling and contributing in a thematic way to core subjects like English and Science, PSHE merits the status of a separate subject. This carries important implications with regard to staffing. In our view, the teaching of PSHE, whatever its location, should be voluntary and dependent on expertise — as is any other curriculum area. An 'anyone can do it'-approach, however convenient, inevitably lowers its status. This fate has already befallen tutoring in many schools — untrained and unwilling staff having been coerced into adopting tutorial programmes, which, not surprisingly, have met with varying degrees of success.

Training is essential for effective PSHE but in an area which has yet to

133

Exercise 5.3: PSHE and the Mainstream Curriculum

Instructions: Thinking about your own subject area (Science, English, Mathematics, etc.), jot down any ideas that occur to you in response to the following statements.

1. The METHODS of my subject (including skills development) might be relevant to work in PSHE in the following ways:

2. The CONTENT area (including facts and concepts) overlaps PSHE in the following ways:

3. The PHILOSOPHY of my subject (i.e. its values and related attitudes, its stance towards knowledge and truth etc.) offers reinforcement to PSHE in these ways:

4. In my view, the subjects most relevant to PSHE work are:

5. In my view, the subjects least relevant to PSHE are:

6. I see my own role in PSHE as:

establish its paradigm or receive direct backing from national organisations this begs a number of questions. What sort of expertise is needed? What makes a 'good PSHE teacher'?

The subject structuring described earlier in this chapter provides a framework to help answer this question. First, in terms of factual knowledge, PSHE teachers need a general understanding of philosophy, psychology and sociology. Such knowledge may be cursory but it entails more than common sense. PSHE teachers also require familiarity with specific content areas, such as health concerns and media analysis, which are relevant to the subject. This factual subject knowledge is useful even if, at the end of the day, teachers are teachers rather than subject 'experts'.

Second, there are fundamental concepts in PSHE which require a theoretical grasp as a prerequisite to practice. Autonomy, for instance, is a much mooted educational aim. But if teachers have not had the opportunity to reflect on its meaning in theory, how can they foster autonomy in the classroom?

Third, while certain skills, such as effective communication, are necessary for all teaching, the focus of PSHE rests on a particular methodology (see Chapter 6). Practice in the strategies this involves is indispensable.

Fourth, while the attitudes of a PSHE teacher should intrinsically be no different from those of any other member of staff, the role of behaviour model may be more prominent. PSHE practitioners are more likely to 'lay themselves on the line' in terms of their attitudes and beliefs. This calls for courage and considerable self-awareness, both of which can be supported through training.

Given the criteria outlined above, whose responsibility is it to enable the development of such expertise? We believe it incumbent upon schools to make provision for training at all levels (see Chapter 8). Ultimately, however, teachers are themselves responsible for their professional development — initially simply by determining their own training needs. The checklist in Exercise 5.4 may help you to ascertain your own strengths and weaknesses. It should be completed individually but discussion with colleagues could help determine training priorities on a whole-school basis.

CONTROVERSIAL ISSUES

We end this chapter with a section which addresses the professionalism of teachers from the perspective of their individual value positions rather than that of subject expertise. Most teachers are confronted with controversial questions but PSHE may be particularly vulnerable to attack on counts of intrusiveness or political indoctrination. Including a section on controversial issues may perhaps seem to deny that all education is controversial but we feel there are a number of general points that need to be made before we move on to the detailed discussion of methodology in Chapter 6.

By dealing explicitly with values and relationships, PSHE is bound to be

Exercise 5.4: Checklist of PSHE Teacher Assets

Instructions: Place a mark on each continuum to show your assessment of yourself in terms of the following skills and attributes. If you are working with a partner, compare your lists and try to help each other think of ways of developing any areas in which you feel weak and of capitalising on those in which you have real strength.

	Low		High
e.g.	. _____	X_____	.

· sense of humour
· counselling skills
· sensitivity
· adaptability
· negotiating skills
· being able to deal with
  conflict constructively
· integrity
· knowledge of adolescent
  psychology
· confidence in using different
  teaching methods
· being sensitive to the
  ramifications of controversy
  in the classroom
· listening skills
· familiarity with resources
· ability to give and receive
  criticism
· understanding of group
  dynamics
· perseverance
· knowledge of one's own
  limitations
· ability to work in a team
  with colleagues
· tolerance
· being able to set realistic
  targets
· being able to say 'no'
· 'public relations' skills
· being willing to share power
· approachability
· being able to learn from
  mistakes
· political awareness
· familiarity with curriculum
  developments

controversial. Moreover, unlike contention in subjects like science, the immediacy and emotiveness of PSHE concerns cause them to be perceived as 'crises' or causes for 'moral panic'. In the mid-1980s, for example, there was widespread anxiety about the health 'problems' of young people, particularly those related to sexual behaviour and drug abuse. Questions of morality and social and political education have also been the focus of differences. Such debate, whether at a philosophical or pragmatic level, involves fundamental, ethical and epistemological questions which we cannot deal with in detail here but which teachers need to reflect on. There are suggestions in the further reading which may be helpful in this connection.

Teachers expose themselves to attack whenever they tackle an issue which is deemed 'controversial'. The questions below may help to 'clear the ground':

· Why is this an issue, here and now?
· For whom is it controversial, and why?
· Why am I tackling this issue — what is my purpose?
· Who decided this issue should be explored and how was that decision made?
· What is the context within which this issue is being discussed?

Expounding on these points briefly: issues are issues because someone decrees them to be so. They may be temporary or ongoing, general or culture-specific. Teachers must decide who is setting the agenda — themselves, governors, parents, students, the media, the government? How much do/should teachers respond to the concerns of others? How much negotiation is feasible, especially with students? To what extent are the educational aims of issue-based teaching openly considered? Apart from the obvious, that a controversial issue is one about which there is disagreement based on value judgements — how do we decide what is controversial and what is not? In many cases an issue is deemed 'controversial' if it threatens the status quo or challenges 'established' values. Certainly, some institutions — the government, the City, the Courts, the media and, in some instances, the Church — have more power to determine what counts as 'controversial' than the average parent, teacher or student. However, we do not operate in a political vacuum. Teachers need to be mindful of recent history, current circumstances and future outcomes, both in general and with respect to their student groups. And they need to ask what they can do to assert their understandings and values alongside those of more dominant agencies. This raises personal as well as political questions: What do I believe in? What do I think about a particular issue? To what extent will I allow my feelings to affect the way I teach?

There are no absolutes to govern our handling of controversy. Moral education, according to a relativist position, would give equal credence to racist and anti-racist views. Such a stance is untenable to us. But, on the other hand, affirmation of certain moral principles begs the question of their selection. Our

137

own commitment is to rational discourse and to balance — although we acknowledge the unequal constraints which affect an individual's contributions. Balance, in this context, is not synonymous with neutrality, impartiality or objectivity. Teachers are already operating in an 'unbalanced' situation, given the prevalence of unsubstantiated 'truths' which pervade wider society. To teach, overtly and covertly, for instance, that white supremacy is natural, that boys are more powerful than girls, that homosexuals are deviants, that the Irish and Jews are inferior, that there is only one true deity and one form of worship — and so on, is, to us, highly controversial and thoroughly anti-educational. How can this sort of 'truth' be redressed? Only, we believe, on the basis of a balanced perspective which relates to the values outlined in Chapter 1. In the light of these, we offer the following guidelines to teachers openly approaching controversial issues in the classroom:

· Demonstrate respect for people, especially your students, irrespective of their opionions.
· Be sincere about (and aware of) your own value position and, if appropriate, admit your view. Be vigilant about relying on reason rather than status in arguing your position.
· Encourage the detection of bias, particularly in areas often taken for granted, including research methods and conclusions.
· Acknowledge the provisionality of 'truth' and the ultimate difficulty, though not the uselessness, of distinguishing fact from opinion. Use evidence where possible and encourage students to assess the objectivity, relevance and validity of supporting material and arguments.
· Try to be informed about the subject under discussion and the nature of ideas pertaining to it. Collect evidence, stimulus materials and so on to focus students' ideas.
· Respect students' rights but point out their responsibilities in terms of engagement with an issue. Use methods, such as structured discussions in small groups, which permit this.
· Attempt to provide 'balance' in terms of representing viewpoints but note that: some issues cannot be simply polarised — 'counter-balance' may be necessary. The status quo is not value-free, nor are students clean sheets. Neutrality, therefore, can mask dissembling.
· Remember the age, experience and abilities of the students and the social and psychological barriers which may inhibit their reasoning.
· Where appropriate, be clear about and refer to the views of the Head, of parents and of governors.
· Be aware of personal relevance and intrusiveness — a discussion on abortion, for instance, may be too traumatic for a recently pregnant student.
· Be clear about procedural rules, such as listening to each other. Agree a contract with students about such procedures.
· Remember that the dynamics of a group, and the interpersonal relation-

ships within it, may affect the outcomes of a discussion — as well as the ostensible nature of the issue itself.
· Encourage autonomous reflection by students to draw their own conclusions.
· Ask your colleagues for support.

As we have already said, PSHE is inescapably controversial. Issue-based teaching within PSHE can be useful in enhancing student motivation, especially where they are involved in negotiating the subject, and in developing communication skills. Possible disadvantages are those associated with a 'one-off' situation, in which an issue gets dealt with in isolation from other aspects of the students' experience. Greater educational benefits will result if connections are made with other issues and aspects of PSHE — and with other areas of the formal and hidden curriculum.

The prerequisite to tackling PSHE controversies is clarity of aims and consistency in terms of methods. The PERM model (Chapter 3) can again be useful here. If your principal aim is 'to develop effective strategies for group problem solving and for critical analysis of existing social set-ups', how will your approach to a controversial issue, such as drug-taking, reflect this? On the other hand, if you are primarily concerned 'to promote conformity to normative needs' your teaching will have a very different slant. Can you justify your handling of controversy in terms of your educational aims?

Without controversy, ideas become sterile. Teachers, particularly those involved in PSHE, are hard pushed to develop good practice in exploring contentious issues. But defensiveness or avoidance is not the solution. There is clear educational common sense in making controversy explicit to students. Our task as teachers is to resist pressures to deny this.

The chapters which follow offer strategies — for the classroom, for the whole school and for training — which may help teachers in their professional practice.

FURTHER READING

Balogh, J. (1982) *Profile reports for school-leavers*, Longman for Schools Council, York
Brennan, T. (1981) *Political education and democracy*, Cambridge University Press, Cambridge
Broadfoot, P. (ed.) (1986) *Profiles and records of achievement*, Holt, Rinehart and Winston, London
Crick, B. and Porter, A. (eds) (1978) *Political education and political literacy*, Longman, York
David, K. and Williams, T. (eds) (1987) *Health education in schools*, 2nd edn, Harper and Row, London
Hirst, P.H. and Peters, R.S. (1970) *The logic of education*, Routledge and Kegan Paul, London
Hitchcock, G. (1986) *Profiles and profiling: a practical introduction*, Longman, Harlow

Kraftwohl, D., Bloom, B. and Masia, B. (1964) *The taxonomy of educational objectives*, Longman, York

Law, B. (1984) *The uses and abuses of profiling*, Harper Education, London

Lawton, D. (1983) *Curriculum studies and educational planning*, Hodder and Stoughton, London

Lee, R. (1980) *Beyond coping: some approaches to social education*, FEU/Longman, London

McCormick, R. and James, M. (1983) *Curriculum evaluation in schools*, Croom Helm, London

McPhail, P. (1982) *Social and moral education*, Blackwell, Oxford

Rogers, B. (1984) *Careers education and guidance*, CRAC/Hobsons Press, Cambridge

Schools Council/Nuffield Foundation (1970) *The humanities project*, Heinemann, London

Skilbeck, M. (ed.) (1984) *Readings in school-based curriculum development*, Harper and Row, London

Wellington, J.J. (ed.) (1986) *Controversial issues in the curriculum*, Blackwell, Oxford

6

The Teaching Methodology of PSHE

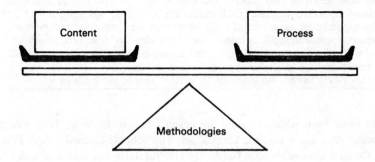

In this chapter we set the scene with a cameo describing a typical first-year lesson in PSHE. We then consider the general tasks of teaching and learning before moving on to address the particular case of PSHE. We end with some examples of student exercises, which help to give a more detailed flavour of practice.

THE TASK OF TEACHING

Teaching is a complex activity made up of a multitude of interactions. Its chief purpose is the enablement of learning, but it does involve other roles. For example, within the classroom, teachers may be expected to act as counsellors, as administrators or as arbitrators. Their wider professional roles may include those of politician, researcher or public relations officer. In this chapter we focus on interactions which are explicitly concerned with learning. However, it is worth remembering that both teachers and learners carry with them thoughts and feelings connected with other roles. These can obstruct or enhance the learning process.

One key to the enablement of learning is accurate matching of student and task. The notion of the spiral curriculum (Bruner, 1960), outlined on p. 102, is a

---

Cameo

It is a sunny morning and form 1S are gathering for the start of another week. Their room, in a now quite shabby post-war building, is brightly bedecked with posters, plants and somewhat dog-eared examples of student work. Ms Peters, the tutor, begins.

First she invites students to share something good that happened over the weekend, in a round. Then they proceed to the main task: to decide on a programme for the remainder of this term's tutor periods. Ms Peters explains that all the other first-year forms are doing the same thing at this time so that staff can work out a common approach. Since the forthcoming module is to be on health careers, the way 1S will explore alternative topics that might interest them is by looking at some of the behaviours that influence their own health. After a blackboard example of what she means by 'influences on health', Ms Peters asks the class to divide into groups. Pairs of groups are first told to brainstorm influences on three separate health topics. The pairs of groups next put their lists together and these are presented to the whole class for comparison and comments. When the common health influences have been identified from each presentation and written on a new sheet of paper, students are asked to vote on their priorities. 'Friends' and the 'media' emerge as leading preferences.

Ms Peters records the votes for 1S to take away to her colleagues.

---

useful basis from which to view the organisation of teaching, both within a particular area and across the curriculum. The Schools Council Health Education Council *Co-ordinator's Guide* (1984), for instance, contains a detailed health education curriculum, showing how health topics can be 'revisited' in greater depth for different year groups. Hopson and Scally (1980) outline another set of possibilities in relation to life skills. Both schemes take account of what Bruner (1971) refers to as 'cognitive matching': the selection of experiences which have the 'best' educational significance for the learner. The principal tasks for the teacher in this respect are to elicit what students know, to determine what they 'need' to know and to present them with opportunities to elaborate their knowledge. A number of considerations are relevant to this process:

· *The nature of the selected knowledge*
Who chose it? What is its source? Does it have a particular form? How does it relate to other content?

· *The development of the students*
Is their physical development (dexterity, onset of puberty, etc.) relevant? Are the stages of cognitive, moral and social development of individual students taken into account? How accomplished are students at 'lower-order' skills (such as writing) or 'higher-order' skills (such as negotiating)? What are the needs of individuals/student groups in relation to their development? What do they already know?

· *The learning process*

How will students interact with the sources of knowledge? What learning strategies seem most appropriate? How are individual learning styles accommodated? How is the learning to be evaluated?

· *The learning milieu*

How are aims/methods affected by whole-school/national priorities? Are the basic resources available (paper, videos, movable furniture, etc.)? Is there a climate of enthusiasm and trust? Is the teacher's behaviour and repertoire of skills appropriate?

Attention to questions like these inevitably requires consultation. It involves agreement over themes, such as study skills, which are not subject-specific. It also demands a detailed picture of students' current progress, say, in the field of communication skills. Teachers therefore have further tasks: those of liaising with colleagues and monitoring and recording student progress.

Another element of the teacher's role concerns motivation. This links both to cognitive matching and to the provision of appropriate learning climates. Clearly, students themselves must bring the intrinsic motivation. But teachers have a direct responsibility to enhance the extrinsic influences on their students' learning. They may choose to do this formally, through the use of rewards and punishments, examination entries and so on. Or they may adopt more informal actions, such as acknowledgement and approval, peer influence and parental pressure. A teacher cannot implant 'natural' curiosity but he can foster it by valuing rather than dismissing or trivialising any signs of enthusiasm.

Another teacher role we wish to highlight is that of behaviour modelling. Traditionally teaching has taken the form of 'instruction'. However, the last 20 years have seen the development of more collaborative relationships in which the teacher is a 'facilitator' (Rogers, 1983). This role requires different understanding and a more flexible set of skills. Within PSHE, consistency between teacher behaviour and teaching aims is all-important, as we saw in the discussion of alternative models. Fundamental principles such as integrity and respect are unlikely to be fostered among students if they are not observable in the actions of teachers. McPhail *et al.* (1972), in their research for the Lifeline project on Moral Education, found that young people were particularly critical of instruction about how to behave in interpersonal relationships when this was not reflected in teachers' own behaviour. 'Do as I say, not as I do', is not readily acceptable nowadays — if it ever was. All kinds of teacher behaviour matter here. For instance, a teacher's own enthusiasm for learning is a powerful model for students: legitimating study, inquiry and interest that might otherwise seem outmoded. Punctuality, fairness and reliability, and the ability to give honest feedback, for example, in marking students' work, are also important models if we want students to show respect and consideration.

Exercise 6.1 takes rather a long time but it provides a useful structure for reflecting on individual approaches to teaching.

Exercise 6.1: What Is My Teaching Style?

This exercise is designed to raise general points about your personal style of teaching by focusing, initially, on your approach to individual students.

1. Take a large sheet of paper and divide it into four columns, headed as follows:

Student trios	Student characteristics	Learning outcomes	Teaching approach
Ⓐ B Ⓒ	outgoing and confident		
A B D			
A C D			
B C D			

2. Think of a class or student group and select four students who are fairly representative of the rest. Group the students in four sets of three and write their initials (or names) in the first column, as indicated.

3. Consider the first trio: A, B and C. Choose two of the three who are most alike and different from the third. Ring the paired initials and, in the second column, jot down a word or phrase to describe their distinguishing characteristic, as shown in the example. Repeat for each set of students.

4. For each pair, in turn, think of a way in which the students are alike in terms of desired learning outcomes. What main educational objective do you have for both of them? Write this in the third column and repeat for each pairing.

5. Go back to the first pair. Ask yourself, 'How are these two students alike in terms of the way I work with them?' In a few words, note your comments and move on to the other three rows. It may help to think, 'IF (column 2), THEN (column 3), BY (column 4).

Comments

Your responses will show that you have your own individual teaching style based on your own theories of teaching and learning. Do you, for example, use a wide range of teaching approaches, or a narrow one? Are some learning goals more universal than others?

The exercise can be applied using more students to obtain a wider range of characteristics. As with most such exercises, this one repays discussion with a colleague.

Adapted from Hunt (1980) in Wooster and Hall (1986).

WAYS OF LEARNING

Gagne (1977) defines learning as 'a change in disposition or capability, which persists over a period of time, and which is not simply ascribable to processes of growth'. Learning, therefore, is more than development and can be facilitated, both through appropriate guidance and by the provision of an appropriate climate. Our approach to PSHE is based on a commitment to 'holistic' learning wherein thoughts, feelings and actions are integrally related and must be addressed in unison. Such an approach inevitably heightens the complexity of the learning process and although no one can ultimately take responsibility for another's learning, it is important for teachers to offer as much clarification and support to students as possible.

One of the most significant points about learning is that there are different ways of doing it. There are no 'right' or 'wrong' ways but different strategies can be more or less effective a) for the particular task in hand and b) for the individual learner. For example, memorising *War and Peace* is not the best way to appreciate the characters' interrelationships nor is an understanding of kinetic energy a necessary precondition for effective mastery of the bicycle. Because people adopt different learning strategies, some may prefer to work steadily in a predetermined direction, organising their thoughts *en route*, while others may 'butterfly' from topic to topic, making intuitive connections and patterns, or may devise complex flow charts and other planning aids.

We do not have space to elaborate on the different taxonomies of learning or classifications of learning style. Suggestions for relevant further reading appear at the end of the chapter. Our main claim is that everybody can get better at learning and can become more aware of their own learning style and the strategies which most effectively complement it. By acknowledging and demonstrating a variety of approaches, teachers can help students become more aware of their own style of learning. They can help them to learn how to learn rather than simply learning how to be taught. This kind of autonomy, as Wall (1977) points out, is 'the most precious cognitive gift of education'. Exercise 6.2, by encouraging you to reflect on your own learning, may help you to recognise different learning strategies.

SOURCES OF LEARNING

The model of learning outlined in Figure 6.1 indicates different sources of knowledge and the possible interactions which are a prerequisite to learning.

Currently, there is a tendency to shift the balance of sources from the teacher and materials to the self and peers. But while we welcome this trend as a counter to traditional models of teaching, we are not advocating that 'student-centred learning' is supreme or, on its own, sufficient. As McPhail (1982) argues:

Exercise 6.2: How Do I Learn?

1. Write down (as in the chart below) ten things that you have learned since you were born. These could be facts, skills, understandings, feelings, familiarities and so on.

2. Next to each one, jot down a few words to describe the context in which this learning took place. Where was it? Did you use any materials? Was someone elsed involved? How long did it take?

3. Write down the principal learning strategy you employed. Did you analyse, copy, practise, memorise, explore connections, or what?

4. Select a) a learning experience that was good/easy/satisfying and b) one that was bad/difficult/frustrating. For each of these, try to identify and write down the main features that made it 'good' or 'bad' and caused you to choose it as an example.

Things I have learned	Context	Learning strategy
1.		
2.		
3.		
4.		
5.		
6.		
7.		
8.		
9.		
10.		

a)

b)

5. Discuss with a partner, or reflect yourself, on the following and any other questions that arise:

· Do you learn best in a particular context? How often are you in this situation?
· Do you find certain learning strategies easier than others? How often do you use them?
· What were/are your main motivating factors for learning?
· How did/do you cope with/adapt to difficult learning situations?
· How does this exercise connect with PSHE?

Figure 6.1: Features of Learning

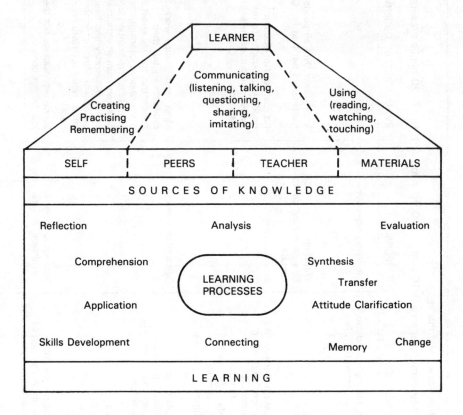

Note: 1. This model of learning assumes that the learner has the motivation, confidence and experience to choose appropriate interactions and strategies to engage with the learning process.
2. 'Teacher' includes anyone who acts as a source of knowledge in a learning situation.

The basic inconsistency of those who advocate social or moral learning only through the individual development of reason and interaction in the peer group (for example, Stenhouse, 1970) is that they accept the importance of interaction but attempt to restrict it to one context — a context in which the participants are equally inexperienced. Such an approach widens the generation gap and encourages children's or adolescents' rejection of adults and their alienation. It is a poor context in which to develop the capacity to put oneself into others' shoes that is fundamental to learning.

Teachers are not only facilitators of learning in the way we have described above. They also generally have more experience, more knowledge and more

Figure 6.2: Outline for a Tutorial Session on 'Influences and Planning' (with a mixed group of First years in an inner-city comprehensive 9.10 a.m. − 10.00 a.m., 3.2.1987, 20 pupils present)

TIME	ACTIVITY	ORGANISATION	PURPOSE	EVALUATION BY OBSERVER
2 mins.	Introduction. T. tells class that they are going to work out their programme for the next half term	Pupils, having moved tables away, sit, listen to T. in a circle	Clarifying objectives	Fine
3 mins.	'One healthy thing I did at half term ...'	Round	Warm-up Re-establishing group climate	Very useful. Not all pupils contributed but that felt OK
3 mins.	*Influences on Behaviour* i) Introduction	i) T. uses a blackboard e.g. 'Influences on drinking behaviour ...', friends money ads drinking thirsty place mood	Scene-setting	Bit rushed. Not enough pupil contributions (allow longer. Encourage fuller discussion)
10 mins.	ii) Brainstorm influences on − a) my eating behaviour b) my personal hygiene c) how I get on with other people	ii) Pupils divided into 6 groups, 2 per topic They write ideas on large sheets of paper	Generating ideas	Most small groups worked productively but their concentration was spoilt by 4 successive interruptions from teachers wanting to make announcements/see pupils (Assembly had been cancelled) Must be firmer about refusing? Note on door?
5 mins.	iii) Whole-group review	iii) Lists compared and pinned up. A new list of common behaviours created	Sorting: looking for similarities, differences, gaps	Some restlessness but the job did get done

Time	Prioritising What behaviours do we want to look at for the rest of this half term?	Negotiation Decision making	Worked well
2 mins.		T. explains this stage	Class now used to this pattern of working. Minimum fuss/disturbance
2 mins.		i) Individuals choose the 3 behaviours they would be most interested in	
3 mins.		ii) With a partner, agree on a joint 'best 3'	
3 mins.		iii) Partners pair up and agree on a joint 'best 4'	
10 mins.		iv) Whole class review the full list of possibilities, noting votes for each behaviour from the 4s	
8 mins.		v) final agreement on top priorities	Ending Too rushed
2 mins.		Replace tables and chairs. Tidy up.	Next class arrived before job was completed. Not everyone helped. (Firmer control)

skills — particularly in areas relevant to the prescribed learning situation. This means that the teacher/student relationship is one of 'temporary inequality' (Miller, D. 1976) whose main *raison d'être* is service to the student. Of course, teachers do not have a monopoly on truth or relevance. However, it is short-sighted if they do not use the knowledge and skills they do possess. Indeed, we would argue that it is mistaken not to encourage student interaction with the widest possible range of sources of knowledge (in and out of school) and, furthermore, that teachers should use as wide a variety of methods as possible in order to foster autonomous learning strategies in their students.

Arguments for variety do not, hopefully, constitute a recipe for chaos! Teachers of all subjects are more likely to accommodate the educational individuality of their students if they utilise different approaches — many of which we would call 'active learning methods'. However, such methods require as much planning and structuring as traditional techniques, if not more. They also demand a high degree of self-awareness and reflectiveness on the part of the teacher as we saw in Exercise 3.2. Detailed attention to timing, tempo, group dynamics and individual differences is a further element crucial to successful practice, as Figure 6.2 demonstrates. You will perhaps recognise the lesson to which these notes relate from the cameo on p. 142.

Just as students become better learners, teachers can learn more about teaching and, inevitably, about themselves — for instance, by asking colleagues to record observations on their lessons, as in Figure 6.2. Given that all learning is a risky business, support is essential, as we argue in Chapter 8. It is particularly important in a field as demanding as PSHE.

THE PSHE FOCUS OF LEARNING

We have suggested that any teaching situation is likely to be more fruitful if a variety of methods are used. For the particular pedagogy of PSHE, however, variety is crucial, given the focus of learning. Whether as a distinct subject, or as an integral component of other curriculum areas, PSHE is characterised by learning about 'self' in relation to 'others'. As we saw in the previous chapter, this focus encompasses the knowledge and skills of communication, decision making, problem solving, reflection and transfer, as well as an explicit consideration of values and relationships.

What is particularly significant about PSHE is the partnership of methods and content. Indeed, the aims of PSHE are virtually unachievable without appropriate methodologies: notably an experiential approach to learning, as described by Claxton (1984). Students can learn psychological or socio-anthropological theory from texts or formal lectures but they are not learning about themselves and how they or others feel, nor are they developing their communication or decision-making skills if they work in this way. The rationale of PSHE implies 'confluent learning' (Brandes and Ginnis, 1986), in which the affective and cognitive domains flow together. Rogers (1983) describes the process thus:

> Let me define a bit more precisely the elements that are involved in such significant learning or experiential learning. *It has a quality of personal involvement* — the whole person in both feeling and cognitive aspects being in the learning event. It is *self-initiated*. Even when the impetus or stimulus comes from the outside, the sense of discovery, of reaching out, of grasping and comprehending, comes from within. *It is pervasive.* It makes a difference in the behaviour, the attitudes, perhaps even the personality of the learner. *It is evaluated by the learner.* She knows whether it is meeting her need, whether it leads towards what she *wants* to know, whether it illuminates the dark area of ignorance she is experiencing. The locus of evaluation, we might say, resides definitely in the learner. *Its essence is meaning.* When such learning takes place, the element of meaning to the learner is built into the whole experience. (author's emphases)

A consequence of achieving harmony between focus and method, content and process, is that within PSHE students learn more about learning. As Rogers indicates, the 'locus of evaluation' resides in the learner. This does not mean that the responsibility for and monitoring of learning is simply dumped on students by the teacher, who abnegates any leadership or guidance role. On the contrary, within the methodology of PSHE, teachers suggest and encourage ways of making their learning more visible to students. This may involve declaring and/or negotiating overall aims with students as well as specific objectives for individuals. Even the simple technique of stating, or writing down, at the end of each lesson, 'One thing I have learned today is ...' helps young people to evaluate their learning. Other examples are given later. What is more, because of the explicit recognition in PSHE that feelings and thoughts are both important, students become aware of all the influences on their learning. This, in turn, may make them better learners. Figure 6.3 shows the four different models of PSHE described in Chapter 3 in terms of their predominant method and focus.

Clearly this representation cannot indicate the whole picture but the criteria relating to content and process are significant ones, especially when comparing ideals and practice. Where should PSHE be plotted ideally? Where would you locate one of your lessons?

The relationship between content and process is complex and can all too easily be seen as a false dichotomy. Unfortunately it is little researched. Sometimes, when exploring group interactions, for instance, the process may in fact constitute the content. What appears to be the case is that most learning, certainly in PSHE, is multi-dimensional. It is also personal. Thus, for some topics and tasks, and for some learners, content and process may be mutually reinforcing — as, for example, when students' decision-making skills improve

Figure 6.3: The Pedagogy of PSHE: a Comparison of Approaches

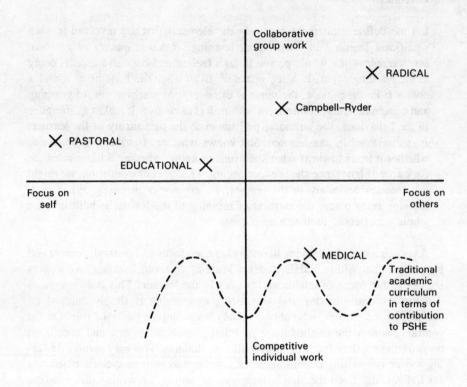

Note: The 'content' axis refers to 'people' (self and others), this being the province of PSHE, but learning about 'things' can also contribute to PSHE, independent of method. An appreciation of the 'wonders of the world', for instance, is an important component of spiritual health.

as a result of taking part in a negotiation simulation. In other cases the matching may be negligible. As Piaget (1932) points out, more empirical research is needed here to establish the links between 'affective' and 'cognitive' matching:

> Apart from the question of the aims of education, it is obvious that it is for experiment alone and not deduction to show us whether methods such as that of work in groups and of self-government are of any real value. For, after all, it is one thing to prove that co-operation in the play and spontaneous social life of children brings about certain moral effects, and another to establish the fact that this co-operation can be universally applied as a method of education.

Figure 6.4: Contrasting Teaching Styles

Student-centred	Traditional
Student role active: · negotiating content and rules of conduct with teacher · controlling student talk · organising display of students' work · sharing the management of resources with teacher · maintaining shared contract of behaviour	Student role passive: · teacher determines content and rules of conduct · pupil/pupil talk discouraged · teacher controls display of students' work · teacher manages resources · teacher maintains discipline and behaviour standards
Subject matter integrated	Boundaries separating subjects
Teacher acts as facilitator/guide	Teacher transmits knowledge/acts as sole authority
Learning predominantly uses active techniques: · collaboration · group work · starts from what students know or are concerned about · not confined to the classroom · regular review and evaluation (of self and group performance)	Learning focuses on memory, practice and rote: · individual and competitive in emphasis · concerned with academic standards · confined to lab. or classroom · accent on tests and grades
Uses intrinsic motivation in students	Motivation mainly external, based on rewards and punishments
Classroom talk often focuses on feelings/cognitive and affective domains given equal emphasis	Classroom talk tends to exclude feelings/neglect of affective domain
Students encouraged to think and talk about what they are learning	Little attempt to focus on student learning behaviors
Process is valued and discussed alongside content	Little attention paid to process

Adapted from Settle and Wise, 1986, and Brandes and Ginnis, 1986

This prompts Piaget to argue for an 'experimental pedagogy'. However, he stresses that 'the type of experiment such research would require can only be conducted by teachers or by the combined efforts of practical workers and educational psychologists'. The following sections of this chapter describe the pedagogy associated with PSHE in a way which teachers may find useful as a basis for their own 'experimentation'.

PSHE CLASSROOM METHODS

A plethora of terms exist to describe the kind of pedagogy we advocate for PSHE: student-centred learning, active methods, experiential learning, confluent education, participatory learning, and so on. The chief characteristics of this pedagogy, as distinct from more traditional approaches, are summarised in Figure 6.4.

153

So far we have argued for an approach which makes the process of learning as clear and explicit as possible (i.e. 'active' in the sense that students are engaged with their own progress as well as with the end-product of their learning). We have also stressed the usefulness of a variety of methods to accommodate different student needs. An immediate difficulty in becoming initiated into these approaches is that of making sense of the terminology. Many of the terms are used interchangeably and not always in accordance with their originator's own interpretation or perspective. Also, some phrases have become labelled as 'jargon' and are thereby prey to criticism — for example, for being trendy, platitudinous or sloppy. This kind of resistance does a disservice to educational innovation but it is clearly important for practitioners to understand the meaning of the terminology they use. This is why we have included a glossary in Appendix 2.

One thing that different versions of the 'new' pedagogy seem to have in common is an emphasis on a particular learning set-up: group work. But what's so special about groups? Have not students always worked in a class group?

We use the term group work to describe teaching strategies which a) encourage students to work collaboratively and share their knowledge and b) provide opportunities to reflect and perhaps improve the interpersonal relationships existing between students. These are both strategies which help students to assimilate the values and skills integral to healthy personal and social development. They also reflect the significance of groups in everyday life. There are a number of reasons why groups are so important. Humans are social animals for whom groups convey identity and purpose. Groups also help in combating the isolation, prejudice and loneliness seemingly endemic in our society. They can support vulnerable members of our communities (the aged, those with disabilities, the bereaved and so on). Indeed, the best chance available to mobilise an effective opposition to the dominant and typically alien institutions of capitalism comes, in our view, from self-help and other voluntary groups (Gibson, 1979). The power of such organisations derives not only from the strength of unity but also from their task-efficiency and adaptability, particularly in the face of set-backs. Structured group work with young people can reinforce such benefits and provide an appropriate vehicle for linking the personal with the political.

Before considering some basic ground rules for group work, we will outline some of its advantages and disadvantages.

ADVANTAGES OF GROUP WORK

· Its methods foster student interaction and hence communication skills — notably oracy and other interpersonal skills such as dealing with criticism.
· There are more sources of knowledge available because students' contributions are encouraged.

- Individual progress can more easily be monitored, through self-evaluation, as well as teacher assessment.
- Both teacher and student are free to explore different roles and take different responsibilities. Hence, they can learn more about themselves and others and develop feelings of worth and esteem.
- Group work provides opportunities to confront prejudice and stereotyping — about race, gender, sexual orientation and handicap, for example. As Salmon and Clare (1984) affirm:

> Collaborative learning offers the possibility of overcoming the barriers to mutual personal recognition. By endorsing the existence of social relation-ships in the classroom and seeking to extend positive feeling beyond existing cliques, teachers may be able to overcome antipathy and incomprehension among pupils and develop mutual understanding.

- Black students are more likely to achieve their potential through working in small group situations (Johnson *et al*. 1984).
- Girls in single-sex groups are freer to develop their abilities (Webb, 1984).
- Group work encourages what Bruner (1966) terms 'reciprocity': an intrinsic drive to join with others in working towards some achievement or shared objective.
- Mixed-ability classes can build on this enhanced motivation, the desire to work together to get things done far outweighing the problem of different abilities and skills.
- Group work is fun. It utilises one of the basic human attributes, that of sociability. As Button (1974) says, 'To be human is synonymous with being in communication and in relationship with other people.' Working in groups is one way of maximising this particular aspect of our humanness.

DISADVANTAGES OF GROUP WORK

- Time. These methods of working need careful pre-planning and, because of the high levels of interaction and engagement, can be exhausting for both teacher and students.
- Participants may initially feel resistant to group work and time is needed to demonstrate its benefits and learn the attendant skills.
- Passive students may feel under more pressure to contribute in group-work situations while confident and more extroverted students are frustrated at having to attend to the needs of the group.
- For those who believe in fostering individual competition, the benefits of collaboration in small groups will seem trivial.
- Teachers need to be able to deal constructively with whatever currents of feel-ing are generated by the group dynamic. Uncooperative behaviour, for

example, is more overt in the group situation than when individual students 'switch off' in class, and it may need confronting more publicly.
· There may be initial discipline problems as students become accustomed to working in new and more flexible ways and are still learning the 'rules' of group-work behaviour.
· Colleagues may be hostile about issues such as increased noise as well as about the implicit challenge to their own teaching approach.

SOME GUIDANCE FOR EFFECTIVE GROUP WORK

The suggestions that follow are necessarily brief and may sound patronising. This is not our intention. While any PSHE teacher is likely to benefit from formal group-work training, we appreciate that such opportunities are limited. We therefore offer a number of practical hints:

1. Be aware that things happen in groups because that is the nature of groups and not necessarily because of your leadership. For instance, they can sometimes be overtaken by group hysteria or by a kind of group apathy or 'stuckness'.

2. Know why you are using a particular method in a group. An exercise just for fun or to wake students up is fine but do not pretend to yourself that it is for a different purpose, otherwise students will be puzzled when reflecting on what they have learnt.

3. Be prepared. Practical considerations such as appropriate materials and writing implements can be crucial, as can alternative materials to use when the activities planned take less time than anticipated. Seating arrangements are also important, though not a shibboleth. Group work can be successful even when the students have to sit around the outside of fixed laboratory benches rather than 'in the round', in a circle of seats, on a carpeted floor.

4. Other important prior considerations include the strengths and weaknesses of individual students; the most appropriate 'mix' of students for any small group or pairs/threes work; the timing/structuring of activities; the way any exercises are introduced and debriefed, and the objectives of any evaluation.

5. Watch out for problems such as marked discrepancies in participation; role-sticking (one student always doing the recording or reporting-back, for instance); personally abusive behaviour; the breaking of confidences; behaviour which risks sabotaging the work of the group; or signs of personal distress.

6. There must be agreed procedures for students to opt out of some activities — either to withdraw completely or to occupy a more neutral role, such as that of 'timekeeper' or 'observer'.

7. Agree a contract with the students with respect to the above 'rules' of conduct. Keep to it yourself and challenge students who break it. The contract might include elements such as agreement to listen to each other, without interruption; keeping confidences and promises; sticking to time limits and so on.

However, it is important that it is perceived as a flexible agreement which can be renegotiated, by consensus, when appropriate. See Hopson and Scally (1980) for further discussion on contracts.

8. Encourage students to take responsibility for their own learning and for their own thoughts, feelings and attitudes. Thus, suggest they use the form: 'I find this exercise boring' rather than 'This (exercise/group/task/subject) is boring', for example.

9. Encourage honesty and acceptance of a diversity of opinions. There is no need to reconcile all differences, especially if students can demonstrate good evidence in support of the view they hold.

10. Be alert! Expect the unexpected and be prepared to abandon your plan and change direction completely! Although it can feel decidedly risky, the best rule is to 'stay with the feelings in the group'. For instance, when students are angry or frustrated, you will be better off abandoning the task (whether or not it is actually the particular task which is at fault) in favour of a direct invitation to talk about whatever is bothering them.

11. Consider your own role. What do you need to do to change from an instructor to a facilitator? Which of your qualities/attributes/skills can you capitalise on, which do you need to keep in check? Will you be an impartial observer or an 'equal' participant in activities? What tasks will you accept and which will you delegate? How will you ensure that you keep to your side of the contract and to these ground rules? How familiar are you with the activities you are imposing on the students? Are you comfortable with them?

12. Learn to manage silences effectively. This involves sensitivity to the difference between 'productive' silence, in which students are thinking or experiencing new emotions, and silence which is due to genuine 'stuckness', embarrassment or boredom.

13. Develop a sense of humour — and particularly the ability to laugh at yourself when things fail to go according to plan!

This book is not a group-work training manual and this list of ground rules is only a summary. (The further reading offers more detailed suggestions which you may wish to pursue. There are also suggestions in Appendix 3 about agencies which offer different forms and levels of training.) Teachers, like anyone else, learn 'on the job' and group-work skills can develop, in part, through trial and error. However, we reiterate our belief in the importance of training, if at all possible. This is both to provide experience of an increased repertoire of teaching strategies and materials and confidence in experimentation and to increase awareness of the processes of group dynamics. Such training must, itself, be experiential, which is an added advantage. For, unless teachers themselves know what it feels like to take part in an exercise, they cannot be sensitive to the feelings of students. Training can also support teachers in adopting a different leadership role: something that is often both personally and professionally threatening. Most teachers rely on their conferred status and subject expertise as a basis for student respect. Within PSHE, given the kind of methodology we have outlined, teachers need to earn their students' respect personally. All this can be hard. But it is immensely worthwhile.

We move now to some illustrations of exercises appropriate to PSHE. These are intended as a 'taster' of PSHE practice, not as definitive examples. Again, we would warn teachers to try them out themselves before introducing them to students.

PSHE EXERCISES: SOME EXAMPLES

We have selected the exercises which follow because they are representative of PSHE practice as well as being adaptable to other teaching situations. We would remind readers that examples of several other exercises have been introduced in previous chapters. The 'methods spiral' in Figure 6.5 indicates a range of approaches illustrative of PSHE pedagogy. It also gives a rough impression of their frequency of use; the innermost plottings being the more commonly used. This is not to suggest that some activities should be more frequently used than others; it is simply a record of our own experience, of our conversations with other teachers, and our analysis of existing resources. What would your own methods spiral look like? Or that of your colleagues?

As far as possible, the source of each specific exercise we have used is identified. However, in many cases the technique has become so much a part of common practice that its exact origins are lost. What is more (and this is in itself an exciting feature of PSHE), teachers frequently improve and adapt techniques to meet their own circumstances and needs so that methods are continually evolving. In an eclectic area like PSHE, whose origins embrace fields as diverse as psychotherapy and environmental health, there has inevitably been a good deal of borrowing. This diversity adds to its richness.

The examples below are categorised according to the key elements of PSHE identified in Chapter 5: the skills of communication, decision making, problem solving, reflection and transfer in connection with the exploration of values and relationships. These groupings are not mutually exclusive; for example, many activities enhance communication. There are also some suggestions about evaluation and student assessment — although the latter raises issues which require much more detailed research and cannot be satisfactorily surveyed here. Please note that some exercises are more 'difficult' than others, either in the intellectual demands they make or in the experience of group working which they presuppose. There are pointers to such factors in the 'Comments' on each exercise.

Throughout this chapter, we have stressed the importance of methods reflecting aims. The PERM model offers a quick and easy tool to heighten awareness of this link in practice (see pp. 69–70). You may find it useful to 'PERM' each of the exercises. This will help increase understanding of what a given exercise might feel like in practice. It will also serve as a checklist to see whether the methods you use match up to your preferred balance of aims.

Figure 6.5: PSHE Methods Spiral

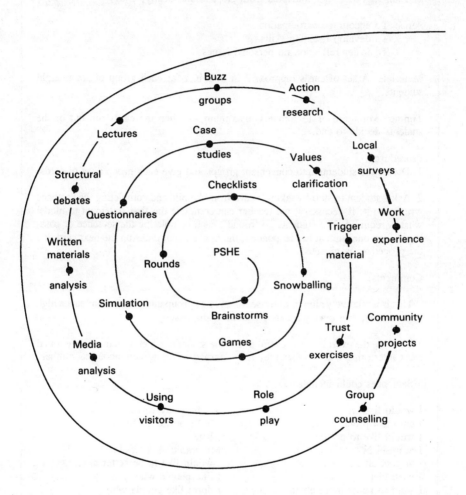

Exercise 6.3: Communication Skills

a) I am ...   (adapted from Hopson and Scally, 1981)

Aims: To encourage participation
      To develop listening skills
      To foster reflection on personal issues

Materials: A set of cards (approx. 3 in. x 5 in.) for each group of six to eight students.

Timing: Minimum of 15 minutes, maximum — when the cards run out or the students decide to end.

Procedure:
1. Divide the students into convenient groups and give each group a set of cards.

2. Ask a student to start by taking a card from the pile and completing the sentence written on it. If necessary, the teacher can complete the first statement to model what is required. The students go 'round', each completing the sentence or passing. When one student has responded, the next student picks up the next card and the procedure is repeated.

Comments:

· This is a relatively simple exercise for any age group and permits students a high degree of control over what they choose to discuss.

· To close the exercise, it is useful to ask the students which statement they found most interesting and whether they have learned anything new about each other.

· Sentences could include:

I would like ...   My best day was ...
I am most proud of ...   My favourite hobby is ...
I would like to go to ...   I hate ...
I'm upset by ...   My ambition is ...
I'm good at ...   I would like to be better at ...
I wish that ...   I like people who ...
I want to know more about ...   I don't like people who ...

but make up your own; the more the better.

PERM here:

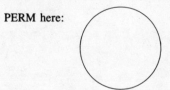

160

Exercise 6.3: Communication Skills

b) Active Listening   (adapted from Clarity Collective, 1985)

Aims: To show the importance of active listening
       To practise communicating, especially listening skills
       To share views about relationships (or any other topic)

Materials: A list of prepared 'trigger' statements (see suggestions below), suitable for the age of students and appropriate to the focus of learning.

Timing: 20–30 minutes.

Procedure:
Students work in pairs, initially, before joining into fours.

1. Each pair selects an issue/'trigger' statement.

2. Ask one of the pair to be the speaker and the other the listener.

3. Ask the speakers to describe their thoughts and feelings on the issue. The listeners can prompt and ask questions but should not voice their own opinions.

4. After four to five minutes, ask the pairs to stop and join up to make fours.

5. Ask the two listeners, in turn, to summarise what their partners said. The original speakers must be satisfied with the accuracy of what they report.

6. Repeat the procedure, the students having changed roles and selected another issue.

7. Ask the students to discuss the activity in fours. What made it easy/difficult to remember what was said? Did the speakers feel encouraged to talk? Are there any points they would like to discuss further? What does active listening involve?

8. Record any feedback (reporting from the small groups) in the whole group.

Comments:

· This exercise needs reinforcement/preparation by other work, such as an exploration of non-verbal communication.

· Trigger statements could include:
   Boys want sex and girls want love.
   Sex without love is immoral.
   It's OK to have two boy/girlfriends at the same time.
   Jealousy is a sign of caring.
   Boys are naturally dominant.

                              PERM here:

Exercise 6.4: Decision-making Skills

a) Time Capsule

Aims: To encourage reflection on physical artefacts of our society
To develop negotiating skills
To practise ways of reaching group decisions.

Materials: Pens and paper.

Timing: Approximately one hour (often more time is needed if the students become really involved).

Procedure: Students work individually to start with and then join up into larger groups.
1. Tell the students that they have each been given the job of deciding on the contents of a 'time capsule'. This time capsule (stipulate size or allow this to be negotiable) can only contain five objects, which should be chosen so as to represent our society to anyone/thing who opens it (e.g. an intelligent alien in 10,000 years' time!) Give students 5 minutes initially to decide what they would put in their capsule. (You might point out that such capsules do already exist.)
2. Ask students to join up in pairs and discuss their selection and to reach a joint decision about the contents.
3. After 10 minutes, ask students to join up in fours and repeat the procedure.
4. After 10–15 minutes, ask students to form larger groups (8s, 10s or whole class, as appropriate) and to reach a consensus within the given time limit (20 minutes or more).
5. Record the final decision (if there is one!) and ask students to return to their original pairs and discuss the following:
    a) How do I feel about the final decision/or lack of one?
    b) How did we make our original decision?
    c) What is different about making decisions in a larger group?
    d) In what (other) ways can a large-group decision be made?
    e) What 'real life' situations require large-group decisions?
6. Take feedback from the pairs, particularly on the last two points.

Comments:
· Probably more suitable for 14+ students.
· These sorts of decision-making/negotiation exercises can be quite unpredictable but invariably give good mileage. Depending on interest in the theme and students' personalities, discussion may become heated, in which case it may be useful to allow students to cool down and follow this by a short group-building exercise.
· Some students will refuse to become particularly involved but their observations in the final feedback will still be useful (they can even be given specific points to observe in the large-group session).
· It is useful for the teacher and/or volunteers to act as observers and to report back to the group on how the discussions proceeded — what kinds of contribution were especially helpful in producing consensus? did a particular group leader emerge? did anyone act as 'timekeeper' etc.
· There are many variations of this exercise, although some are only suitable for more able students since they depend on a technical knowledge base.

PERM here:

Exercise 6.4: Decision-making Skills

b) The Kidney Machine

Aims: To consider the ethical implications of controlling the fate of others
To assess the criteria used in making a decision
To look at students' behaviour in groups

Materials: Copies of 'The Situation', the 'Biographical Record', the observer checklist and the self/group assessment checklist for each student.

Timing: Approximately 40 minutes.

Procedure: The class should be divided into 'committees' of 6/7 students per group and seating arranged accordingly.
1. Ask for a volunteer 'observer' for each group and give him an observer checklist. The observer will need to find a comfortable but non-intrusive position.
2. Ask each student to read their copy of the situation sheet. Check if there are any procedural queries and set the time limit e.g. 20 minutes.
3. Give out the biographical records and leave the committees to reach their decision.
4. Give regular time checks but refrain from becoming involved in dialogues with groups.
5. After 20 minutes, stop the committees and record their final verdict. Give out the self/group assessment checklist and ask individuals to complete them privately. (2/3 mins)
6. Meanwhile, ask the observers to prepare to feedback their observations and to 'chair' any ensuing discussion. Allow 10 mins for this.
7. Whole-group feedback:
a) what decision did your group take and how do you justify it?
b) how did your committee operate as a group?

Comments:
· Suitable for 16+ students who are used to group work.
· Some groups may get stuck or give up. Still keep to the time limit. They may return to the task and it is interesting for them to discuss their group behaviour afterwards.
· Students may refuse to accept the responsibility of making a decision (e.g. on moral grounds). It is worth pointing out that life and death decisions are being made all the time on their behalf. By whom? With what qualifications? Who should have such power? What about global issues like economic impoverishment, genocide, war?
· The observer role is crucial but difficult. The observers should be in control of the feedback discussions but shy students may find this threatening. Advise them to go through each checklist question in turn and invite comments on them one by one.
· The specific feedback is confidential to each group and should not be raised in the whole-group discussion. Students need to be clear about this.
· It could be useful to bring the group together with a closing round, e.g. 'During this exercise, I felt ...' or 'If we did this exercise again, I would ...'.

PERM here:

Exercise 6.4: contd.

The Kidney Machine

The Situation
A new type of kidney machine has recently been installed in the local hospital. The machine functions as a kidney for those who have lost the use of their own and who are therefore likely to die. By being connected to the machine for 24 hours per week, patients can remain alive indefinitely (unless they die for some other reason).

There is only *one* place available for using the machine but local doctors have submitted the names of five candidates. Your job, as a committee, is to select one patient on the basis of the attached biographical information and brief psychological report. You *must* make a decision in the time available and you must also be able to justify the criteria you have used to reach your decision.

Biographical Record

SALLY: Aged 46.
Married for 22 years with two teenage children. Research biochemist at the University Medical School, working on a cancer immunisation project and apparently on the verge of an important breakthrough.

Sally is obviously dedicated to her work but this commitment has caused family problems. Her husband seems resentful of both her illness and the extra time she spends working. Sally seems mentally unstable and prone to fits of depression.

MICHAEL: Aged 27.
Married for 5 years with one 3-year-old child. Wife is 6 months pregnant. Currently employed as a car mechanic for a local garage and attending the technical college for a car mechanics' class. He hopes to start his own business one day.

Michael is devoted to his family and appears to be an excellent husband and father. His school and college records are just satisfactory and his ideas for the future seem to be vague hopes rather than plans. His wife was a secretary but neither of them wants her to work while they have a young family. There are evidently some financial problems. Michael seems unconscious of the seriousness of his illness.

EILEEN: Aged 30.
Married for 11 years with five children. Husband owns and operates a bar and take-away restaurant. They have just bought a house in the suburbs which Eileen intends redecorating completely. She was an Arts student. Eileen seems keen to take up interior decorating.

Eileen is deeply religious and speaks of little else, except her children. Her husband works very hard but spends as much time as possible with the children. Eileen's mother, who lives with them, handles most of the child care. Eileen is dedicated to her work for various charities but seems resigned to her illness and possible death.

JOHN: Aged 19.
Single but with a steady girlfriend whom he hopes to marry soon. He is currently studying for a degree in philosophy and literature and hopes to continue in this field, eventually becoming a lecturer himself. He is very active politically

Exercise 6.4: contd.

and has been responsible for organising several student protests. His mother died recently and his father looks after John's two younger sisters.

John has obvious academic potential but seems determined not to 'toe the line'. He openly disregards his father's wishes but has taken full advantage of financial and emotional support from his family. John is deeply resentful and bitter about his illness and his marriage plans seem full of rebellion rather than deep commitment.

SEVDA: Aged 34.

Single with no children. Presently occupied as a manager for a large manufacturing company. Her work record is excellent and she has introduced many useful schemes for improving production. She has several hobbies, including music and tennis, and spends two nights a week running a telephone counselling service for young people. After her parents died, ten years ago, she took responsibility for bringing up her four younger brothers and sisters.

Sevda is highly independent and ambitious. She is hard-working and has many acquaintances but few, if any, close friends. She seems to have unlimited energy and enthusiasm for life, yet appears resigned to her death.

Self and Group Assessment Checklist (on a separate sheet)

1. In what way did you affect the decision made by the group?
2. Were you unhappy about the final decision?
3. Were you able to express your views?
4. Do you feel you were able to contribute as much as you would have liked?
5. What significant contributions do you feel you made?
6. What was the single most important issue that was discussed in the group?
7. Who do you think had most influences in the group?
8. Do you think there were any significant features about the way in which the group worked?

Observer Checklist (separate sheet)

1. Who led the group and made the decision to start?
2. Who influenced the group most?
3. Was there agreement on *how* to make the decision?
4. What attitudes/values emerged?
5. What were the criteria for decisions about individuals' choices?
6. Was the final decision unanimous?
7. Were there any significant features about the way in which the group worked?
8. What was the single most important issue that was discussed in the group?

Exercise 6.5: Problem-solving Skills

a) Sharon's Problem   (adapted from the Clarity Collective, 1985)

Aims: To practise some of the skills involved in solving problems
      To consider alternative courses of action in real-life problems

Materials: A copy of the story for each participant and large sheets of paper hung around the room.

Timing: Approximately 45 minutes.

Procedure:
1. Ask each student to read the story and decide what Sharon should do.
2. Brainstorm (for about 5 minutes), as a whole class, suggestions for Sharon's alternative courses of action.
3. Composite the suggestions, if necessary, and write each on the top of a separate sheet of paper. Draw a line down each sheet and label the two halves: 'positive outcomes' and 'negative outcomes'.
4. Ask the students to walk around the room and write possible outcomes in the appropriate columns. Encourage them to fill in as many as possible (in approximately 15 minutes).
5. Take each list in turn and, as a whole group, try to eliminate any actions which, in the light of the possible outcomes, seem unrealistic or unreasonable.
6. Divide the students into small groups (three to five) and ask them to decide on the 'best' solution.
7. Record these solutions as a whole group.
8. Ask the students to think of the skills they used to solve this problem. What other problems could be solved in a similar way?

Comments:
· This technique is more appropriate for older students and those used to working together in this way.
· The process can be used to solve many problems raised by the group or individuals themselves.
· Write your own story (or get students to write one) that is more suitable for them.

PERM here:

Sharon's Problem

Sharon is 16 years old and lives with her 17-year-old brother, Mark, their mother and her mother's boyfriend. The young people are both still at school. Mark is studying hard for his A-levels. He hopes to become a doctor. Sharon and Mark often row, mainly because Sharon resents the greater freedom that her brother enjoys. The adults let Mark do almost anything he wants because 'he's such a sensible boy'. Sharon and her friends were recently in trouble at school and now her mother and boyfriend are much stricter with her and say they don't trust her any more.

One weekend a party given by some school friends is raided by the police, who find various illegal drugs and make several arrests. Sharon was at home by herself but Mark went to the party. He managed to get away before the police caught him. Now, however, the police keep returning to question Mark because two of the boys who were arrested have said that he was there and that he provided some of the drugs. Mark wants Sharon to swear to the police and their folks that he was at home with her all evening and that he has never had anything to do with drugs. He has told her that if he gets convicted he will never be allowed into medical school.
   What should Sharon do?

Exercise 6.5: Problem-solving Skills

b) Local Pollution Map   (adapted from Dorn and Nortoft, 1982)

Aims: To identify potential sources of pollution in a locality
        To assess the severity of problems
        To undertake/assess courses of action about environmental issues

Materials: Large maps of the local area. Coloured pens. Phone directories.

Timing: Map activity: 30–40 minutes.

Procedure:
1. Brainstorm causes of pollution (both substances, e.g. lead, and happenings, e.g. accidents).
2. Group these according to type (e.g. radiation, chemical) and allocate each a colour.
3. Ask students (working in groups of 4–6) to colour their map showing the potential sources of pollution in the locality. The phone directories may help to identify products of factories. (Do not forget roads, sea pollution, air routes and farming!)
4. Ask each group to report back on the *main* pollution risk in the area. How did they decide this was the biggest risk?
5. Whole-group discussion — how can pollution be lessened/prevented: a) at a personal level; b) at a local level; c) nationally?
6. Ask each group to discuss and recommend a proposal for reducing pollution in the area.

Comments:
· This exercise, which may be part of a piece of action research for 14+ students, requires preparatory and follow-up work.
· Students' work/suggestions could be presented in letters to the local paper or council or used as a basis for questionnaires to the public.

PERM here:

167

Exercise 6.6: Reflective Skills

a) Shifting Sub-groups

Aims: To elicit students' opinions on a given topic
    To encourage reasoned discussion about different values
    To change tempo/revitalise students

Materials: Either a) a prepared list of statements on a theme
or b) paper/card for students to write one statement each on an agreed theme.

Timing: 10–30 minutes, depending on theme, mood, ensuing discussion.

Procedure: This exercise involves physical movement around the classroom so it should be uncluttered by furniture or belongings.
1. Explain that each of the four corners of the room represents a different stand-point, as indicated:

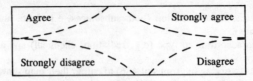

2. Read out one of the statements (either prepared according to the age/interest of students or collected anonymously) e.g.
    'Boys have more opportunities in life than girls',
    'By the year 2000 nuclear weapons will have been disarmed',
    'Nicking things from shops is OK',
    'Last term's PSHE course was useful'.
3. Ask the students to move to the corner of the room which best represents their opinion about the statement.
4. Either a) ask for volunteers from each of the corners to explain why they moved there. This might lead to an informal, open debate on the issue, or b) ask students to pair up with someone from a different corner and discuss their opinions.

Comments:
· Statements, questions, predictions can be collected from sources such as newspapers, magazines or the school handbook for this activity.
· Sometimes it is more appropriate to imagine two halves of the room indicating agree/disagree or positive/negative and ask students to move accordingly, with a 'don't know' position between them.
· Students may be reluctant to move initially, particularly if they are unused to physical exercises of this sort. The first statements need to be clear and the procedure conducted rapidly until the students get into the swing of it. This sort of exercise is more threatening than, say, completing a questionnaire, because of the visible commitment to position. It may be important to reassure students that they will not be 'branded' in any way nor will their reactions be recorded.
· At the end of the activity it is useful to encourage students to reflect on anything that surprised them about their views or about those of others and whether they have changed in any way.

PERM here:

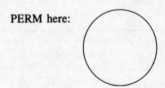

Exercise 6.6: Reflective Skills

b) Life-space Designs   (Adapted from Button, 1981)

Aims: To encourage students to reflect on 'significant others' in their lives
        To encourage personal sharing between students

Materials: Pens and paper.

Timing: 20–30 minutes.

Procedure: Initially, the students work alone. It is very important that the teacher demonstrates this exercise himself, not only for clarification but also to foster a climate of trust.

1. Explain to the students that we all have different relationships and that some are closer, or more significant, than others. Ask each student to draw a life-space diagram, using initials, to show their own current relationships (friends, family, acquaintances, etc.).
    Shorter lines indicate closer relationships and vice versa. For example:

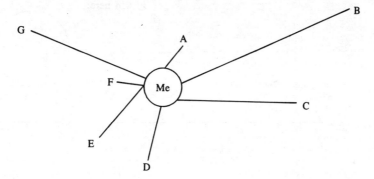

2. After about 5 minutes, ask students to pair up and discuss their diagrams with a partner. Emphasise that they can share as much or as little as they wish — they need not show each other their diagrams or identify the initials.
3. After 10–15 minutes, draw the students together as a whole group. Explain that there is no 'optimum' number of lines or correct distances; we are all different. Emphasise, also, that this diagram represents how they feel now. It may be completely different tomorrow, or next week or next year. Students may be interested in making these comparisons. Ask them to reflect on:
    a) any changes they would like to make, e.g. for some people to become closer and others less close,
    b) if they learned anything about themselves,
    c) how they felt about doing the exercise.
Students may, or may not, wish to respond publicly to these questions.

Exercise 6.6: contd.

Comments:

· Any age group.

· It is important that this does not develop into a competitive exercise along the lines 'I've got more friends than you'. The initial climate is crucial.

· This exercise is best used as one stage in a structured programme of work on interpersonal relationships. The development of such a programme will depend on students' ages and on the dynamics within the group.

· Although most students are perfectly able to monitor their feelings and disclosures, it is possible that some might find the exercise upsetting, particularly following a recent relationship crisis. Teachers need to be alert to this possibility, although often peer support is effective. Clear 'opting out' procedures are essential in such circumstances.

PERM here:

Exercise 6.7: Transfer Skills

a) Role Swap   (adapted from Bond, 1986)

Aims: To encourage students to put themselves into other people's shoes
      To consider the consequences of different behaviours
      To reproduce situations outside the classroom

Materials: A list of appropriate situations (see below).

Timing: Approximately 30 minutes.

Procedure:
1. Ask each pair to decide who is A and who is B and to choose (or give them) a description of a situation.
2. The pair discuss for five to ten minutes details of the context and how A would behave in the situation.
3. B acts out how A would behave, with A prompting or guiding his behaviour.
4. Ask the pair to discuss what happened, especially how A felt seeing his own behaviour being enacted by someone else. What advice would they give to people actually in this situation?
5. Repeat the procedure with A acting out B's behaviour in the same or a different situation.
6. Ask the pair to discuss how it felt doing this role play.

Comments:
· Any age group but with students who have some experience of group work.
· After any role play or simulation the participants should be given a chance to de-role, otherwise they may continue to feel and act towards each other as though still 'in character'. For a short role play, such as this, de-roling could simply be a class round, e.g. the students, in turn, complete the sentence, 'My name's ... and I feel (or I like) ...'.
· Situations could include:
  'Breaking bad news' — how would you tell someone bad news?
  'A lover's tiff' — how would you behave in an argument with someone you are fond of?
  'Helping a friend' — how would you set about helping a friend in trouble?
  'Saying sorry' — how would you behave when you have let a friend down?
  'Making friends' — how would you approach a stranger you would like to get to know better?
  'Getting home late' — how would you behave to your parents if you were very late getting in at night?

PERM here: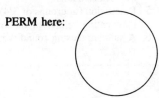

Exercise 6.7: Transfer Skills

b) Calorie Count

Aims: To relate theory (i.e. information on food energy levels) to practice (i.e. individual day-to-day behaviours)
To share feelings about personal eating habits and, if desired, to share strategies for changing behaviour

Materials: Copies of food composition tables. Additional/background information, e.g. HEA leaflets, diet sheets, recipes, food labels, etc.

Timing: Two sessions, approximately 40 minutes each.

Procedure: The emphasis is on individual work but students will share experiences and feelings in small groups.
1. Give out food composition tables. Set 3 or 4 problems to familiarise students with the table. E.g.
    a) which are more fattening, crisps or cornflakes?
    b) how much milk would give you 300 kcal? What is this in pints?
    c) devise a lunch which adds up to 500 kcal.
    d) what is the calorific value of an average breakfast of 2 rashers of bacon, 1 fried egg, 1 helping of beans, 2 slices of buttered toast and 1 cup of tea?
2. Ask students to record everything they eat for three days (or whatever time seems suitable) and to work out their daily calorific intake. It may help to provide a tabular framework. E.g.

Day

Type of Food	Approx. Weight in lbs/ozs	Energy (kcal) per oz	Energy (kcal) per helping

3. Next session, ask students (in groups of 3/4) to compare their diets and their calorific intake. The recommended intake for adolescents is 2,880 kcal for boys and 2,150 kcal for girls. Ask them if they are happy with their diets. Do they want to increase or decrease their calorie intake?
4. Whole group brainstorm. What do we need to consider if we want to change our eating habits?
5. Discussion (in groups of 3/4). Ask students to share ideas about how to change their eating behaviour or how to help someone else to do so.
6. A suitable closing round would be: 'The food I would find hardest to give up is ...'

Exercise 6.7: contd.

Comments:

· Any age group.

· This particular exercise is an example of transferability but would only constitute a small part of work on the theme of food. It is assumed, therefore, that students will have an understanding of energy related to food, and are familiar with relevant measures, e.g. calorie, ounce, gram, litre and pint, and their interrelationship.

· Some students may need help with the arithmetic involved.

· Other exercises which would be useful for this theme could be 'influences on eating behaviour' (pp. 148–9); 'force-field analysis re changing diet' (pp. 203–4); 'media analysis collage' re food and appearance (p. 49).

· This exercise could be adapted to take account of specific nutrients using more comprehensive food tables (*Manual of Nutrition*, HMSO, 1976) or appropriate computer software (*NUPAC* — ILECC, 1986).

· The idea of this exercise and approach is not to tell students what they should eat but to encourage them to apply given information to their own practice and to work out their own feelings about their eating patterns.

PERM here:

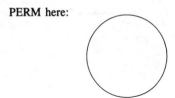

Average weights and measures of commonly used foods (HMSO, 1976)

Milk	for 1 cup of tea	1 oz
	for 1 glass	7 oz
Cheese	1″ cube	¾ oz
Steak	average	6–8 oz
Bacon	1 large rasher	1 oz
Sausage	1 large sausage	2 oz
Meat pie	1 individual pie	4 oz
Eggs	1 egg	2 oz or 50g
Butter or margarine	for 1 slice bread	⅛–¼ oz
Lettuce	2 large leaves	½ oz
Potatoes,		
boiled	2 medium	4 oz
mashed	1 scoop	2 oz
Tomato	2 medium size	3 oz
Orange	1 medium (with peel)	4 oz
Apple	1 medium	3 oz
Bread	1 thick slice from	
	small loaf	1 oz
	1 thick slice from	
	large loaf	2 oz
Flour	1 tablespoon, rounded	1 oz
Porridge oats	1 tea cup	3 oz
Breakfast cereal	1 helping	¾–1 oz
Biscuits,		
dry	three	1 oz
plain sweet	one	⅓ oz
Coffee, instant	per cup	1/10 oz or 2 g
Tea	per cup	1/6 oz
Beer	½ pint	10 fl oz or 285 ml
Wine	1 wineglass	2½ fl oz or 70 ml

FOOD ENERGY LEVELS (kcal/oz) (HMSO, 1976)

Food	Energy kcal	Food	Energy kcal	Food	Energy kcal
Milk		**Meat contd.**		**Preserves etc.**	
Cream, double	127	Liver, fried	69	Chocolate, milk	150
Cream, single	55	Luncheon meat	89	Honey	82
Milk, liquid, whole	18	Pork, average, raw	92	Jam	74
Milk, condensed, whole, sweetened	91	Pork chop, grilled	94	Marmalade	74
Milk, whole, evaporated	45	Sausage, pork	104	Sugar, white	112
Milk, UHT	18	Sausage, beef	84	Syrup	84
Milk, dried, skimmed	101	Steak and kidney pie, cooked	81		
Yogurt, low-fat, natural	15	Tripe, dressed	17	**Vegetables**	
Yogurt, low-fat, fruit	27			Beans, canned in tomato sauce	18
		Fish		Beans, broad	19
Cheese		White fish, filleted	21	Beans, haricot, dry	77
Cheese, Cheddar	115	Cod, fried in batter	56	Beans, runner	7
Cheese, cottage	27	Fish fingers	51	Beetroot, boiled	12
		Herring	66	Brussels sprouts, raw	7
Meat		Kipper fillets	52	Brussels sprouts, boiled	5
Bacon, rashers, raw	120	Salmon, canned	44	Cabbage, green, raw	6
Bacon, rashers, cooked	127	Sardines, canned in oil, fish only	62	Cabbage, green, boiled	5
Beef, average, raw	75			Carrots, old	6
Beef, corned	62	**Eggs**		Cauliflower	4
Beef, stewing steak, raw	48	Eggs, fresh	42	Celery	3
Beef, stewing steak, cooked	63			Crisps, potato	152
Black pudding	87	**Fats**		Cucumber	2
Chicken raw	65	Butter	210	Lentils, dry	86
Chicken, roast, light meat	40	Lard; cooking fat; dripping	253	Lettuce	3
Ham, cooked	77	Low-fat spread	104	Mushrooms	2
Kidney, average	26	Margarine, average	207	Onions	7
Lamb, average, raw	95	Oils, cooking and salad	255	Parsnips	14
Lamb, roast	83			Peas, frozen, raw	14
Liver, average, raw	46			Peas, frozen, boiled	11
				Peas, canned, processed	22

FOOD ENERGY LEVELS (kcal/oz) (HMSO, 1976) contd.

Food	Energy kcal	Food	Energy kcal	Food	Energy kcal
Peppers, green	3	**Fruit** contd.		**Cereals** contd.	
Potatoes, raw	24	Plums	9	Spaghetti	107
Potatoes, boiled	22	Prunes, dried	46		
Potato chips, fried	72	Raspberries	7	**Beverages**	
Potatoes, roast	44	Rhubarb	2	Chocolate, drinking	104
Spinach	6	Strawberries	8	Cocoa powder	88
Sweetcorn, canned	22	Sultanas	71	Coffee, ground, infusion	1
Tomatoes, fresh	4			Coffee, instant powder	28
Turnips	5	**Nuts**		Coca cola	11
Watercress	4	Almonds	160	Tea, dry	0
		Coconut, desiccated	171	Squash, fruit, undiluted	34
Fruit		Peanuts, roasted	162		
Apples	13			**Alcoholic beverages** per fl oz	
Apricots, canned (including syrup)	30	**Cereals**		Beer, keg bitter	9
Apricots, dried	52	Barley, pearl, dry	102	Spirits, 70% proof	63
Bananas	22	Biscuits, chocolate	148	Wine, red	19
Blackcurrants	8	Biscuits, cream crackers	125		
Cherries	13	Biscuits, plain, semi-sweet	130	**Puddings and cakes, etc.**	
Dates, dried	70	Biscuits, rich, sweet	133	Apple pie	80
Figs, dried	60	Bread, brown	63	Bread and butter pudding	44
Gooseberries, green	5	Bread, starch reduced	66	Buns, currant	93
Grapefruit	6	Bread, white	66	Custard	33
Lemon juice	2	Bread, wholemeal	61	Fruit cake, rich	94
Melon	6	Cornflakes	104	Jam tarts	109
Oranges	10	Custard powder; instant pudding; cornflour	100	Plain cake, Madeira	111
Orange juice, canned, unsweetened	9	Crispbread, rye	91	Rice pudding	37
Peaches, fresh	10	Flour, white	99	Soup, tomato, canned	16
Peaches, canned (including syrup)	25	Oatmeal	114	Trifle	45
Pears, fresh	12	Rice	102	Marmite	49
Pineapple, canned (including syrup)	22			Ice-cream, vanilla	47

Exercise 6.8: Evaluation Exercises

a) Field of Words   (see Clarity Collective, 1985)   See page 178.

b) Rounds, using sentence stems, e.g: I have learned that ...
                                                                Next session I want to ...
                                                                I have most enjoyed ...
                                                                I would have preferred ...

c) Graffiti: each student writes comments anonymously about the session on card/paper. These are then stuck around the room or on boards. Students mill around and read them.

d) Consequences: i) brainstorm (whole group) of criteria/issues to be evaluated
     ii) small groups (3–5) select one issue (this may need negotiation as it is preferable for groups to choose different topics)
     iii) each group writes title/topic on top of A2 (flip chart paper), then writes a comment on the bottom of the sheet. This is folded under and the groups pass on their sheets to the group on the left.
     iv) the procedure is repeated until all groups have written a comment under each heading
     v) the comments are then displayed and read out, being discussed if necessary.

e.g.   **GROUP DYNAMICS**   **TIMING**
                    everyone contributed   too rushed
     ———————————————   ———————————————
                teacher talked too much   not enough time
     ———————————————   ———————————————
                it was fun but noisy   good pace
     ———————————————   ———————————————
         enjoyed pairs work more than   we would have liked
                        big group   longer on ...
     ———————————————   ———————————————

e) DIY evaluation   See page 179.

f) Group assessment checklist   (see Button)   See page 180.

g) Positive strokes

     i)   students have a sheet of paper pinned to their backs
     ii)   students mill around and write positive comments on the paper — as many as they like
     iii) after a certain time (e.g. 10 minutes) students unpin their sheets and read them
     iv)   no feedback necessary but students may like to close with a round saying which comment pleased them most and/or how they felt having positive things said about them.

Exercise 6.8: Evaluation Exercises

a) Field of words

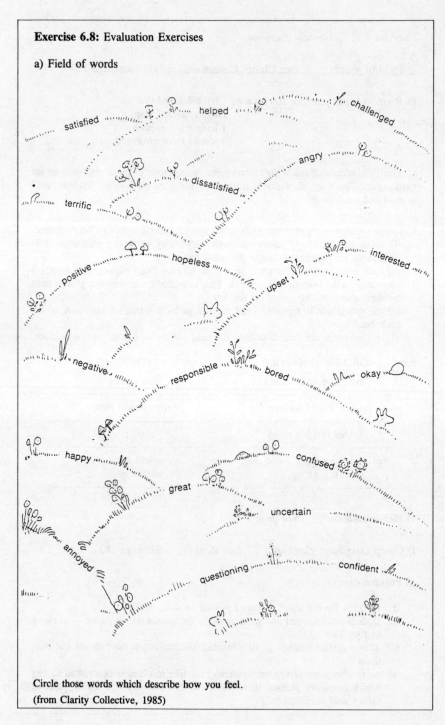

satisfied   helped   challenged
angry
dissatisfied
terrific
hopeless   interested
positive   upset
negative   responsible   bored   okay
happy   confused
great
uncertain
annoyed
questioning   confident

Circle those words which describe how you feel.
(from Clarity Collective, 1985)

Exercise 6.8: Evaluation Exercises

e) Reviewing PSHE: a DIY evaluation exercise

Aims: to involve all course members in selecting the areas they wish to
evaluate
to publish the full range of responses while allowing some degree of
anonymity

Procedure:
1. In 3s, brainstorm areas to evaluate from the course.
2. Record suggestions from all groups.
3. In 3s, select 3 priority areas from the list and record choices.
4. Decide as a whole group how many areas to evaluate and allocate one area to
each small group.
5. Groups fills out sheet below, writing 2 positive and 2 negative statements
related to their area of evaluation. (It is a good idea to begin each statement
with 'I or we ...')

	Area to be evaluated	Agree	Reservations	Disagree
+ ve				
+ve				
−ve				
−ve				

6. All sheets are displayed and each course member ticks all four statements on
each set.
7. The original 3s take back their own sheet and prepare a comment for the whole
group on what has been entered on the sheet.
8. There is further discussion in the whole group over what has arisen.
9. Close with a round, giving everyone a chance to say something about the
evaluation process if they wish.
(Acknowledgements to Linda Kelly)

Exercise 6.8: Evaluation Exercises

f) Personal roles within the group

	MEMBERS OF THE GROUP								
1. Suggests things to do.									
2. Gives instructions.									
3. Looks after members of the group.									
4. Asks questions about what the group should do.									
5. Is always willing to fall in with others.									
6. Helps the group to decide.									
7. Delays decisions.									
8. Leads the fun.									
9. Makes the group cross.									
10. Listens to other people's trouble.									
11. Gets things done.									
12. Puts spanners in the works.									
13. Leads the group when we are threatened.									
14. We make fun of him/her.									
15. Calms down trouble inside the group.									
16. Tries to get us to be serious.									
17. Represents the group to people in authority.									
18. Keeps us cheerful.									

Rate each member from 0 to 10 — Not like him 0/Very much like him 10
(Adapted from Button, 1981)

CONCLUSION

Educational aims are generally widely accepted. It is their translation into practice which causes difficulties. Our aims, for instance, are in many ways at variance with the competitive, individualistic stance of traditional education as well as with the prevailing ethos of society and the values of many of its sub-cultural groups. Most strikingly, the deliberate movement away from didacticism in PSHE contrasts with everyday notions like the 'boss', 'expert', 'supervisor'. In spite of this we are convinced that PSHE offers genuine opportunities for intellectual stimulation, for the growth of physical confidence, for emotional and spiritual reflection and for improved social relationships. It confers specific benefits on individuals and promises a better world for everyone.

We believe that PSHE has a dynamic role in combating sexism and racism. Further research, however, is desperately needed here, particularly on the role of different methodologies in furthering equal opportunities. PSHE provides a forum where the effects of sexism can be explored and its basis challenged. Girls are the obvious beneficiaries of such analysis. But boys are also constrained by their socialisation so that they often find it difficult to express their feelings constructively, for example, and are labelled 'weak' if they opt out of competitive sports. The advantages of increased empathy and collaborative support between, as well as within, the sexes are less tangible than academic 'success' but no less important in the long run.

For black students too the potential of PSHE is rich. Some studies (for example, Jones, 1986) have shown that black students perform better when active learning methods are used. However, it is important not to ignore the expectations of black parents who, conscious that their children may be underachieving as a result of racist attitudes, see the most obvious solution as encouraging success in traditional terms. If, as we believe, one of the effects of racism has been to deny black children full educational opportunities, we are bound to heed the demands of the black communities. There need not be a conflict of aims but full consultation with parents is essential. Not only can small group work in PSHE provide opportunities to challenge the roots and manifestations of racism, it can also build young people's confidence so that they, themselves, are able to assert their own rights.

Children with special educational needs, including the physically handicapped, are another group which might expect to benefit from the adoption of PSHE methods and approaches. Because of its focus on relationships and communication skills, and its commitment to fostering characteristics like self-esteem and respect for others, PSHE confronts the issues of inequality and handicap directly. It also, through role play and simulations, for example, possesses the means to put 'normal' students into the shoes of those less fortunate than themselves.

PSHE, then, is not about tokenism, nor is it about conforming. Rather its purpose is to challenge existing understandings of the world and of relationships and to equip students with their own reasoned analyses of where they stand and what they value. Because of this and because of its methods, it turns out to be an area that students enjoy and find rewarding. However, the formal status of PSHE, compared to subjects which have more conventional modes of teaching and assessment, is one that is far from resolved. So there is still some way to go to improve the learning process for all students. It is one thing to adopt more child-centred teaching methods: as Kyriacou observes, 'the current shift makes good psychological as well as good educational sense'. But these may be affected by changing priorities at other levels in the educational system and by the immediate climate of the school. This is our subject in Chapter 7.

FURTHER READING

Barnes, D. (1975) *From communication to curriculum*, Penguin, Harmondsworth

Bond, T. (1986) *Games for social and life skills*, Hutchinson, London

Brandes, D. (1982) *Gamesters handbook two*, Hutchinson, London

────── and Ginnis, P. (1986) *A guide to student-centred learning*, Blackwell, Oxford

────── and Phillips, H. (1979) *Gamesters' handbook*, Hutchinson, London

Bruner, J. *et al.* (1956) *A study of thinking*, Wiley and Sons, London

Butterworth, C. and Macdonald, M. (1985) *Teaching social education and communication: a practical handbook*, Hutchinson, London

Button, L. (1974) *Developmental groupwork with adolescents*, Hodder and Stoughton, London

Clarity Collective (1985) *Taught not caught: strategies for sex education* (British edn, Dixon, H. and Mullinar, G.), Learning Development Aids, Wisbech, Cambs.

Collins, N. (1986) *New teaching skills*, Oxford University Press, London

Douglas, T. (1984) *Groupwork practice*, Tavistock, London

Gagne, R.M. (1977) *The conditions of learning*, 3rd edn, Holt, Rinehart and Winston, London

Hopson, B. and Scally, M. (1980, 1982, 1985) *Lifeskills teaching programmes I, II, III*, Lifeskills Associates, Leeds

Houston, G. (1984) *The red book of groups*, The Rochester Foundation, London

Jacques, D. (1984) *Learning in groups*, Croom Helm, London

7

The Healthy School

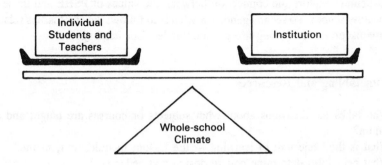

Developments in the pedagogy of PSHE are echoed in several recent initiatives:
in pre-vocational courses, in assessment and in modularisation. Together, these
innovations reflect a formidable shift in educational practice which — if not
diverted by the counter-tendencies implied in the national curriculum — could
mark a new phase in the history of comprehensive schooling. What is salutary
to observe, in this connection, is the way in which PSHE values and approaches
are now being embraced not simply in a wider range of teaching contexts but
in organisational set-ups generally. Indeed, notions like 'organisational health'
and the 'healthy school' are increasingly being recognised as the foundation for
successful adaptation and growth. Crucial to both concepts is harmony between
values and relationships at every level of school life. The connections will be
elaborated later. To begin this chapter we look at the process of organisational
change.

THE AGENDA FOR CHANGE

Understanding how schools work and change is not an easy task, as Handy and
Aitken (1986) make clear. Nor is the experience of diagnosing needs and
supporting innovation. This is partly because schools are forced to embark on

change piecemeal. There are more fundamental difficulties too. To start with, it is not always clear to what extent change is either necessary or desirable — or on whose authority it is happening. This is complicated by the sheer range of diverse needs and interests represented (students, teachers, parents, employers, local authority representatives, HMI *et al.*). Having to reconcile all these different interests frustrates the idealists and makes compromise inevitable. Cost, both in financial and in human terms, puts another kind of brake on substantial kinds of change, especially in a period of deliberate contraction. This is a particular problem in institutions which, compared to industry, lack a clearly identifiable end-product whose costs and benefits can readily be measured in the short term and used as an index of future profitability.

Here we shall examine the limits and possibilities for change in schools and, in particular, explore the connection between the values of PSHE and those of the healthy school. To set an agenda for what is to follow, the chief issues related to organisational well-being are grouped under four headings below.

1. Timetabling and Resources

· Who takes the decisions about what subjects or courses are taught and by whom?
· What is the basic unit of learning — the lesson, module, unit, theme?
· What principles determine course design and pedagogy?
· How much choice are students given over what they learn and how is that arranged?
· What arrangements, if any, exist for out-of-school studies, e.g. work- or community-experience, residentials, extra-curricular activities?
· What time is available for staff consultation, working parties, parent-teacher meetings, team development?
· Who is responsible for designing new course materials and for integrating IT (information technology) requirements?
· How swiftly can the curriculum respond to the need for new units for work; for example, to follow up controversial TV programmes?
· How are curriculum matters monitored and evaluated — and in the light of whose values?

2. Co-ordination

· Who defines particular subject, topic, unit boundaries for different groups of students — and on the basis of what principles of selection or integration?
· Who is responsible for managing students' learning to avoid overlap and maximise opportunities for reinforcement?
· How are policies re anti-sexism and anti-racism determined and monitored?

- How are students grouped and special needs identified?
- Are alternative study routes clearly identified and students fully counselled about their options?
- What forms the basis of staff affiliation — teams, departments, year-groups?
- What opportunities are there for staff to plan, trial and review new resources and programmes for learning?
- What role is there for tutors and for the pastoral system in the overall system?
- What opportunities exist for INSET in cross-disciplinary fields like information and study skills, profiling, pastoral casework?
- How are cross-curricular areas like PSHE managed?

3. Assessment

- Which students study for what awards — GCSE, TVEI, RSA, B/TEC, City and Guilds 365, CPVE, AS- (advanced supplementary) and A-levels — and on what basis?
- What form of profiling or record of achievement exists?
- How are these different forms of assessment managed and integrated — and by whom? What role do students, parents, staff play?
- Who holds students' records? Where and how are they updated — and by whom?
- Who are records for and what purposes do they serve? Are they publicly available or confidential?
- How are they resourced? What role is there for IT?
- Who guides students in their learning and counsels them about alternative routes and rewards?
- How is all this monitored and evaluated — in the light of what values and principles for learning?

4. Leadership

- What roles are occupied by members of the leadership hierarchy?
- Who is responsible/accountable to whom?
- Where does the buck stop?
- How are decisions made, implemented and monitored?
- Who is involved — staff, students, parents, governors, advisers?
- How are new programmes and procedures evaluated and staff development needs identified?
- Who determines priorities for curriculum planning and assessment?
- Who provides any school-based INSET, when and how?
- Who communicates with parents and others outside the school — and how?
- How is a balance ensured between aspects of the hidden curriculum and those of the formal structures of learning?

Balancing the different interests involved in these four areas of organisational life is obviously difficult. It requires several simultaneous juggling acts to take account of very different sets of needs: those of students, staff, parents, LEA advisors and councillors, local residents, employers, the DES, as well as those of the senior management team who are actually responsible for the task. The job of managing the image and reputation of the school and ensuring that external and internal message systems are in harmony is perhaps paramount. This involves a judicious regard for the optimum balance between stability and change.

Recent research on school effectiveness (Reid *et al.*, 1987) is quite unequivocal in its assessment of the most important elements contributing to organisational health. These are the principles of consistency and collaboration, backed by values like trust, openness, clear communication, respect and support for others. The same principles inform the HEA Health Skills dissemination project whose aims, Jen Anderson, the Project Director, describes as being 'holistic':

> to make sure that our philosophy and practice are reflected at each stage of the project. Personal, social and health education must be holistic too — the promotion of health must happen not only in the curriculum, but must be reflected in the corridors and staff-rooms of schools, in relationships with parents and with the community of which that school is a part. (*TES*, 29.5.87)

The project's whole-school philosophy is summed up in Figure 7.1.

As well as being centrally embedded in the Health Skills project, the values underpinning the health-promoting school are central in human relations theories. Thus, in characteristically American terms, Benne and Muntyan (1951) pinpoint 'five norms of participation' in their paper on 'Democratic Ethics and Human Engineering':

collaboration
task-orientation
educational for the participants
experimental and research-oriented
anti-individualistic (yet providing scope
for individual creativity)

While acknowledging the similarity between these norms and those of PSHE, we are bound to admit that there is not much empirical evidence supporting their validity. In the suggestions that follow we shall therefore rely a good deal on experience of 'good' practice. Those who wish to broaden their knowledge of alternative curriculum structures may find some guidance from the references

Figure 7.1: The Health Skills Project Whole-School Approach

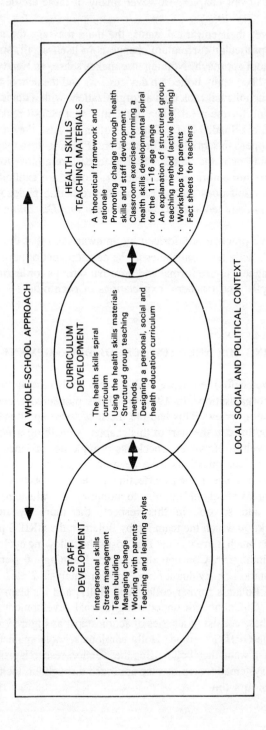

A WHOLE-SCHOOL APPROACH

STAFF DEVELOPMENT

· Interpersonal skills
· Stress management
· Team building
· Managing change
· Working with parents
· Teaching and learning styles

CURRICULUM DEVELOPMENT

· The health skills spiral curriculum
· Using the health skills materials
· Structured group teaching methods
· Designing a personal, social and health education curriculum

HEALTH SKILLS TEACHING MATERIALS

· A theoretical framework and rationale
· Promoting change through health skills and staff development
· Classroom exercises forming a health skills developmental spiral for the 11–16 age range
· An explanation of structured group teaching method (active learning)
· Workshops for parents
· Fact sheets for teachers

LOCAL SOCIAL AND POLITICAL CONTEXT

at the end of this chapter. However, many of these are descriptive rather than analytic.

Whatever their empirical status, the main message the texts convey is that, even if a particular curriculum change is in itself small, success depends on a whole-school approach. Nothing else makes sense, as Handy and Aitken (1986) point out: 'Too many bolted-on devices . . . and the school begins to look more like a kitchen utensil rack than an organization, with a device for every purpose but no menu for the meal.' The problem is that utensil racks have a propensity to become overloaded and collapse — often because they are unbalanced. This is what happens in schools if, for example, PSHE is introduced without adequate staff training or if the values PSHE teachers are aiming to encourage in their students are not embraced elsewhere or, worse, are explicitly rejected because the school itself does not have a health-promoting philosophy. As DES/HMI comment in their report on *Good Behaviour and Discipline in Schools* (1987a):

Effective practice is informed by an awareness that the whole range of the school's activities contributes to the development of pupils' maturity, and by a willingness to use formal and informal settings for learning and for enhancing pupils' and teachers' expectations of each other.

REVIEWING THE NEED FOR SCHOOL DEVELOPMENT

How do we begin, then, if we wish to see schools moving towards more healthy forms of organisation? In 1977 the ILEA pioneered a checklist approach to whole-school review. This had the merit of focusing attention on the kinds of question outlined at the start of this chapter (something which, at that time, was itself a novelty). However, checklists provide no guidance on how to proceed once the various questions have been answered: how to determine priorities; how to co-ordinate policies affecting different aspects of the curriculum or different areas of school life; how to monitor and evaluate progress towards new goals — and so on. In this respect, the more dynamic action-research framework, on which the team led by Bolam in the GRIDS project (1984) based its ideas, is much more useful. This posits the following cycle: Problem Analysis → Fact-finding → Conceptualisation → Planning of Action Programme → Implementation → Evaluation → Problem Analysis 2 etc.

One of Bolam's former colleagues, Holly, and his team have more recently produced 'Guidelines for undertaking internal development through evaluation' (1986). These consist of a series of action steps, as Figure 7.2 shows. However, as with the GRIDS method, Holly cautions schools against attempting to take on too much when they begin using these action-research procedures. He recommends a 'systematic, step-by-step approach throughout, tackling one area of the curriculum at a time'.

Figure 7.2: The Research-based Development Process

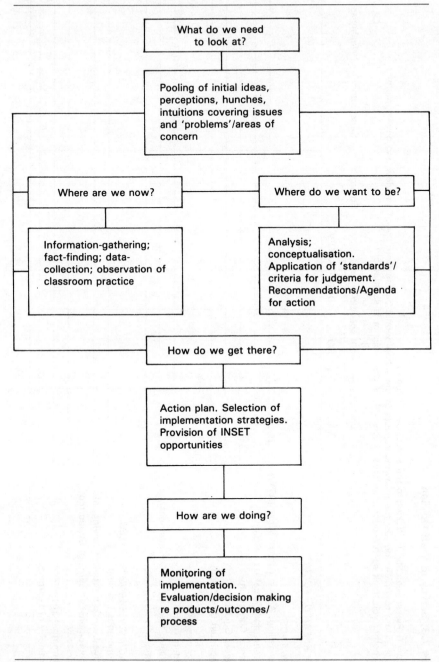

Source: Reid *et al.*, 1987

Figure 7.3: Survey of Staff Opinion

Section 1. Please indicate (by ticking in the appropriate column):
(i) the extent to which you feel the following aspects of the school would benefit from specific review and development
(ii) whether you think each aspect is an area of strength or weakness or is satisfactory

	(i) would benefit from specific review			(ii)		
	YES	NO	DON'T KNOW	Strength	Satisfactory	Weakness
KEY AREAS OF FOCUS						
GUIDANCE						
Counselling: Active Tutorial Work (ATW)						
Personal and Social Development						
Pastoral Curriculum						
Careers Guidance						
Negotiated Curriculum						
ASSESSMENT						
Graded Tests						
Profiling: Records of Achievement						
Continuous Assessment						
TEACHING/LEARNING STYLES						
Autonomous Learning						
Active Learning: problem solving, etc.						
Resource-based Learning: Supported Self-study						
Information Technology						
Continuity of Learning						

Holly also offers a model questionnaire (Figure 7.3) which can be used to gather staff opinion about what areas of the curriculum should have priority in any review. You might find it useful to go through this in terms of your own school's needs in PSHE, if possible comparing your priorities with those of colleagues. Where there are differences, notice in particular what source these spring from. (They could arise from differences in values, in experience, in responsibility, or in beliefs about the ideal school.)

If the whole staff were to fill in this questionnaire it is certain that different teachers would turn out to hold different views about what makes an ideal school (as about the role of PSHE!). This is to be expected. What might not have been so obvious is the extent to which these different views inform not simply ideals about pedagogy and the curriculum but also attitudes towards the more informal activities of the school. But we must now move from ideal types to practical realities.

PREPARING FOR CHANGE

Having conducted a review along the lines suggested above, the next step is to implement any policies for change. This requires preparation on a number of levels:

1. Organisational health

Before any kind of organisational development is initiated, it is crucial to ask whether your school is healthy enough to stand change. What is the balance of arguments for and against the proposed innovation? Will staff readily agree? Is there sufficient stability and security within the staff group? Do people trust each other — or will they experience the idea of change as threatening and manipulative? What other pressures are staff having to face up to — industrial action, salary erosion, parental demands, etc.? Can sufficient time be found to ensure adequate pre-planning as well as time for monitoring and evaluation of the proposed changes? Does the project build on existing strengths and harness willing staff energies?

2. Ownership and the co-ordination of change

While there may be a role for the willing enthusiast or charismatic innovator in getting developments started, identifying new initiatives too closely with one person or sub-set of staff should be avoided at the planning stage (even though a named person eventually has to carry responsibility for implementing or co-ordinating the change). This is because of the importance of getting full staff

191

collaboration. Ideally, as many staff as possible (and reasonable) should be encouraged to feel that they have a stake in the proposed development and share responsibility for its success or failure. They should participate not just in the preliminary review of needs but also in any decision making about priorities and strategies for implementation. This might mean weekly working-party meetings occupying some of the time available while others conduct assembly or students come into school late. One London comprehensive adopted the following model for co-operative planning in devising its social education curriculum.

HOW WE DID IT

Co-operative Planning of the Course — The Process

The course planning team divided amongst itself the major subject *areas* we were to cover, i.e. Religious, Moral, Sex, Health and Political Education. Other inputs were made by the Resource Committee in the areas of study skill and library user education while the Head of Careers worked as a full member of the team in the development of careers guidance and understanding of the world of work within Social Education.

Our focus on autonomy as an aim and on *process* rather than *content* — *how* you decide rather than *what* you decide — is the unifying factor which turns these various 'sources' into a coherent experience for students.

The dual role of the members of the course planning team also helped the development of a coherent course. Each member of the team had two jobs.

Area Specialist	Year Co-ordinator
* reads professional literature, attends courses	* identifies 'critical incidents' within that year, e.g. induction year 1, adjusting to option groups year 4
* invites specialist advice	
* researches pupil material	
* is responsible for the development of that area year 1–5	* plans material to support tutors in working through those 'incidents'
* presents model syllabus objectives for whole team discussion, e.g. sample RE syllabus	* jointly plans programme year 1–5
* works with team to integrate 'specialist course'	* commissions, collates and co-ordinates specialist inputs into units planned in her year
* shares planning, writing, and evaluation of integrated course, bringing specialist perspective to bear	* works with tutors in preparing lessons
	* works with tutors, students and course planning team in evaluating programme

---

This is an interesting example of PSHE values at work in the organisation at large. It also illustrates the critical role of co-ordination, on which the successful development of PSHE and other cross-curricular initiatives depend. The co-ordinator should ideally be a senior member of staff who can act as a catalyst and resource person, stimulating debate and discussion across the curriculum, identifying needs, planning and negotiating with others, and monitoring what is happening in the school at large. She should play a leading role in organising any new developments and particularly in running any school-based INSET.

3. Facing uncertainties and ensuring the possibility of reassessment

Once begun, it is important that the aims of a new project are constantly open to criticism and improvement and that there is a possibility of honourable retreat if, after a reasonable trial, the changes prove unsuccessful. Failure can happen when staff development needs are underestimated, when student uptake for a project is too low or when changes in examining policy undermine the pedagogy of a new course. The involvement of a senior staff member in the working party and an organisational structure which can respond swiftly and flexibly to unforeseen difficulties are of great importance in enabling reassessment to take place effectively. A climate of trust and co-operation among staff is also vital so that it is possible to back off or alter direction without anybody losing face. Open management, good informal staff relationships, pleasant social surroundings and regular opportunities for meetings can all help in this connection.

One thing is crucial: everyone concerned needs to be realistic about the extra burdens likely to be created. This will ensure that teachers are not too rapidly demoralised once change is under way but perhaps not yet proceeding smoothly. One way of minimising the risk of disappointment is for all the participants to have a chance of voicing their doubts at the planning stage, and for these to be carefully examined then. The experience of technicians, caretakers, the school secretary, evening institute and community department colleagues will be especially valuable for, frequently, it is communication difficulties and practical details which make the difference between success and failure. Uncertainty and lack of confidence can continue for a considerable period, as Hanko (1985) points out in her study of teachers' reactions to the integration of pupils with special educational needs into ordinary classrooms. This makes positive leadership and the fostering of staff support groups a priority, whether on an in-school basis or outside.

4. Managing conflict

Wherever there is a danger of disagreement over a new project it is important to rehearse counter-arguments to the complaints of those who are hostile or uncommitted. For example, potential opponents on the staff should be given full information and reassurance at the planning stage and then supported closely in any new teaching roles they have to undertake. Often, opposition is a symptom of uncertainty and lack of confidence. Given a chance to voice this and to discover that their concerns are shared by others, most staff begin to feel safer and more willing to have a go. Parents or other members of the community who are likely to resist change also need reassurance and a chance to voice their uncertainties. This can be done by arranging special meetings. Alternatively, some schools offer an open invitation to parents to come in and examine resources or sit in on lessons if they have any doubts about what their children are being exposed to. If resistance is deep-seated, it may require more positive initiatives still. Some useful suggestions are made in the *Handbook on Parental and Community Involvement in Health Education* (quoted in David and Wiliams, 1987). For example:

1. Consulting parents about the curriculum

Questionnaires for parents to prioritise topics which could be dealt with in health education . . . followed up by a meeting to clarify and discuss the results and to feedback similar information from staff and pupils.
Consulting individual parents about the selection of appropriate health education modules for their child.
Meetings to canvass parental preferences for a range of audio-visual and written health education resources.

2. Information about health education

Letter to parents outlining purpose and content of health education curriculum
Meeting to view resources to be used in the classroom, so parents can provide support at home
Class open days for parents to view work done in health education

3. Parents in the classroom

Parents work alongside children . . . maybe acting as a group discussion leader or providing support
Pregnant mother and/or mother and baby talk and demonstration in child care
Variety of parent talks about hobbies or professional activities related to health

4. Health education activities at home

Parents help children keep health diaries etc.
Parents collaborate with children in collecting information

5. Workshops for parents

On all areas of the school curriculum, including health education
OU course on 'Parents and Teenagers'
Invite a range of health professionals to talk about topics and services
Parents explore own attitudes to and knowledge about health
Parents and children together in 'quit smoking' groups

6. Special events

Parents' group writes a 'children's health handbook' on common childhood
ailments, problems or tips for coping
Parents make video on health topics
Parents work as voluntary home–school link workers

The key to success in all of these (and similar) projects is careful advance information and the chance for conflicting views to be heard openly and answered
honestly. However, where such attempts to inform and advise parents fail or
where resistance is grounded in deep cultural or spiritual objections, parents
should be given the right to withdraw their children from the offending activity
— or, as a last resort, to change schools.

5. Managing resources

A precondition for success in any process of innovation is adequate resourcing.
Sufficient cash is needed not only for the start of a new scheme but also to keep
it running. Time also must be carefully budgeted, for example, to secure adequate
training and opportunities for team support; to build in materials-writing, feedback and evaluation sessions, and so on. Other kinds of resources are also
important. Depending on the innovation concerned, the requirement may be for
the help of an outside consultant; for an increased supply of specialised
stationery; for new folders to record student progress; for filing cabinets; for
computer facilities to access or store information; for a television studio for
student productions, etc. Having the appropriate insurance cover and permis-
sions, for instance, for work- or community-experience projects, may also be
crucial if students are not to be disappointed — or parents over-anxious. A recent
example of the neglect of resource considerations is the introduction of the
GCSE examination in 1986 — even though, thanks to the dedication of already
hard-pressed teachers, it has not turned into a totally damp squib. As the teacher
unions argued, ideally such a radical shift in assessment requires smaller classes,
time for testing, assessing and recording, and for moderation meetings inside
and outside school — changes which, in turn, require additional staffing and
supply cover. The new-style coursework requires extra equipment and
materials, new textbooks, and accommodation (Gipps, 1986). TVEI offers a

different model, of an innovation which was well resourced at the pilot stage (the extra capitation for each TVEI student in fact being almost four times that allocated by LEAs normally).

6. Involving school governors

Given new powers under the 1986 Education Act, governors can expect to be closely involved in any curriculum developments in their schools. They will be especially sensitive to proposals in the area of PSHE, as was clearly demonstrated in the cases of Brent and Haringey in Outer London in the mid-1980s. Many of the suggested ways of involving parents outlined above are equally valid for governors. There are other possibilities too. Their interest in a new project can be awakened by involving them in key policy makings (as, in any case, is required by law). They can then be given responsibility for carrying any decisions to subsequent staff or parent meetings, as spokesperson for the planning group. Taster workshops, for instance to explain a school's sex education policy or to permit governors to pre-trial workshops on AIDS education, have proved particularly effective in the PSHE area (see Tambini, 1985, and Hovey, 1987).

7. Publicity and whole-staff involvement

Even where a piece of curriculum development only affects a small number of staff and students, it is useful to keep everyone informed of what is happening and to make sure that their interest and awareness is maintained. This can be encouraged through displays of students' work, items for staff meetings, open days, opportunities to experience demonstrations of new teaching approaches or new audio-visual materials. All of these should help reduce undue rivalry or suspicion in colleagues. They should also ensure that staff are kept in touch and are thus better able to comment on or to counsel their students about the new projects. Well sign-posted notice-boards which are regularly cleared of out-of-date bumf and attractively located (i.e. not all on the wall behind a row of regularly occupied seats or under the pigeon-holes!) are a great asset to effective in-school communication. Weekly staff information sheets (including details about meetings, examinations, visitors to the school, sports fixtures, parent-teacher events, INSET opportunities and so on) are also valuable. On matters of major importance there is probably no substitute for a whole-school conference/teach-in — preferably off the school premises and lasting for at least two days.

For some developments, especially those likely to impinge in any way on the local community, it may be valuable to seek suitable coverage in the media (press, radio, television). This offers three main advantages: a news story is a useful way of giving information to parents and others who may be interested or involved in a project; it contributes respectability and prestige to innovations, and enhances the students' sense of value and pride in their work. There may also be opportunities to contribute to professional journals and conferences, to address relevant LEA panels or to share experiences with colleagues from other schools in a learning network. All of these are ways of maintaining enthusiasm and morale and of valuing new pieces of work. The lists of relevant journals and of subject and other associations in Appendix 3 may provide a useful resource in this connection. The Community Education movement has pioneered other useful strategies for public understanding. These have included hearings and open meetings, school improvement councils, citizens' groups, education funds and partnerships, education road shows and information exchanges and task forces. But, after years of effort to involve low-income and minority parents (those least likely to participate in schools), they have concluded that, with the growing centralisation of power in Britain, 'If citizens are not given a voice in the decision-making process, it will be difficult to get them involved in schools' (Lindner, 1987). This, of course, reinforces some of the points made earlier about the importance of participation for organisational health.

8. Support, review and evaluation

Once changes are under way, staff centrally involved in any innovation, as well as those more marginally affected (ancillary staff, caretakers and media resource officers (MRO), for example), need a chance to monitor and review their progress, to iron out any difficulties and to offer each other practical support. At this stage it will not be sufficient for difficulties simply to be reported and discussed; tangible changes and the necessary support will be required to take effect as quickly as possible. These could be relatively minor, as when the MRO needs staff to adjust their delivery times for the printing of new worksheets. Or they might require a more fundamental reappraisal, as when contradictions emerge; for example, in the way different teachers treat the theme of sexuality, say, in PSHE, in Biology and in English. The interest of senior staff is crucial at this, just as at every other, stage. It may also be necessary to provide extra staff back-up from time to time. One comprehensive, for instance, always has its six senior staff timetabled to be free while the rest of the school have the weekly Social Education lesson. This means that if there are crises, particularly where staff are inexperienced and reluctant to handle topics on their own, there is generally someone available to go in and work with them. Another school has made it possible for the PSHE co-ordinator to spend time each week with year teams, in a specially designed PSHE resource area, reviewing and preparing for their teaching.

MANAGING THE PARA-CURRICULUM

The suggestions for managing innovation outlined above deliberately reflect a collaborative and democratic approach to school organisation, reflecting our values for PSHE and the healthy school. The same values need to be echoed in the para-curriculum. They should be explicit in relation to language and equal opportunities policies and in areas like Special Educational Needs. But they may be less easy to specify in other areas of school life. The following exercise will help to clarify those features essential to maintaining a healthy school ethos.

Exercise 7.1: Design a School

On your own, or in four separate groups, brainstorm the characteristics of:

    a)   A healthy school
    b)   An unhealthy school
    c)   A school which appears to be healthy but in reality is not
    d)   A school which appears to be unhealthy but in reality is healthy

If the exercise has been shared between four groups it is especially interesting to compare the 'apparently healthy' and the 'really healthy' scenarios.

Which set of characteristics comes closest to describing your present school?

The descriptions in Figure 7.4 were produced by a group of students interested in the links between health education and the tutoring and counselling aspects of teaching.

To achieve a healthy ethos, it is desirable to ensure that every aspect of the school's life is consistent with its overall values. Among these, the area of relationships is crucial. This includes the day-to-day communications between students, teachers and other adults. These can be measured in a number of ways. Some are obvious, like the form of address students and teachers adopt towards each other, rules about eating in class and talking during lessons. Others are more subtle, like the handling of racial incidents, gender messages in textbooks and so on. Richardson *et al.* (1980) ask some pertinent questions on this score. We have added others:

What proportion of the *teachers* in your school:
· have visited another school during the last year to look at aspects of the other school's curriculum or organisation?
· have watched at least one of their colleagues teaching during the last year or taken part in a team development meeting?

198

Figure 7.4: The Healthy School: Real and Apparent

The healthy school	The apparently healthy school
· anti-racist/anti-sexist curriculum · well-designed eating facilities and healthy menu — no chips or buns · toilets on every floor and good washing facilities · happy atmosphere: respect and responsibility · uniform · a health education co-ordinator · a counsellor · INSET for PSHE · a garden · a full, balanced curriculum · assemblies twice a week · a theatre · a good car-park for cars using lead-free petrol · full resources · decent buildings and furniture · a core curriculum including maths, humanities, science, RE, PE, PSHE and technical subjects · good sports facilities/showers	· clean and tidy surroundings, no graffiti · a 'tough' head · 'good' discipline · a quiet atmosphere · strict school uniform, no make-up or jewellery · no staff turnover · streaming · a good attendance record · a traditional curriculum · no PSHE co-ordinator · a swimming pool — but it's closed pending repair (no money!) · pupils have day diaries but they are not completed by staff/commented on by parents · tutorial time but nothing much goes on apart from homework and gossip
The unhealthy school	The apparently unhealthy school
· no playgrounds · no tutor periods · no timetabled PSHE · unhealthy food: no choice, chips with everything · no mention of taboo subjects: sex, drugs, alcohol, racism, sexism · poor communications with parents · special educational needs completely ignored · no multi-cultural curriculum · girls-only needlework/boys-only woodwork · poor internal communications · no back-up for staff · no INSET · low morale · poor resources · no space for recreation	· run-down buildings and untended grounds but an ecology garden · an inner-city/remote rural setting but good community links · mixed ability teaching but good group work and careful monitoring of special educational needs · a noisy atmosphere but lots of student-centred, active learning · no school uniform but smart dress · a high percentage of students on free school dinners but good dinners, cooked on premises · no on-site sports facilities but use of local gym and playing field · few lavish resources but lots of visitors, advisers, guests and work-/community-experience

· have taken part in a small planning meeting with colleagues during the past week?

· have participated in any decision-making meetings with respect to curriculum matters?

· know their counterparts in neighbouring schools?

- know the names and personal circumstances of all or most of their colleagues and of the non-teaching staff?
- know the names and personal circumstances of all or most of the students they teach or tutor and have spoken with their parents within the last year?
- have been involved in a case conference or some other form of inter-agency liaison concerning a student they teach?
- have received a written or spoken note of praise or encouragement from a colleague during the last seven days?
- believe or know that the head and/or at least one of the deputies knows something of their hopes and plans with regard to future career; their ideals and values with regard to education; their views and feelings on current school policies; and their personal circumstances?

What proportion of *students*, during the last week:
- have been off the school premises for legitimate reasons?
- have talked with or listened to an adult other than a teacher?
- have written a letter?
- have made a telephone call?
- have worked on a topic selected by themselves?
- have spoken to the head?
- have talked informally with a teacher on a subject other than work?
- have received a written note of praise or encouragement from a teacher on a piece of their work?
- have talked informally with a member of the non-teaching staff?
- have spent time on the school premises after school hours with groups other than their peers?

A period of industrial action and strained relationships with LEA employers is clearly not the best time to expect teachers to take up all of the options for collaboration and professional development implied above. However, it would be a pity if any new contractual arrangements were to inhibit the possibility of this kind of openness to what is happening in other schools or the willingness of teachers to support each other and to communicate with colleagues and parents. Indeed, more flexibility should ideally be written into teacher contracts, precisely to permit a balance of school and community-based work; better liaison between home, school and welfare agencies; more effective educational and careers guidance; wider opportunities for educational enrichment out of school hours — and so on. In our view these kinds of relationship are essential, not only for practice in PSHE but also for the well-being of those who work in, and with, schools generally.

The scale opposite, devised by John Watts — ex-head of Countesthorpe — with students on a school-community project, provides a check on how far your own school is moving towards meeting such ideals.

Exercise 7.2: School–Community Involvement

Instructions: For each aspect of community involvement, put a tick on the scale representing the current degree of involvement in your school. The pattern of ticks will give a profile of your school's overall performance. Ask other staff, parents and community workers to try the task and see whether they share your perspective. What steps can you take to increase community involvement?

Type of involvement	Low level	1 2 3 4 5 6	High level
· parents in school	by appointment		open access
· staff home visits	forbidden		every home visited
· community participates in decisions of school	confined to governors		management of curriculum
· community contributes to resources	only through rates		direct contributions
· school uses resources within community	not at all		widely
· school involved in community issues	not at all		actively
· school used by community at all hours	not at all		throughout year
· staff participate in decisions	decisions imposed		full participation
· staff development	no chance		good chance
· inter-agency collaboration	crisis contact		regular liaison
· students participate in learning	teacher-directed		full participation
· curriculum reflects community	LEA/National directive		rooted in local life
· women's issues	stereotypes maintained		anti-sexist policies implemented
· anti-racist issues	perceived as irrelevant		anti-racist policies implemented
· school organisation	hierarchical		equal representation

Source: Adapted from *Network*, May 1987

MANAGING FUTURE SOCIAL MOVEMENTS

If changes in the direction of greater school–community liaison and better interpersonal communication matter now, they are increasingly likely to be of significance in the years to come, as more of the social movements we identified in Chapter 2 become a reality. One head, Moon (in Day and Moore, 1986), predicts the following quite dramatic shifts in schooling by the end of this century:

- a reduction in contact time to 10 hours a week
- developments in video and information technology permitting independent study
- the collapse of age-related learning
- the widening of the curriculum
- a greater role for ancillary teachers
- a move from information transmission to roles involving the management of learning
- greater use of community resources
- the blurring of the boundaries between education, work and training
- a shift to student-centred assessment
- team teaching and collaborative learning
- the removal of some of the present impediments to learning, for example, the built-in expectation of failure, tedious movement between lessons, the ubiquitous bell, mass arrival and exodus, etc.

In his own school, as at several of those described in the SCDC Report (Watkins, 1987) on *Modular Curriculum*, such innovations are already under way. What is more, with current changes in assessment (for example, OCEA, the Northern Record of Achievement, Graded Tests and student profiles), and the transformation of pre-vocational training opportunities for 14 to 19 year olds, the impetus for change is likely to accelerate — to some extent regardless of schools' wishes; that is, unless central directives outlaw any further innovation.

Exercise 7.3 invites you to consider the balance of positive and negative forces for change operating in your own school.

LEADERSHIP

Sound leadership, good teamwork and effective staff training will be essential in this next phase of educational advance, for the challenge is no less than to 'probe the deep-seated interconnections between teaching "codes", the hidden (or para-)curriculum and the school's culture, climate or ethos' (Holly in Reid *et al.*, 1987). Contributing to this set of tasks is something for which PSHE teachers are particularly well qualified, given their training in collaborative styles of communication and rational, action-research based modes of working. In fact, like an earlier generation of counselling-trained teachers, trained PSHE co-ordinators are increasingly being recruited to senior management positions. For if it is true that management is 'philosophy in action' then leadership in PSHE — as in wider aspects of schooling — involves a common set of

Exercise 7.3: A Force-field Analysis: Influences on Change

The following exercise helps to devise strategies to achieve a desired goal by analysing relevant influences on the change.

1. Decide the main area of innovation you wish to address, such as:
   · the organisational health of the school
   · public relations in the local community
   · whole-school communication
   · involvement of governors and parents
   · reviewing internal assessment procedures
   · improving staff meetings
   · managing resources
   · publicity

2. State your objective as specifically as possible, e.g. to gain governor support for the implementation of a PSHE programme.

3. Decide on the positive and negative forces (at each level) which may help or hinder the achievement of this goal. For example:

Positive forces		Negative forces
Reluctant to make a fuss and 'rock the boat'. Have taken on many campaigning issues recently.	**within self**	Confident about advantages of PSHE. Scale III postholder with 10 years experience. Have led successful PGCE sessions. Involved in PSHE training.
Competition with pastoral heads who want more time for ATW. One deputy strongly opposed to PSHE.	**within immediate staff group**	ATW programme in 1st and 2nd years, well-tried, motivated tutor teams. Staff meeting held to discuss PSHE — general enthusiasm.
Chair of governors is hostile. Other issues e.g. GCSE seen as priority. Little cash left for INSET. School has been receiving a 'bad press' recently.	**within wider context**	Workshop for parents scheduled. Training offered by LEA. Local employers accepting of PSHE elements of work experience.

4. Give each force a value: 3 — strong; 2 — medium; 1 — weak, and add up the +ve and −ve columns.
Do the positive forces outweigh the negative? If so, go ahead, but the next stage, 5, may help. If the balance is roughly equal, try 5. If the negative forces are far greater, you may have to reconsider, or postpone your goal.

5. Take each force in turn. Preferably with a partner, acting as a consultant, devise strategies to minimise the negative forces and maximise the positive.
   For example: Prepare a written paper about the advantages of PSHE.
   Sidestep the chair of governors and concentrate on winning support from others.

Exercise 7.3: contd.

Repeat stage 4 as though each of your strategies had been implemented. Your goal ought now to appear much more feasible!

6. Set target dates for the completion of each of your tasks.
7. Do them — and good luck!

Source: adapted from Lewin, 1939

---

requirements: knowing the task, knowing the situation, knowing the followership, knowing oneself (Stoner in Day and Moore, 1986). More pragmatically, leadership for curriculum change involves the capacity to identify realistic areas of action. The flow chart in Figure 7.5, produced by Millman and Weiner (1985) in their work on anti-sexist strategies, offers one style of approach. You might wish to follow their suggestions exactly or to adapt the diagram to analyse possible developments in PSHE. Note, however, that having found an appropriate route through the figure does not in itself tell you how to proceed with any detailed planning.

Another useful instrument is the checklist (see Figure 7.6) for the GRIDS project (Bolam in Oldroyd *et al.*, 1984).

It should be clear from these two instruments that effecting whole-school change is a major undertaking and one which requires keen analytical skills, imagination and creativity as well as sensitive interpersonal relationships. For if the various procedures look neat when expressed diagrammatically or in a questionnaire the reality is a good deal less tidy. There are likely to be delays and frustrations to overcome; problems of cash and commitment; conflicts of loyalty; disappointments about resourcing and staff training; bouts of student resistance and parental suspicion — all of which have to be resolved. The role of the Head or project co-ordinator will be paramount in steering a course through these obstacles.

Perhaps the crucial element in successful leadership is the ability to take colleagues with you so that they give their assent to any proposed changes. According to Hirst (1982), this depends on four qualities:

· willingness to learn new practices (VOULOIR),
· knowledge of what to do (SAVOIR),
· knowledge of how to do it (SAVOIR FAIRE),
· access to the means to do it (POUVOIR).

These are dispositions which we should ideally wish all teachers to possess. But in some schools they are not too evident at first glance since they demand a much greater degree of sharing of responsibility and openness to collaboration than has hitherto been the norm. Apart from difficulties in terms of attitude, there can be practical constraints. In hierarchically organised institutions, for example, innovation can threaten settled patterns in several ways — it can affect staff

Figure 7.5: Reducing Sex Differentiation in the Secondary School

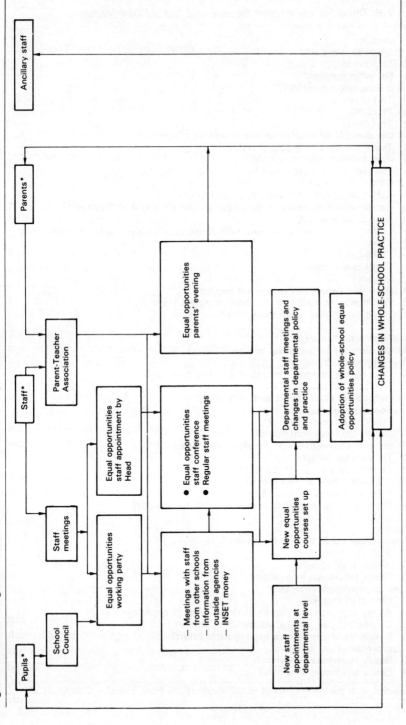

Note: *If you are a pupil, member of staff or parent, place yourself in the appropriate box on the top line. By following the arrows, you can identify possible areas of action open to you if you want to reduce sex differentiation in the secondary school.

Reproduced with the permission of SCDC Publications from Millman and Weiner (1985)

Figure 7.6: Checklist for Internal Review and School Development

The innovation
1. Is it *centrally* relevant?
   (a) To whom?
   (b) For what purpose?
2. Will it bring major benefits?
   (a) To pupils?
   (b) To staff?
   (c) To others?
3. Will the changes be substantial and extensive in terms of:
   (a) Teacher behaviour/teaching style?
   (b) Pupil behaviour/learning style?
   (c) The rest of the staff/school?
4. Is it simple and flexible?
   (a) Can staff understand what they have to *do*?
   (b) Can it be broken down or are all parts essential and interdependent?
   (c) How adaptable is it?
5. Are its underlying values congruent with those of the main people concerned, e.g.
   (a) The staff?
   (b) The pupils?
   (c) Significant others?
6. Is it feasible?
   (a) What additional resources will it require?
   (b) Will it alienate staff (e.g. by threatening job status)?
   (c) Will it require too much extra time?

The implementation strategy
1. Will the planning be 'adaptive' and continuing?
   (a) Participation by whom?
   (b) Opportunity to adapt innovation goals and content?
   (c) Feedback on progress?
2. Will staff training be relevant and continuing?
   (a) Specific and practical
   (b) Provided by practitioners?
   (c) On-the-job/classroom-based?
3. Will there be opportunities to develop local materials?
   (a) To learn by doing?
   (b) To develop a sense of 'ownership'?
4. Will a 'critical mass' be developed?
   (a) A *team* of involved participants?
   (b) Thorough discussion/information for non-participants?

The setting
1. Is the change agent viewed favourably?
   (a) Status/authority?
   (b) 'Leadership' style?
   (c) 'Track record' on innovation?
2. Is the 'organisation' receptive?
   (a) High staff morale?
   (b) *Active* support/commitment of Head (head of department etc.)?
   (c) General support of local education authority?
   (d) Readiness of teachers to expend extra effort?
3. Is the 'organisation' adaptive?
   (a) Ready to change behaviour?
   (b) Ready to change timetable?

Reproduced with the permission of SCDC Publications from Bolam in Oldroyd *et al.*
(1984)

loyalties; departmental responsibilities; resource allocation; technical and secretarial support; career development opportunities and so on. These cannot be ignored. However, the fact that such difficulties can be overcome is amply evidenced by the radical new structures to which we have already referred — especially in the worlds of pre-vocational and community education.

MONITORING AND EVALUATION

As well as being able to help others overcome obstacles and having a greater than usual amount of energy, determination and courage, educational change agents need another set of skills: those of critical evaluation. To date, in British schools, most teachers' experience of evaluation is limited to the formal assessment of student performance or the validation of Mode 3 courses (Adelman and Alexander, 1982). However, evaluation as we conceive it, both for management purposes and for programmes of PSHE, involves ongoing appraisal of course organisation and of the teaching-learning process and its outcomes — for students, for teachers and for the school. It means asking questions about the teachers' skills of organisation and pedagogy as well as about students' learning. It also requires clarity about possible outcomes and about what purposes the assessment procedure is intended to serve.

Any evaluation process needs to take account of these starting questions (see further Harlen and Elliott, in McCormick, 1982, and Figure 7.7).

Given a clear sense of the purpose of a review, the main issue is how to conduct the evaluation. This will partly depend on who it is for. If it is for the LEA, for example, as part of a GRIST project, it will need to be relatively brief and to concentrate on immediate and highly visible changes. If it is for research purposes a much wider range of techniques suggest themselves, which may be part of an ongoing process of review lasting up to a year or more. In either case, the most realistic instrument is normally a short checklist or questionnaire (see, for example, McGuiness, 1982; Hamblin, 1986; Bell and Maher, 1986; Clemett and Pearce, 1986).

However they are conducted and whatever interview schedules or checklists they involve, evaluation studies demand considerable resources of time. The fact that the evaluators are often participants in the change process does not make things any easier (see Carr and Kemmis, 1986).

None the less, the end-point of any process of curriculum or organisational evaluation should be the same: information about the balance of present strengths and weaknesses and future needs for stability or change. This can then lead to the formulation of new action plans — including the specification of staff development needs and any adjustments to students' programmes of learning.

Figure 7.7: Questions for Evaluation of PSHE

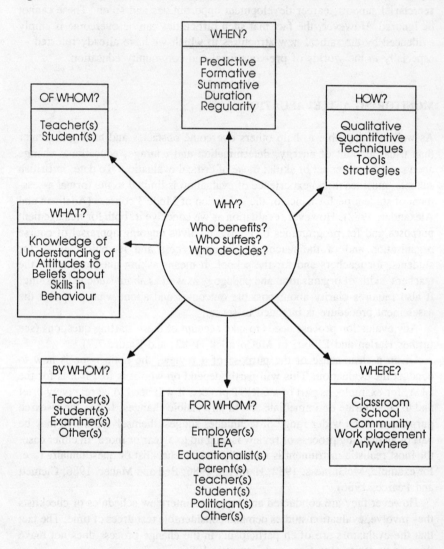

CONCLUSION

The next chapter looks at staff development as perhaps the most crucial ingredient in the cycle of organisation development. But we conclude with a model connecting our desired outcomes for PSHE with the values of healthy organisational life. It is worth noting that the outcomes are outcomes for staff as well

Figure 7.8: A Four-tier Model of Desired PSHE Outcomes for Staff and Students

Individual outcomes
self-confidence
problem solving improved
less dependent learning

Peer group outcomes
collaboration, sharing good
practice, risk-taking, communication
skills, disclosure and feedback, challenge
to stereotyped thinking and prejudiced attitudes

Institutional outcomes
healthier climate, hidden curriculum
congruent with formal organisation, clear
aims, whole-school co-ordination and support,
visible participative, decision-making processes,
collective support for the institution, procedures for
change and innovation involving students, parents, community

Wider outcomes
involvement of school members (students and staff)
with community (parents, governors, employers, agencies),
social and political literacy and motivation for involvement/
engagement, democracy, accountability, 'healthier' society

as for students and that gains in health for one group are, in our view, automatically gains for others and for the institution as a whole.

This chapter has argued that for PSHE practice to be successfully developed, schools themselves need to be healthy. This is so that the values of the school and those of the PSHE curriculum are mutually reinforcing and also because organisational change depends crucially on the kind of values central to PSHE. As Figure 7.8 suggests, where this relationship does occur, there are positive outcomes in terms of individual, organisational and community health.

FURTHER READING

Bell, L. and Maher, P. (1986) *Leading a pastoral team: approaches to pastoral middle management*, Blackwell, Oxford

Blackburn, K. (1983) *Head of house, head of year*, Heinemann, London

Bolam, R. and Medlock, P. (1985) *Active tutorial work: training and dissemination — an evaluation*, Blackwell for the Health Education Council, Oxford

City of Salford Education Department (1983) *Schools looking at themselves*, Salford

Clemett, A.J. and Pearce, J.S. (1986) *The evaluation of pastoral care*, Blackwell, Oxford

Easen, P. (1985) *Making school-centred INSET work: a school of education pack for teachers*, Open University with Croom Helm, London

Handy, C. and Aitken, R. (1986) *Understanding schools as organizations*, Penguin, Harmondsworth

Hargreaves, D. (1982) *The challenge for the comprehensive school, culture, curriculum and community*, Routledge and Kegan Paul, London

Heller, H. (1984) *Helping schools change*, CSCS, University of York

Holt, M. (1983) *Curriculum workshop: an introduction to whole curriculum planning*, Routledge and Kegan Paul, London

Inner London Education Authority (1984) *Improving secondary schools*

McMahon, A. *et al.* (1984) *Guidelines for review and internal development in schools: a secondary school handbook*, Longmans for Schools Council, York

Oldroyd, D. *et al.* (1984) *School-based staff development activities: a handbook for secondary schools*, Longmans for Schools Council, York

Reid, K. *et al.* (1987) *Towards the effective school: the problem and some solutions*, Blackwell, Oxford

Richardson, E. (1973) *The teacher, the school and the task of management*, Heinemann, London

Skilbeck, M. (ed.) (1984) *Readings in school-based curriculum development*, Harper and Row, London

8

Staff Development/INSET for PSHE

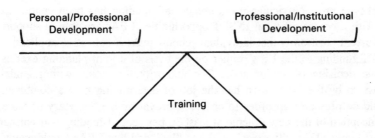

Our account of healthy whole-school strategies for innovation and of new roles for teachers arising from developments in PSHE, PVE and assessment highlight the importance of staff development — whether in the interests of teacher professionalism or enhanced school functioning. This is a need also acknowledged by the government, albeit for different reasons. However, in contrast to the sort of training associated with the introduction of the GCSE, what we have in mind is not a once-off transmission process. We believe the INSET ideal to be something much closer to the notion of '*éducation permanente*': a process which involves regular individual, team and whole-school reviews and a range of negotiated opportunities for staff development, not just once in their careers but on an ongoing basis.

CURRENT INSET ARRANGEMENTS

Since it is not clear which of the 'thousand flowers' seeded by the 6/86 GRIST arrangements will bloom most luxuriantly, this chapter will often refer to earlier types of INSET framework. We have two main aims: to outline what is involved in identifying INSET needs and opportunities and to look at various models of delivery for INSET courses.

211

Accounts of earlier responses to INSET needs, as identified in the James Report on *Teacher Education and Training* (DES, 1972) can be found elsewhere (Bolam, 1982; Ashton *et al.*, 1983; NAPCE, 1986). The typical arrangement was characterised by sponsorship for individual teachers who sought to improve their prospects by attending diploma, certificate or higher degree courses at local colleges of HE, at polys or at universities. Unless they required full-time secondment or time off for study leave, teachers were virtually free to determine their own INSET — regardless of the needs of their school or local authority. Funding, including the salaries of seconded teachers, the cost of supply or replacement teachers, fees and travelling costs, plus advice from the relevant adviser, came from the LEA. The authority, in turn, was able to claim 90 per cent of the cost back from central government on a pooling arrangement.

Since April 1987, although pre-shadowed by the two-year TRIST arrangements which secured special funds for LEAs to assist and promote TVEI-type cross-curricular programmes, all funding has been centralised — and with it control of what INSET opportunities LEAs are able to support. So the current position is that individual schools make a collective application for INSET funding to the LEA, either on the basis of a joint planning exercise or on the decision of senior staff. The authority, operating within guidelines drawn up by the DES, then has the job of determining how a combined bid should be presented in order to ensure approval by the Secretary of State. At the inception of the new scheme at least 30 per cent of funding was earmarked for 19 'national priority areas', with the likelihood that LEAs would eventually determine additional priorities on the basis of local conditions and needs. However, while the DES was prepared to give 70 per cent funding to courses in the national priority areas, local priorities only attracted 50 per cent backing.

The result of the GRIST arrangements will be dramatic for all concerned — not least financially. For example, they are likely to mean:

· the collapse of support for teachers wishing to pursue long courses at universities and elsewhere, with short (i.e. 20-day or less) courses becoming the preferred norm. Year-long secondments are thus likely to disappear, with teachers paying their own fees for higher degree and other higher-level courses. There is understandable anxiety that this could lead to an emphasis on rather narrow forms of training at the expense of deeper personal and professional development.

· more INSET will be school-based and school-focused, using the expertise of existing staff (on the cascade model) or buying in advisers and consultants from outside (on the organisation development model).

· externally run short courses will operate in the market-place, with 'best buys', 'value-for-money', 'loss-leader' tags and intense competition between the providers — whether universities, polys, colleges of higher education, the LEAs themselves or independent consultancies.

· concentration of courses on nationally identified priorities, which currently include CDT, mathematics and computing, physical science, multi-cultural initiatives, drug education and special educational needs.

· longer term, once regions have developed a more co-ordinated policy, the proliferation of schemes for cross-centre course accreditation, offering the posssibility that, say, six to eight modules, appropriately sequenced and assessed, might add up to a diploma or masters degree.

From the point of view of schools, in spite of the anxieties being voiced by teacher associations about centralised direction, the new structure may afford some potentially useful opportunities — assuming a) that there are sufficient INSET courses on offer and b) that there is a democratic structure within schools enabling staff to share in determining their own INSET needs, individually or on a team basis. These opportunities include the prospect of:

· providing cross-sector training (primary/secondary/further)
· complementing and improving on existing provision to make it more responsive to schools' needs
· setting training objectives within overall school plans for curriculum development
· selecting appropriate staff to be trained and a timetable for their release which fit in with whole-school priorities
· negotiating follow-up roles and activities
· designing new teaching programmes (including opportunties to produce new materials)
· designing appropriate monitoring and evaluation schemes, including peer and self-assessment techniques
· sharing concerns, learning and opportunities for support across neighbouring schools

Whatever we feel about such developments, the GRIST arrangements are likely to require a major shift in attitudes and approaches in schools. This may not be easy, for a number of reasons:

· lack of expertise, resources and time
· lack of sustained commitment, given conflicting priorities and pressures
· lack of incentive in terms of cash or promotion
· staff turnover and/or low morale
· the sheer complexity of the managerial issues involved
· unwillingness to tolerate change and alternative strategies
· unwillingness to be sufficiently thorough and honest at the stage of review and evaluation of needs
· lack of experience

MODELS OF INSET

So what are the current alternatives in INSET? Figure 8.1 outlines the features of four different models of INSET. The independent and the competitive models (C and D), which were the norm until recently, have as their main justifications the furtherance of learning for its own sake and the individual development of teachers. Models A and B, on the other hand, are both school-focused. They therefore have implications not just for the staff involved but for the whole organisation. Figure 8.2 weighs up the advantages and disadvantages of the different schemes. There are, of course, many variations, in detail. What is more, any one individual may find himself engaged in more than one type of INSET. For instance, a PSHE co-ordinator might be a member of a central training programme run by the LEA, as well as being a part-time student on a higher degree course at the local university. In addition, he might be leading some team training for first-year PSHE tutors at his school.

As we have already noted, models C and D are both likely to receive less offficial backing in the current INSET climate. They are also less likely to contribute to whole-school processes of change. In what follows, we shall therefore concentrate on models A and B. However, before moving on to explore aspects of the two types of school-focused INSET, it is worth pointing out the rich variety of external training opportunities that are available — many of which can result in valuable changes in individual teachers' practice. The alternatives include:

1. Involvement in Initial Training/INSET:

including, acting as co-tutor to PGCE or B.Ed. students on teaching practice
interviewing prospective students
assessing students' project work
job exchange with college or department of education staff

2. Secondment:

including,   i) to LEA advisory teams
ii) to research/development projects, for example, preparing and trying out new teaching materials or assessment instruments
iii) to study for a higher degree

Figure 8.1: The Spectrum of INSET Approaches

	A. COLLABORATIVE	B. MANAGERIAL	C. COMPETITIVE	D. INDEPENDENT
1. Scope	– whole school/team development	– sub-group/school development	– individuals, classroom skills	– individual, personal development
2. Location	– school-based, school-centred	– school- or externally based system-centred	– school-focused but externally supervised/ monitored	– out of school
3. Focus	– curriculum, pedagogy, team & professional development	– organisation development and staff development for specified roles	– curriculum, pedagogy in classroom settings	– a specific academic or other area of interest/skill development
4. Ownership	– collegial	– managerial	– individual	– private
5. Initiation	– bottom-up, working teams	– top-down, senior staff/ INSET co-ordinator	– hero innovator	– individual, with or without sponsorship
6. Role of Expert Consultant	– process helper, ideas person, counsellor	– change agent, trainer, legitimator, network co-ordinator	– resource-provider, assessor, career agent	– gatekeeper of knowledge skills, evaluator/assessor
7. Mode	– self/group evaluation dialogue, negotiation	– school-based review training/staff development package focused on co-ordination & communication skills cascade training	– observation, hypothesis formation, data-gathering, analysis, evaluation	– mix of receptive/active learning/report writing some peer learning but 'expert' assessment
8. Duration	– ongoing, at different levels, in response to needs	– cyclical, based on a gradualist policy of spiral development	– limited, one-off	– fixed and limited
9. Evaluation	– peer review of objectives & outcomes	– self-evaluation peer review	– pre, post tests participant observer	– examination with tutor's report

Figure 8.2: Advantages and Disadvantages of Different INSET Models

Advantages	Disadvantages
1. Collaborative Approaches (Model A)	
· start from teachers' perceived needs with issues and problems with which they identify. Thus · high levels of motivation and commitment can be maintained · willingness to share and experiment with new ideas · teachers 'own' their own INSET so have a high investment in successful outcomes · goals and agendas agreed collectively so priorities are likely to reflect what most staff want · acknowledge and work within the practical constraints (of resources and personnel) of particular set-ups · generate high levels of sharing and trust across the staff at all levels, thus improving confidence and morale · 'solutions' are negotiated and staff are collectively responsible · can lead to personal as well as professional development — especially in the area of human relations skills	· depend on the existence of change agents among the staff who are capable of identifying development needs and taking responsiblity for initiating INSET · risk being manipulated by management in the name of democratic consultation · may get squeezed by pressures of time or cash · depend on staff willingness (and creative timetabling) to work for shared goals, abandoning present curriculum hierarchies · without sensitive leadership and/or effective agenda-setting risk of unbalanced developments · make 'failures' highly visible so staff may feel vulnerable to adverse assessment · may require high levels of personal disclosure and willingness to admit difficulties (both at variance with teacher norms) · without external consultant, risk of inward-looking, limited response to change
2. Managerial approaches (Model B)	
· work with committted teachers who know what they want and why · generate high levels of commitment and motivation · focus on the perceived needs of teachers back in the school to develop content and process skills · maximise opportunities for sharing/comparison between schools and so facilitate creativity · empower key teachers to use newly acquired skills for training programmes in their own schools · efficient use of expertise · focus on learning to learn means development process is never complete, no static 'solutions'	· risk that those who benefit from training are rejected by colleagues back at school · distancing from actual structure and constraints of own school · school itself may not be receptive to changes · there may be competition for staff's attention from other curriculum developments · key trained personnel may move/be promoted so their skills are not passed on to others · expensive in staff cover if teachers are out for a whole day each week (or longer)

Figure 8.2: contd.

Advantages	Disadvantages
3. Competitive approaches (Models C and D)	
· permit in-depth, long-term investigation of key problems	· staff may be suspicious of 'hero innovator'
· encourage examination of previous research/development policies in the relevant area	· actual school problem being studied may have changed when teacher returns and/or their new skills/perceptions may be irrelevant to where most staff feel their problems lie
· high-level academic supervision available	
· may enhance career prospects because of opportunity to gain qualifications and to meet influential mentors	· academic emphasis may ignore the very practical constraints operating in everyday school life
· further understanding of school-based issues/arrangements and offer a test-bed for academic theories	· no support/follow-up for returning teacher guaranteed
· develop critical awareness, willingness to challenge common-sense understandings of schooling and, hence, potentially open up new perspectives for more radical change	· do not address whole-school issues/needs
· encourage comparison of school strategies between peers and thus enhance transfer of training	· ignore possible advantages of collaborative approaches to learning and change

3. Award-bearing courses:

(possibly in parallel with 1 and 2)
including, Masters Degrees, full- or part-time Research Degrees
Open University post-experience courses
Diplomas and Certificates, for example, in Counselling and Careers Guidance, in Health Education or in Human Relations

4. Non award-bearing courses:

as provided by Teachers' Centres, HE, Universities, usually on specific topics or skills, with or without a school focus; for example, courses in computing and CAL (Computer Assisted Learning); anti-racism/anti-sexism; ESL; assertion training; special educational needs and so on

5. Support groups:

formal or informal, single interest-focused or mixed; for example: groups for probationers, Special Educational Needs, black and women teachers

Although we shall not examine these alternatives further here, teachers interested in finding out more for themselves might begin with the list of training agencies in Appendix 3.

Apart from the IT/INSET model which is being developed in a number of regions, one of the features that distinguishes school-based from externally provided INSET is that, whereas the latter tends to take the form of a course or fixed unit of experience, a wide variety of different kinds of experience and involvement are available within the school-based option. These are listed by Oldroyd and his colleagues in their pioneering work for the Schools Council (1984) as follows.

1. Whole school:

Staff conferences
Working parties
Career counselling/staff appraisal
Organisation development training programmes
Cross-disciplinary support teams

2. Sub-groups:

Induction programmes for probationary teachers
INSET for pastoral teams
Department-based training
Teams review/support
Inter-school INSET
Visits to other schools

3. Individuals

Specific piece of action research
Team teaching
Teacher exchanges between schools
Mutual lesson observation
Support from advisory team or other external consultant

Examples of these different types of INSET are usefully described in the case studies collected in the report referred to above. Some of their advantages over external INSET courses (even when these do in fact focus on the school) are immediately apparent; for instance, their flexibility and focus on school-based needs.

USING A CONSULTANT

A major question facing providers of school-based INSET is whether to engage an external consultant, either to advise on the setting up of their INSET programme or actually to run parts of it. The person concerned could be an adviser, a college lecturer or an independent 'expert'. In an article in the *British Journal of Inservice Education* (1977), Eraut defines a consultant as follows:

> any external agent from within the education system who involves himself in discussing the educational problems of a class, department or school with a view to improving the quality of teaching and learning.

And he outlines a 'preliminary typology of consultant's roles':

1. The Expert
2. Resource Provider
3. Promoter
4. Career Agent
5. Link Agent
6. Inspector/Evaluator
7. Legitimator
8. Ideas Man [*sic*]
9. Process Man [*sic*]
10. Counsellor
11. Change Agent

Matching these roles against the range of school-based INSET opportunities, it is evident that particular roles or combinations of roles are more relevant to some activities than others — and some will suit some personalities more than others! What role a consultant adopts, either formally or informally, will also depend on what he was brought in to the school to do — and how. For instance, a person whose original contact with the school was as a teaching practice supervisor might find himself being approached to lead some staff training workshops on profiling or graded assessment — as a resource provider and link with a current research project. Alternatively, a university teacher with expertise in training methods, who happens to be supervising an M.Phil. thesis being undertaken by one of the deputy heads, might find himself being invited to visit the school to legitimate a particular INSET programme and to train workshop leaders. In the present climate of change, first-hand contacts of this kind appear to be extremely important since, in many instances, LEA advisers and heads have no other way of knowing who or what training expertise is on offer in their area. This means that the market-place in opportunities referred to earlier is in reality more like a lucky dip!

But by whatever route they arrive, when consultants formally contract to work with a school, a number of important issues needs to be addressed — on both sides. There are three main questions to be worked on.

1. Who is the client?

Is it the Local Authority, which, say, following an inspection or in relation to 1/86 training for CPVE, wants a department or a school as a whole to improve its performance? Is it the Head, who, independently, has similar motives — in which case where does the LEA stand? Is it a sub-group of staff, who, while pursuing a serious piece of development work in relation to their own area of the curriculum, are hoping to subvert some other part of the school system or to sabotage another group's INSET plans? Is it a particular head of department with a bee in his bonnet? Or was the request to the consultant, as we would hope, the product of a joint staff negotiation?

2. What is the extent of the consultant's involvement?

At what point in the training process is the consultant to be involved? How will he relate to the member of staff responsible for co-ordinating INSET? Should he help in evaluating needs, designing staff roles or producing ideal job specifications? Should he impose his own definition of what staff require — with or without prior discussion? Can he insist on a joint planning exercise, and on a post-experience evaluation — regardless of the extra time and costs involved? What kind of preliminary documents and follow-up report will he write regarding the INSET?

3. What authority does the consultant possess?

What is the source of the consultant's credibility and are his skills acknowledged as appropriate? How will he be introduced to the staff? How much detail will they receive in advance about the activities they are likely to be taking part in? What will happen about those who are reluctant (or refuse) to take part? What is the force of any recommendations made during the INSET programme and backed by the consultant? Does he have the right to make judgements on individual staff members and, if so, to whom? To whom is the consultant accountable and how is his consulting evaluated?

LEVELS OF NEED

In the PSHE area we would expect there to be two different levels of INSET need: for senior management and those with co-ordinating responsibilities and for teachers who need support in developing new classroom approaches. Given the particular features of teaching in PSHE, training for both groups should be experiential. However, the issue of whether the two groups should have their training needs met separately or whether there are advantages in joint INSET groups is important to consider, just like the issue of using a consultant. There is not any one right answer to these alternatives: only the 'best' answer for a given institution, at a specific stage. Perhaps the optimum solution is a mix of approaches, sequenced over time to take account of developing staff needs and curricular changes. This might take the following form:

1. A whole-school workshop to identify needs, clarify strengths and weaknesses, agree to a programme of goals and targets for development (one to two days with an external consultant)
2. An ongoing programme of school-focused training for PSHE staff (run weekly by the school's PSHE co-ordinator)
3. A central training opportunity for the PSHE co-ordinator focusing on the skills of negotiation, curriculum design and evaluation (run by the LEA advisory team, weekends twice a term)
4. A variety of external short courses on specific aspects of PSHE for individual teachers (one night a week termly or day courses)
5. A whole-school programme of review and evaluation sessions to monitor all cross-curricular developments and re-evaluate training (run termly by a deputy head and the PSHE co-ordinator)

One thing is clear, in the new INSET framework, '*laissez-faire* . . . may need to be replaced by a clearer definition of its role in servicing the overall curriculum needs of the institution' (Darley and Helsby, 1984). This means an end to '*ad-hoc*ery' and 'crisis management' and closer attention to staff consultation and selection for training. It also means finding ways of mobilising staff interest and commitment: not an easy task in a climate in which promotion chances are blocked and pay depressed. With these traditional motivators in eclipse it will be necessary to hold out new prospects to staff — for instance, a sense of achievement in tackling difficult cross-curricular problems, responsibility for one's own work and ownership of the results, the satisfaction of enhanced teaching skills or improved relationships with students, colleagues and community. For, however organised, ultimately the success of any training must depend on the teachers involved.

The staff are the central resourse, their expertise and creativity tapped through individual encouragement and through working in teams. The changes in role

221

and exchange of ideas which are the essence of teamwork make it one of the most dynamic forces for development. (Kenwood and Clements in Day and Moore, 1986)

INSET PEDAGOGY

Bearing in mind the crucial fact of staff commitment and motivation, it is worth looking at INSET pedagogy. If we ignore the distance learning methods which are currently being explored by the Open University and others, basically there is a choice between two models of teaching/learning: one which is subject-centred, the other centring on students' needs. While we would not wish to dismiss the usefulness of some knowledge content in the training of teachers for PSHE, more important, as we have already indicated in Chapter 6, is practice in experiential approaches. As well as providing first-hand experience of what it feels like to be involved in different forms of group work, this enables teachers to discover ways of adapting their existing teaching skills so that they feel confident in a new-style role. As with classroom practice, a supportive climate within which teachers can share their hopes and anxieties, as well as their ideas, is fundamental to PSHE training. Hence, personal and professional development go hand in hand.

The outline programme on page 223 gives a flavour of what the experiential approach involves.

You will notice the similarity in structure to the first-year tutorial programme on pp. 148–9: a further instance of consistency at all levels of practice in PSHE. However, it is worth repeating a point made in the previous chapter; to be successful, experiential approaches themselves require a number of preconditions. In fact, they demand no less than that 'the culture of the staff group is transformed into a permanent, supportive, workshop setting' (Holly in Reid *et al.*, 1987). What this means practically is summed up by Stibbs (1987):

1. Regular opportunities for consultation at all levels
2. Participation in decision making
3. Encouragement of innovation and creativity
4. Genuine delegation and shared responsibility
5. Meaningful job descriptions
6. Ready support for those in difficulty or under stress
7. Induction schemes at all levels
8. School-based training
9. Encouragement of off-site training
10. Systematic professional appraisal and guidance

As Stibbs adds, none of these can be effectively acted upon without 'a management characterised by genuine commitment to staff care and development,

AIDS Workshop: Outline Programme

Time	Activity	Purpose	Group Size
5 mins	Introductions	To explain the purpose of the workshop	Whole group in a circle
5 mins	*Opening activity* Name round. Participants give their name, and role within the school	To enable the group to get to know each other better	
10 mins	*Fear in a hat* Each participant completes the following sentence on individ- ual pieces of paper. 'My biggest fear about AIDS is . . .' The pieces of paper are collected, shuffled and read out by participants. Main points are written on a flip-chart, and discussed in pairs.	To share anxieties about AIDS in a non- threatening manner	Individuals

Pairs |
| 25 mins | *Checklist of information* True/false questionnaire. Participants fill in individually. Discussion in 2s. Join with another pair, look at questions they are unsure about, and are then given the booklet to check information. | To check information | Individuals

2s
4s |
5 mins	*Feedback* Each 4 reports back on answers they are still unsure of.	To clarify any points where there is still disagreement	Whole group
20 mins	*What should we do as teachers?* Discussion on how and where such issues should be included in the curriculum, and by whom. Points recorded on large sheets of paper, and then reported to large group.	To start to consider how AIDS should be tackled in the classroom	Small groups
5 mins	*Closing round* The most interesting thing about this workshop . . .	To evaluate the session	Whole group

Acknowledgements to ILEA HEPD team

genuine sympathy with staff needs and problems, and genuine willingness to share responsibility'.

This is a tall order, especially when we consider how radical such conditions are compared to present practice. Things are not made easier by the large number of different aspects of school life currently subject to very substantial transformation — each carrying its own INSET needs. These are on top of the adjustments necessitated by falling school rolls and other population movements and by the shortages of teachers in key subjects. The problem in some schools must be how to get anything to happen at all, never mind the all-embracing model of staff development we have described. However, the goal is worth striving towards if at all possible for it brings rewards not just for the institution but, as we have hopefully demonstrated in earlier chapters, for the teacher too — professionally and personally.

CO-ORDINATING SCHOOL-BASED INSET

There are two intertwined processes involved in school-based INSET on the collaborative model: individual and school development. For the best results these need to be kept in balance, as Holly (in Reid *et al.*, 1987) emphasises: 'For far too long . . . we have had . . . overdeveloped individuals in underdeveloped schools. The reverse is now in danger of happening in some schools. What is required is an equilibrium of investment.'

Crucial to balancing schools' and individual teachers' needs is the work of the INSET co-ordinator whose role it is to manage, support and encourage appropriate in-school change processes. As we saw in the previous chapter, such a person ideally needs to possess highly developed interpersonal skills. These are likely to be required in several different contexts:

· liaising with the LEA and external support agencies
· co-ordinating all in-school development activities
· chairing the school INSET steering group meetings
· representing the school at project conferences or workshops
· training the staff in evaluation
· resourcing

All of these are major responsibilities, especially as experience suggests that the team leader becomes 'not only an enabler, but also a gate-keeper (the barometer of staff stress and strains), a fixer, a nurse and internal consultant' (Holly in Reid *et al.*, 1987). Having an outside source of support and counsel is crucial for such a person or team. Hence the valuable role that advisers or consultants can occupy, at a distance from schools. Hence, too, the justification for the central or managerial model of staff development. This offers the possibility that when senior staff meet, for example as a group of PSHE co-ordinators on a course specifically designed to provide leadership training in this area, the individuals concerned have an opportunity to share experiences and problems and to learn from each other's successes and disappointments.

The tasks of the PSHE co-ordinator are threefold:

1. to identify INSET needs
2. to decide on and implement suitable INSET programmes
3. to evaluate and provide ongoing support for these activities

We outlined the cycle necessary for a whole-school review in Chapter 7. Such an exercise should provide the necessary data to order INSET priorities — those of individuals, of teams and of the school as a whole. There may also be an opportuntiy to link the definition of INSET needs to creative staff appraisal and role consultation (see Trethowan, 1987). This is certainly an advantage in supporting the career needs of more senior teachers, although it is inevitably time-consuming if conducted across the whole staff (and may meet with resistance or suspicion in some quarters). However, one of the hopeful developments that we see emerging form school-based staff development is a more constructive attitude towards staff sharing their difficulties. In other professions, notably social work, this is the very basis of professional learning and growth (see Atherton 1986). It seems all the more disappointing that in a profession which spends so much of its time managing students' learning difficulties it should be so hard for staff to feel secure in sharing their uncertainties.

To spare staff the embarrassment of talking openly about their problems, as well as to save time, many schools use a questionnaire to get teachers to identify their training needs, as in the example in Figure 5.4 (p. 136). Ideally, the outcome of such a personal review should be a meeting with the head or INSET co-ordinator (perhaps with the relevant adviser in attendance). Here, as with most professionals working in other sectors of the economy, each teacher would have an opportunity to review their present job specification and to negotiate any new responsibilities. A follow-on from that discussion would be the identification of any INSET needs, which might perhaps include a period of consolidation or withdrawal from the teaching profession.

Having attempted to balance individual, team and whole-school development needs, the person co-ordinating INSET has to decide on priorities for any one term or year. The next step is to decide which INSET can be met internally and which will mean sending staff to external agencies. It may be useful to have an LEA adviser or some other external consultant available at this stage of the process, both to help weigh up alternatives and to consider their likely outcomes. Simply knowing what you can expect from a particular amount of INSET time invested is crucial to making these decisions effectively. Figure 8.3 attempts to give a rough guide. There are of course infinite variations in what is possible. Our outline simply contrasts some common alternative forms of course organisation.

225

Figure 8.3: Training Objectives for INSET re PSHE

Time	Content	Possible Objectives
1–3 hours	Discussion of what is meant by PSHE; its location in the curriculum and underpinning by whole-school values	Clarification of links and boundaries between PSHE and the pastoral system; para-curriculum; vocational and academic curriculum
1 day 5–6 hours	EITHER A. General: 1. Discussion of concept and definitions as above 2. A look at models of PSHE and related materials 3. An introduction to active learning approaches OR B. Specific: Focusing on a particular topic, e.g. health education	1. As above 2. Understanding of alternative curriculum models and need for consistency between aims, methods and assessment techniques 3. Understanding rationale for active learning and relating this to present knowledge and skills 1. Raised awareness 2. Information re resources and approaches
2–3 days 10–18 hours	1. As above 2. Opportunity to practise basic group work or face-to-face skills 3. Design of learning materials and evaluation techniques 4. An examination of student needs and interests 5. Focus on specific topics, e.g. working with mixed-ability groups; assessment in PSHE; integrating equal opportunities work; parent/governor workshops; anti-racist strategies	1. As above 2. Enhanced professional skills and awareness of personal strengths and limitations 3. An understanding of the application of knowledge and skills 4. Design of co-ordinated PSHE curriculum from year to year 5. Raise awareness and information re resources and approaches
20+ hours	Higher level skills, e.g. co-ordination and greater familiarity with resources and methods	As above, at a higher level

The relative advantages and disadvantages of the different patterns are weighed up in Figure 8.4.

Figure 8.4: Advantages and Disadvantages of Different Forms of INSET Given the Same Amount of Time Distributed Differently

Advantages	Disadvantages
1. THREE DAYS INTENSIVE	
· high profile · strong group commitment/cohesion · easy to timetable/administer · focuses interest/concern · efficient in time/resources · likely to keep clientele · offers (false) hope of easy evaluation · makes reflection on the learning easier · permits intensive work	· tiring · one-off, quickly overtaken by next 'flavour of the month' · less time for negotiation or developmental work/reflection · composition of group more restricted · cannot take much account of students' starting points · need for a variety of tasks/activities but can degenerate into a circus/hotchpotch
2. ONE DAY FOLLOWED BY FOUR TIMES HALF A DAY	
· high-input, high-impetus cascade possible · action research encouraged · developmental reflection encouraged · possibility of ongoing support for members · high profile · possible certification, e.g. as Diploma or MA module	· hard to timetable · hard for staff to maintain a focused interest in the group and its development · not very flexible · missing any one session could defeat the purpose entirely · possible loss of momentum/morale for participants
3. SIX HALF DAYS	
· permits time for group development · time for reading/practice/reflection · time to negotiate future work · reasonably visible status/identity	· risk of fluctuating attendance · vulnerable to unforeseen emergencies · restricted to people who can be freed for the specific slot · risk of impact disappearing fast
4. TWELVE SESSIONS OF ONE AND A HALF HOURS	
· can be responsive to changing needs of group and issues arising (internally and externally) · provides basis for a valuable support group for members · focus for ongoing review of practice · easier to timetable (so likely to attract a wider clientele) · well designed, it offers easy-to-assimilate chunks/clear outcomes and easy assessment · does not disappear from the agenda as fast as other models	· lead-time wasted each meeting for group building · seen as peripheral/low-status compared to more intensive courses · fluctuating attendance (unless certificated) · risk of high drop-out · lack of continuity and depth · actual contact time (with all present) too short for balance of imput/activity/reflection · risk of sessions being cancelled at last moment so loss of impetus

Note: The above models all assume a school base, within timetabled time; so individual 'best buys' will depend on specific institutional constraints and possibilities. There are common problems for each model (for example, when the only available space is the dinner hall just before or after lunch!) and also risks dependent on members' status (dealing with 'emergencies', taking phone calls, being diverted to other duties etc.).

A fuller impression of what different amounts of training can offer can be gained from the outline programmes below:

1) is an outline of a week's programme
2) is for a one and a half hour workshop on PSHE
3) is for a two-day workshop on Active Learning Methods

You will notice that these programme outlines always contain a brief review session at the end. This provides useful feedback to course organisers about the immediate impact of their work. However, longer-term feedback is also important: for example, how durable was the training? what changes occurred as a result of the INSET?

1. Programme of a Week's Course on Experiential Approaches to Personal and Social Education

13–18 July

Time	Sunday	Monday	Tuesday	Wednesday	Thursday	Friday
9.00		Communication skills	Group discussion skills	Gender	Small group	Small group
					Constructing a classroom exercise	Goal setting
12.30		L	U	N	C	H
2.00		Small group	Small group	///////	Drawing and fantasy	Ending
4.30	Registration	Small group	Constructing a classroom exercise	///////	Drawing and fantasy	Ending
5.00				///////		///////
6.30	Meeting	D	I	N	N	E R
	Dinner					
7.30	Why are you here?	Goal setting	Small group	Goal setting	Small group	
9.00						

Acknowledgements to Arthur Wooster *et al.*, School of Education, Nottingham University

2. Programme of PSHE Staff Workshop

Staff workshop   30 March 1987
Personal Health and Social Education (PHSE) Pastoral Curriculum

Time	Activity	Group Size	Purpose
1.55	Aims of Workshop	Whole	Clarification
1.57	Round, At the moment I feel . . .	Whole	Warm up/Ice
	OR Good news — something good that's happened to me . . .		breaker
2.00	PSHE checklist	Individually	Decision
	Complete		making
2.03	Discuss with another person similarities and differences	2s	Sharing ideas
2.10	Report back — one person from each pair One we agree with and one we disagree with — Reasons.	2s	Sharing ideas
2.20	Pick a number		
2.22	PSHE Identify needs in each year	Small groups (3s)	Clarification
	BRAINSTORM — What do children need to know (with reference to topic) in Years 1 & 2, 3 & 4, 5 & 6		Fitting things together
2.28	Prioritise list and record up to 10 on chart (BE SPECIFIC)	Small groups	Negotiation Co-operation
2.38	Put charts on wall		
2.40	Personal voting Put a tick by the ones you think are most important (prioritise 5 for each year)	Individual	Recording choice
2.45	Collect charts and write on card the most important needs for each year. Report back.	Group	Recording group choice
2.50	Evaluation What process have we used? Why?	Group	Analysis of group process
2.55	What would we like to see happen next — short-term.	Small groups 3s	Forward planning
3.00	— long-term BRAINSTORM		
3.05	Short-term goals Long-term goals	Whole	
3.10	Closing Round, What I found useful . . .	Whole	
3.15	Plenary What we would like to see happen next — short-term — long-term	1 person from group report back to staff NOT group leader	
	MEETING OF GROUP LEADERS		

Acknowledgements to Janet Packer

229

3. Programme of Active Learning Methods Workshop

Day 1

Time	Activity	Purpose	Tasks/Who
9.30	*Introduction*	To say hello	
	'Lucky Dip round' —	To share expectations of active learning	
	I think active learning is ... (with introductions to 5 people and 1 thing about job)		
	Introduce programme and our definition of active learning	To share our aims and our views of active learning	Written on flip-chart
9.50	*M.U.D.* (Memory, Understanding, Doing, see Belbin *et al.*, 1981) — *A Model for Learning*		
	Brainstorm — how do you learn something new?	To identify learning *strategies*	Whole group record
10.00	How do I learn — sheet	To focus on learner's own strategies	Individually → Pairs
10.05	Q. Are there any strategies that you have not used much?		
10.15	Feedback	To record any additional strategies	Whole group
10.20	M.U.D. input	To explain a simple model of learning	
10.25	M.U.D. Task — classification of learning strategies (N.B. Add two of own to each column)	To use the M.U.D. model	In 3s
10.40	Give out hand-outs	To provide background information	
10.45	Coffee		
11.05	*Advantages of Active Learning* 'Diamond Nines'	To prioritise the advantages of using active learning methods in the classroom	Individually → New 2s → 4s
	Feedback	To discuss issues	Whole group

Programme of Active Learning Methods Workshop: *Continued.*

Day 1

Time	Activity	Purpose	Tasks/Who
12.15	Review of methods	To record a list of activities	Whole group
	— What have we done?		
	— How appropriate are these methods for your own teaching	To relate to own teaching situation	In 2s
12.25	Find the person	To finish the morning and remember names	Whole group (N.B. hand-out)
12.30	LUNCH		
1.30	*Individual Learning Styles* Opening round : Name and 1 word to describe how I learn	To start the session and focus on individuals	Whole group
1.35	'What's my learning style?' — (Life skills II)	To reflect on one's own learning style	Individually (instructions flip-chart)
1.50	Q. Are you surprised by your own scores?	To share	In pairs
1.55	Discussion in small groups	To discuss issues and implications	In 3s
	1. Which style do you think is most common in this group? 2. Which style do you think most common for your students? 3. Is there a 'best' style? 4. Which style do schools encourage?		
2.10	Grouping according to style (in the manner of the style!)	To look at variation within whole group	Various groups
	1. Discuss the pros and cons for your own style 2. Choose 2 advantages and 1 disadvantage to feedback	To reflect on the pros and cons of each style	Give sheets of advantages and disadvantages Whole group

Programme of Active Learning Methods Workshop. *Continued*

Day 1

Time	Activity	Purpose	Tasks/Who
2.30	Tea		
2.45	Force field analysis	To develop strategies for improving learning To act as consultants	Individually → pairs
3.20	Review of methods	To continue record of activities	Whole group
3.25	Round : What I have learned today	Consolidation of day	
3.30	Close		

Day 2

Time	Activity	Purpose	Tasks/Who
9.30	*Raising Some Issues* Jigsaw 1) Title 2) What has this got to do with active learning	To warm up To get into groups To look at 'triggers'	The Cobb Book pictures
9.45	Graffiti — statements about reading material	To raise issues	In small groups Sheets headed CPVE and Active Learning, Race and Active Learning, Gender and Active Learning
10.15	Implications of current developments	To discuss the implications of particular trends in education	In 2s/3s
10.35	Feedback	To record comments	Whole group
10.45	Coffee		
11.05	*Active Learning Simulation* Character groups	To develop roles and strategies	Cards with role and context
11.20	Meeting		In 4 groups
11.50	Character groups	To debrief meeting To summarise main arguments	
12.05	Feedback	To record issues arising	Whole group
12.20	Review of methods	To continue record of activities	

Programme of Active Learning Methods Workshop. *Continued*

	Day 2		
Time	Activity	Purpose	Tasks/Who
12.30	Lunch		
1.30	*Making Sense of Learning* 'The Salmon Line'	To look at factors which affect learning	Individual → pairs
2.25	Tea		
2.35	*Evaluation* 'Consequences' Brainstorm criteria for evaluation Each group writes one comment	To evaluate the course, publicly but anonymously	Small groups
3.10	Personal evaluation	To reflect on own learning	Individually
3.20	Review of methods	To continue record	Whole group
3.25	Closing Round	To close the session	
3.30	Close		

Acknowledgements to Lesley Campbell and Barbara Patilla

EVALUATING INSET

Monitoring and evaluation begin as soon as a particular INSET programme is under way. But there are a number of issues to be considered first. These are summarised in the set of questions which we have adapted from the DES document, *Making INSET Work* (1978). The first set of questions concerns the purposes of the evaluation exercise:

WHO wants to know and WHY?
· the teachers who participated in the activity
· the school as a whole — i.e. the staff meeting
· those to whom the school is accountable — e.g. the Head, parents, governors, the LEA
· the external consultant, if any, or his employer

WHO will carry out the evaluation?
· a teacher or group of teachers
· the Head or INSET co-ordinator
· an LEA adviser
· an independent evaluator
· the external consultant — or someone from his institution
· a working party representing different staff interests
WHAT will be evaluated?
· the aims and value of the starting intentions
· the achievement of participants' hopes and expectations
· changes in curriculum or pedagogy
· the extent to which the INSET matches the needs for professional development outlined in the teacher's appraisal interview
· whether the course provided value for money
· whether it was instructive and/or enjoyable
· whether participants are keen to continue with further training
· student gains

There are then a set of decisions to be made about HOW any monitoring or evaluation should be conducted. There are several alternatives, each at different levels of sophistication (see Reid *et al.*, 1987). However, it is becoming clear that evaluation in the sense used with reference to GRIST can be something relatively unsophisticated. Simple indices of 'change' and 'satisfaction' would appear to suffice — and, indeed, to be all that is possible in the short time span available. In addition to any checklist or questionnaire approach that attempts to gauge these reactions for the school, perhaps the best we could recommend is that each teacher becomes his own ongoing monitor and researcher: regularly checking and evaluating lessons, materials and training opportunities, in the light of his own and the school's wider needs.

We have already hinted at the importance of choosing practical evaluation techniques; a further set of questions in the DES Report addresses some useful considerations here:

Are the proposed evaluation methods *feasible*?
· in terms of the time available
· in terms of cost
· in terms of their acceptability to those involved
What professional *safeguards* will be guaranteed to participants?
· who will have control over any data collected and reported?
· will staff have a right to reply to any report of their views/activities?
· wil! these views be incorporated in any final report?
· will the acceptability of the data collection methods and reporting of results be negotiated in advance?

Figure 8.5: How Do We Evaluate INSET?

DIY evaluation at the end	videoing sessions
graffiti sheets	self-assessment at all levels
6 months/10 years later	by relating to our aims
writing a report	has it been fun?
using numbers/forms	what have I learnt?
rounds	have expectations been met
are children changed?	ask parents/employers etc.
who gets promoted?	our own feelings
tutors' review	have we recruited more potential trainers?
ask participants to make a personal record	is classroom practice changed?
what did it cost?	will we be asked to do more INSET/consultation work?

What back-up *resources* will be available and will they be sufficient?
· equipment, paper, postage, filing cabinets, IT
· secretarial assistance
· working space with suitable furnishing
· special time allocation to those carrying out the evaluation

An interesting case study of the way many of these factors influenced the planning and evaluation of one particular INSET course in 'Education for Health and Personal Relationships', organised in Sheffield, is described by Cox and Lavelle (1983). You might like to brainstorm some of the possible forms INSET evaluation might take in your area of work. The list in Figure 8.5 was produced by a group of trainers. As the questions in Figure 8.5 illustrate, it is important to be clear about what criteria will be used for reviewing the gains from INSET — either for participants or for trainers. It is also necessary to choose the appropriate time for a review. Similarities with the evaluation exercises listed in Chapter 6 are clear.

DISSEMINATION OF INSET

The final stages of any INSET programme, and a preliminary to the next cycle of development, involve the dissemination of results from the training and the continued support of course members. Allocation of time for reports back in staff meetings; the circulation of written reports to all staff; contributions to local authority newsletters; articles in relevant journals; team-building activities and investment in appropriate resources — are all crucial here. So, for some purposes, may be teachers' involvement in the kind of external support groups advocated by Hanko (1985). These have proved exceptionally valuable for teachers needing to resolve their anxieties about working with students who have

235

behavioural or learning difficulties. There is no reason why they should not be equally useful for those whose concerns are more curriculum-centred, like teachers of PSHE.

Professional associations, NAPCE and the Institute of Health Education, for example, can provide occasional support in the shape of local or national workshops and LEA or even regional networks — perhaps based on a teacher's centre or suitable HE establishment. They enable practitioners to keep in touch by newsletter, to meet to examine resources, to exchange experiences, to arrange visits to each other's schools and so on. The kinds of database held by some of the agencies listed in Appendix 3 are a further source of information of 'good' practice.

INSET AND ORGANISATION DEVELOPMENT

In both this and the last chapter we have emphasised the need for consistency between approaches to PSHE in the classroom and approaches to whole-school review and staff development. We have also stressed the neeed for experiential models of learning and for collaborative structures of decision making. The connection is explained by Kirk (1987):

> If experiential learning is an integral part of a well-planned and structured staff development programme, aimed at helping teachers to enchance their own understanding and inter-personal and other skills and to manage change more effectively, then the transmission of similar attitudes and activities to the classroom will follow naturally and the whole culture of the institution will be affected.

Looking at staff development from a Local Authority standpoint, Jane Jenks, Warden of the ILEA Health Education Teachers' Centre, also argues for coherence (November 1986). She suggests that new approaches to INSET are creating four key areas of need:

· A need to focus co-ordination of INSET need assessment and support on the school
· A need to arrive at a shared understanding of effective processes for bringing about change involving different INSET providers and schools/colleges
· A need for staff development teamwork across the Authority to support the development of this shared understanding
· A need to institute a pattern of career development which promises opportunities for individuals/teams to share their experience and good practice on a wider basis, possibly through a staff development team

Clearly, this authority-wide view of INSET is seen as the basis for wider achievements. According to Darley and James (1984) INSET represents 'the key to the raising of awareness and the improvement of competence and catalyses the attitudinal changes which are essential prerequisites to effective curriculum reform'.

For many purposes, no doubt, the school-based and school-focused INSET offerings generated in response to the 6/86 GRIST arrangements will provide the 'best buy'. But we should like to stress the considerable advantages in promoting individual and organisational change of some external courses, especially for teachers who are in Authorities which cannot offer central programmes for PSHE.

CONCLUSION

The INSET pattern eventually adopted by particular schools and authorities will necessarily reflect local needs and opportunities. We hope it will also balance individual and whole-school development. But perhaps most important of all is that INSET for PSHE should itself be modelled on the kinds of values, processes and hoped-for outcomes which we have identified as belonging to its core.

In the next chapter we look at the way this PSHE core and related staff development needs operate in further education establishments.

FURTHER READING

Bolam, R. (1982) *School-focused in-service training*, Heinemann Educational, London

Carroll, S. and McQuade, P. (1985) *The staff development manual*: vol. 1, *Delivering the curriculum*; vol. 2, *Staff development in action*, (1986), Framework Press, Lancaster

Cox, K. and Lavelle, M. (1983) *Learning from experience: problems and principles of developing an INSET course*, Department of Educational Management, Sheffield City Polytechnic

Day, C. and Moore, R. (eds) (1986) *Staff development in the secondary school*, Croom Helm, London

Donoughue, C. *et al.* (1981) *In service: the teacher and the school*, Kogan Page, London

Easen, P. (1985) *Making school-centred INSET work: a school of education pack for teachers*, Open University with Croom Helm, London

Hanko, G. (1985) *Special needs in ordinary classrooms*, Blackwell, Oxford

Lambert, K. (1986) *School management: materials and simulations for in-service training*, Blackwell, Oxford

McMahon, A. *et al.* (1984) *Guidelines for review and internal development in schools: a secondary school handbook*, Longman for Schools Council, York

NAPCE (1986) *Preparing for pastoral care: in-service training for the pastoral aspect of the teacher's role*, Blackwell, Oxford

Nuttall, D. (1981) *School self-evaluation: accountability with a human face*, Longman for Schools Council, York

Oldroyd, D. *et al.*, (1984) *School-based staff development activities: a handbook for secondary schools*, Longman for Schools Council, York

Ruddock, J. (ed). (1982) *Teachers in partnership: four studies of in-service collaboration*, Longman for Schools Council, York

Trethowan, D. (1987) *Appraisal and target setting: a handbook for teacher development*, Harper and Row, London

9

PSHE in Further Education

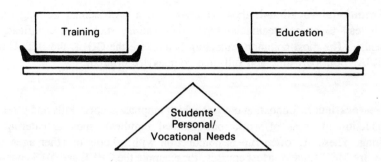

This chapter is not a postscript, nor do we wish to give the impression that further education (FE) is a poor relation of schools. But the set-up in FE is different and explicit PSHE is elusive to the point of non-existence. In this chapter, we merely wish to indicate features of FE which are likely to prove significant for the development of PSHE. There are many instances of good practice in this area but, as yet, no recognised forum for sharing them. We hope this will not always be the case.

First, some boundaries and distinctions are important. The chapter will concentrate on non-advanced further education (NAFE) rather than advanced courses (AFE) such as those leading to degrees and higher diplomas. Hence, we are looking at Colleges of Further Education, not Universities or Polytechnics. As in the preceding chapters, the focus is on formal, accredited educational establishments rather than adult education institutes, youth centres, youth clubs, community projects and so on. PHSE, as such, is not an established entity in FE. However, PSHE-type activities do take place under a number of guises. You can probably recognise examples in the institutions with which you are familiar.

Before focusing on PSHE issues and organisation specifically, we shall outline the overall FE system and raise some general issues. Recommendations for further developments are suggested in the conclusion to the chapter.

THE FE SET-UP

This is so complex that it is hard to plunge in without fear of total submersion! A relatively tangible starting point is to describe the sorts of course on offer. These can be grouped into five categories.

1. Academic: those courses which lead directly to a nationally recognised qualification, i.e. GCSE or A-level. These are comparable with school syllabi and primarily related to higher education. Both full- and part-time courses are available.

2. Traditional vocational: those courses with a professional training remit which lead to a craft/technician-type qualification, such as a certificate in carpentry. The most common validating bodies are the CGLI, the B/TEC and the RSA. Both part-time and full-time courses are offered.

3. Pre-vocational: foundation courses which emphasise core skills and offer an introduction to areas of work (occupational families), such as catering or retailing. These are often run in conjunction with schools or other agencies. Many are MSC-funded. Most courses, for example the CPVE and YTS courses, are one or two years full-time.

4. Short vocational: entrepreneurial-type courses, often designed in direct response to the demands of industry, offering short, intense and highly specific periods of training, for example, in information technology. These are often sponsored by industry and may be certificated by the college or by an external body.

5. Leisure: courses offering opportunities to pursue interests, like yoga, wine-making or conversational Spanish, mainly for adults, which may or may not be linked to professional needs. These are mostly part-time evening courses.

At present, approximately 90 per cent of courses offered in FE are designed and validated by the B/TEC, the RSA and the CGLI. About 10 per cent of courses are pre-vocational. This balance, however, is in some upheaval. Numbers applying for traditional vocational courses are falling, particularly for part-time, day-release training. Meanwhile, there is a potential growth area in recurrent (or continuing) education for adults should sufficient funds become available. 'Access' courses, to prepare students for university entrance are another recent development. These are designed for students who have not followed a traditional academic route, maybe because of earlier educational discrimination, such as against black women. Finance is again a problem and depends partly on future university funding.

A second way of describing the FE set-up is in terms of the numbers and features of the student population. In 1984 there were 1.6 million students in 570 FE colleges in England and Wales (DES, 1986). Approximately three-quarters of these were part-timers and about half were in the 16 to 19 age range. Numbers for men and women were about equal.

The figures above indicate the most significant feature of the FE population: its heterogeneity. Although particular courses may attract a more specific, or 'type-cast', student, overall the mix is considerable, in respect of age, ethnicity, gender, ability, financial status, vocation and motivation. Because FE is voluntary, students' reasons for enrolling are both varied and changeable. Some of the issues which arise from such diversity are discussed in the next sections.

GENERAL ISSUES IN FE

This section lists issues which seem relevant to current concerns and development within the FE sector. Some are likely to have widespread repercussions while others may only have high priority in certain colleges or LEAs. The list is in no particular order and is intended as an overview of the present situation rather than as a set of strategic recommendations.

· FE funding and discrepancies in grant allocation are the most serious limiting factors on curriculum developments. These lead to a waste of resources, both financial and human.
· Course changes, in response to government, industry or LEA pressures and financial constraints have led to problems of departmental reorganisation (even closure), staffing and co-ordination. Separate departments within a college can be as big as schools and, seemingly, as autonomous. This makes the job of co-ordinated provision almost unmanageable, either within colleges, within LEAs or nationwide.
· The increased and unnegotiated influence of the MSC, following the government circular, *Training for Jobs* (DOE, 1984), has caused widespread concern about the 'industrialisation of education', the instrumental approach advocated by the MSC being in direct contrast to that espoused by FEU schemes, such as *A Basis for Choice* (FEU, 1979).
· The rationalisation of educational provision for 16 to 19 year olds (and even 14 to 19 year olds) is necessitating increased school/college links. Thus, organisational developments, such as the establishment of tertiary or sixth-form colleges, are giving rise to difficulties in the areas of staffing and conditions of service and in the progression from the accreditation of specific courses such as CPVE and TVEI.

241

· Staff development and training in FE have been an issue for some time (see Haycock's Reports, ACSTT, 1977, 1978a, 1978b). This is still an *ad hoc* situation, with about 40 per cent of FE lecturers having no pre-service training, although opportunities for attending in-service, day-release teacher training courses have been greatly extended. The situation is complicated by the large numbers of part-time staff involved.

· Assessment and accreditation procedures are changing dramatically in the wake of recent curriculum deveopments. The new 'rhetoric of competence', for example, requires staff to adopt new procedures such as profiling.

· Changing patterns of employment, notably the high level of youth unemployment, are reflected in both the student and the staff populations and, inevitably, in course provision.

· Power and control over the curriculum is becoming a more visible issue. What is/should be the influence of government, government-sponsored bodies, industry and employers, LEAs, governors, parents and students?

· Research within the FE sector is haphazard and receives little funding or national support. The FEU has pioneered many innovations within FE but they are not widely disemminated. Cantor and Roberts (1983) list seven areas of research which demand attention: teaching methods, learning and careers guidance and counselling, equal opportunities for women and girls, the special needs of the disadvantaged and physically handicapped, provision for ethnic minorities, the organisation and administration of FE, comparative further education.

· Equal opportunties provision for women has, at long last, been recognised as an issue. This raises questions about the predominantly male ethos of FE colleges, stereotyping on traditional courses, sexism among staff, the low aspirations of female students, family circumstances and the provision of nursery and crèche facilities.

· Racism is an equally important concern which affects course structure (content and methods) and career opportunities and is even manifested overtly by students and staff in some instances.

It may be useful for those teaching in FE to rank this list according to apparent priorities in your college. Does this match your personal priorities? If not, how can you shift the balance? We shall now consider the specific relevance of such issues to PSHE.

PSHE ISSUES IN FE

Our rationale for PSHE (values, principles and desired outcomes) is the same for the FE sector as it is for schools. However, there are different points of emphasis. First, the heterogeneity of the client group has implications for both teaching approach and for back-up/guidance services. FE students will have had very different previous educational experiences. Many will have been cast as 'failures' and will be wary of this label being reinforced. Others, however, will expect continuity from their schooling. Clearly, then, there needs to be a range of flexible and negotiated teaching methods which give students opportunities to express their individual needs and to share their ideas. This point links to what might be called the 'developmental tasks of young adulthood'. Many FE students will be dealing simultaneously with occupational issues, such as getting a job, or promotion; with family matters, such as establishing a long-term relationship or becoming a parent; and with wider problems, such as finding somewhere to live and adopting a role within the community. FE students are adults, by and large. Teachers, therefore, need to heed their experiences and to respect their maturity, while also not neglecting the need to address the personal and social dimensions of their learning. This concern is completely at odds with narrow schemes of training. Many of these are designed to impart knowledge and skills, and nothing more. Such an approach is anathema to our view of education. Not only will all students learn more if their individuality is valued and the social context of their learning recognised, but also, we feel, it is incumbent on educational institutions to accept some responsibility for the health of their students.

Traditionally, FE colleges have concerned themselves with student welfare through the installation of guidance and counselling services. Most colleges have student services officers and/or counsellors whose job it is to deal with a multitude of problems, ranging from grant and legal enquiries, course options and careers guidance, work-load and study skills, interpersonal and family difficulties, to specific health concerns, such as pregnancy and drug abuse. The commitment and competence of the majority of such staff is not in question. Often they are seriously overworked — as might be expected, given the crisis-management approach to perceived problems. We do not dispute the need for this sort of 'pastoral care' — especially for individual students in trouble. However, a more pro-active approach, in which lecturers and tutors use allocated time to explore common concerns, makes far more sense, in our view — educationally, economically and socially.

PSHE already exists within some FE courses: A-level Sociology and Psychology, City and Guilds' 'Services to People' and General Studies, for instance. It is unfortunate that staff working in these areas tend to be isolated within their own departments and have little opportunity to discuss their work. The National Association for Teachers in Further and Higher Education (NATFHE) Health Education Committee organises a biennial conference which offers one forum for such exchanges. Given their clear emphasis on training, it is interesting that courses such as TVEI, YTS and CPVE advocate a core curriculum which encompasses personal development or related themes. While one might legitimately wonder whether this masks a form of socialisation deliberately designed to produce 'good' (i.e. compliant) employees, there are opportunities here for PSHE. For instance, these schemes openly acknowledge the importance of adaptability and learning how to learn. Such sentiments, although probably deriving from a different ideological stance, are not at all incompatible with PSHE and many FE teachers have welcomed such opportunities for increasing students' decision-making and transfer skills.

The last issue we want to highlight in terms of PSHE is that of the hidden curriculum. Sexism and racism in the curriculum have been mentioned. Other factors are just as important. Some colleges, for example, have grossly inadequate lavatory facilities for women. Many college canteens, even in inner-city areas, pay no attention to the dietary needs and preferences of different ethnic groups. There are also more general features of college ethos which impart all sorts of messages to students. For instance, there is often no staff/student interaction beyond the classroom; security staff can have an ominous presence; the students' union has little influence; there are no extra-curricular acitivities; counselling and medical services are inadequate, and so on. You might generate a list which describes the ethos of your particular college. It is also worth thinking, realistically, what the equivalent might be to the list of features describing the 'healthy school' in Chapter 7. As we saw there, such features have a marked effect on the healthy development of students (and staff!) and deserve much more serious attention.

THE ORGANISATION OF PSHE IN FE

Our concerns about the organisation of PSHE in FE match those already described in relation to schools. PSHE is cross-curricular but also merits separate status. This requires co-ordination — difficult in schools but wellnigh impossible in some colleges of FE. However, PSHE proponents can take note of a number of more optimistic developments. Modularisation, for example, has been introduced in some colleges, with the effect of breaking down rigid departmental boundaries and improving communication procedures. In addition, some colleges have inter-departmental officers, such as multi-ethnic co-ordinators, health and safety, and staff development officers, as well as broadly based departments, such as Communications or Sport and Recreation, which 'service' other areas.

Given the size of FE colleges and their traditional industry-oriented ethos, enthusiasm for PSHE seems unlikely. Pioneers will, therefore, need to find as much support as they can. There will always be some staff working in the area — so the first task is to find them. Figure 9.1 shows possible courses of support in FE in relation to the influence of current developments.

These developments will not feature in the same way in every college but there are bound to be sympathetic and identifiable staff working in some of the six areas.

One area that has to be clarified before working with colleagues to develop PSHE is the distinction between education, training and counselling. Figure 9.2

Figure 9.1: Sources of impetus for PSHE development in FE

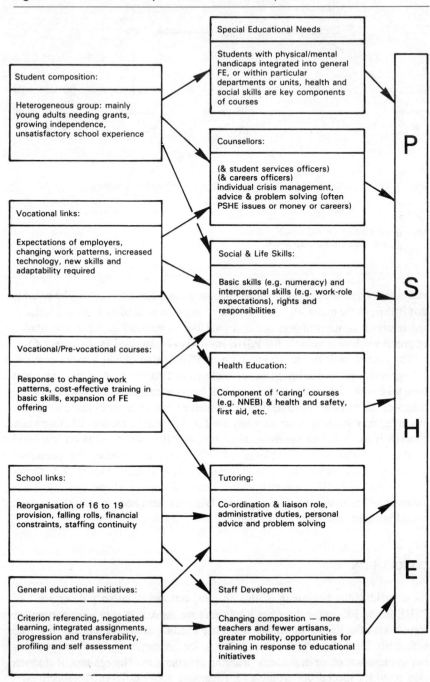

Figure 9.2: Staff Roles in FE

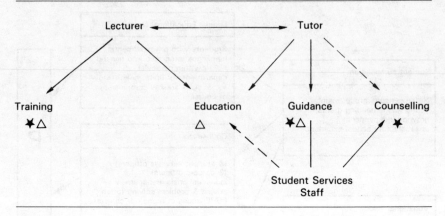

key: ✱ emphasis on individual work
△ emphasis on group work

makes this point simply, and can be used as a basis for discussion. The point is that PHSE, as the name suggests, is a function of the educational roles of lectures and tutors; it is not training, nor is it guidance or counselling. The importance of group work as a vehicle for PSHE must also be stressed (see Chapter 6).

The second task in the organisation of PSHE is to obtain a more general, college-wide, picture using grids, as outlined in Chapter 5. Any such research must take note of the ways terms are used, both by individual staff members and from one institution to the next. Terms such as 'pastoral care' and PSHE, for example, may be unfamiliar to many staff and therefore mistrusted. Our main concern is to challenge the assumption that PSHE is for students on low-level courses or who have 'problems'. PSHE can, and should, be presented positively, untarnished by a traditional welfare image. Figure 9.3 shows possibilities for PSHE organisation in colleges. There are advantages and disadvantages of each, as we have suggested. What teachers need to consider is what would be 'best' for their own situation.

CONCLUSION

As we said at the beginning of this chapter, our rather cursory description of PSHE in the FE sector does not imply that we think this area unimportant. In some ways, the FE set-up makes it a more exciting arena for aspects of PSHE to flourish. The voluntary student population, for instance, suggests that negotiation has an important place in students' learning programmes. The age-mix of students also provides special opportunities for learning about different perspectives.

Figure 9.3: Possible Organisation of PSHE in FE Colleges

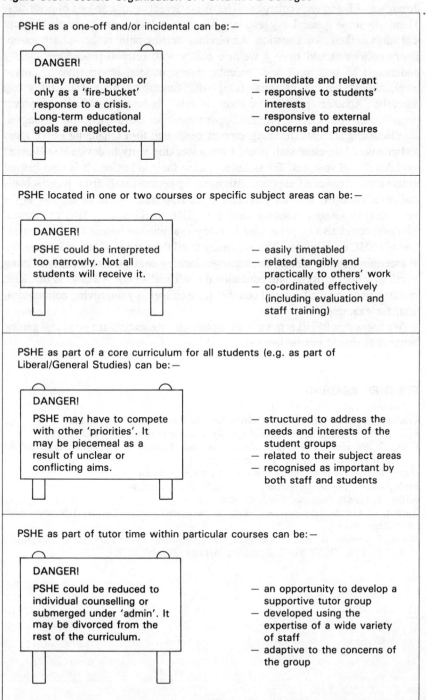

PSHE as a one-off and/or incidental can be:—

DANGER!

It may never happen or only as a 'fire-bucket' response to a crisis. Long-term educational goals are neglected.

— immediate and relevant
— responsive to students' interests
— responsive to external concerns and pressures

PSHE located in one or two courses or specific subject areas can be:—

DANGER!

PSHE could be interpreted too narrowly. Not all students will receive it.

— easily timetabled
— related tangibly and practically to others' work
— co-ordinated effectively (including evaluation and staff training)

PSHE as part of a core curriculum for all students (e.g. as part of Liberal/General Studies) can be:—

DANGER!

PSHE may have to compete with other 'priorities'. It may be piecemeal as a result of unclear or conflicting aims.

— structured to address the needs and interests of the student groups
— related to their subject areas
— recognised as important by both staff and students

PSHE as part of tutor time within particular courses can be:—

DANGER!

PSHE could be reduced to individual counselling or submerged under 'admin'. It may be divorced from the rest of the curriculum.

— an opportunity to develop a supportive tutor group
— developed using the expertise of a wide variety of staff
— adaptive to the concerns of the group

Clearly it will take considerable time and effort before PSHE is valued throughout FE and each college will have a different agenda and set of priorities. There are some general suggestions, however, which individuals could adopt and adapt to their own situation. An obvious starting point is the welfare set-up. Every college should have a welfare policy with referral procedures clearly understood by both staff and students. Every student, irrespective of course level, should have a personal tutor with timetabled individual and group tutorials. Another possible avenue is via 'in-house' staff development programmes. These could provide opportunities for sharing teaching strategies, for discussing students' learning support needs and for exchanging PSHE ideas and practice. Interested staff could form a working-party to devise PSHE-taster modules for all students, for instance during their induction. It is also helpful to use other sources of support. Advisers, inspectors, staff from local schools and other colleges, and other agencies (see Appendix 3) can be used — at the very least, to set up a resource bank for PSHE work. Senior staff, or external advisers, could also be persuaded to lobby examination boards for the recognition of PSHE components. The prelimary to all these types of action is research: to ascertain students' needs, to exchange teaching strategies, to identify existing PSHE practice, to formulate educational goals and so on. A bonus is that such research may carry all sorts of benefits for a college, by improving communication, for example.

We know that PSHE is not a 'soft' option. Its credentials are good and getting better. FE should not be left out.

FURTHER READING

Collins, N. (1986) *New teaching skills*, Oxford University Press, London

FEU (1980) *Developing social and life skills*, Longmans for the FEU, York

Grey, G. and Hill, F. (1988) *Health action pack*, National Extension College (for the Health Education Authority), Cambridge

Hamblin, D. (1983) *Guidance: 16–19*, Blackwell, Oxford

McMahon, T. (1986) *Developing tutor skills*, FEU, London

Miller, J. (1982) *Tutoring*, FEU, London

Turner, C. (1978) *Inter-personal skills in further education*, Further Education Staff College, Bristol

White, R., Pring, R. and Brockington, D. (1985) *The 14–18 curriculum: integrating CPVE, YTS, TVEI?* Youth Education Service, Bristol

Conclusion

We hope, having accompanied us through the various balancing acts that make up this book, you have been able to clarify your views on PSHE. When we set out on our own investigation, two years ago, we attempted to answer the question 'What is PSHE?' by addressing a series of philosophical, sociological and psychological questions, suggested by Lawton's scheme of cultural analysis. This led us to distinguish four models of PSHE and a technique (the PERM model) for identifying the different elements in practice. We went on to consider the relationship between PSHE and other aspects of the formal and the hidden curriculum and set out a procedure for co-ordinating it with work in other subject areas, using grids. Moving on to teaching methods, following the lead established by the various Health Education projects and active tutorial programmes, we saw the pedagogy of PSHE as being based on active group work and provided examples of a range of typical exercises and evaluation techniques. Finally, as an extension of the values underlying our view of PSHE, we discussed the importance of healthy whole-school relationships and support for staff development. The appendices suggest avenues for more detailed exploration and offer suggestions on resources for PSHE.

However, the journey is far from being at an end. We ourselves are conscious of a substantial list of questions and issues that remain. You will no doubt be aware of others. The agenda includes:

- the place of formal assessment in PSHE
- the criteria for evaluating student performance in PSHE
- the status of PSHE in the 'national' or 'entitlement' curriculum
- PSHE in the primary and further education fields
- the role of PSHE for students with special educational needs
- the influence of PSHE pedagogy on student achievement, especially that of students from ethnic minority groups and girls
- the place of PSHE as a force for innovation in mainstream subjects
- the co-ordination of PSHE, e.g. in modularised curricula
- training in PSHE and similar cross-disciplinary fields
- who should teach PSHE
- accountability to parents and governors
- the ideology of PSHE in relation to social class values

To tackle these issues effectively will inevitably mean more research, more collaboration, more teamwork and more time! It will also depend on more accounts of successful practice and more effective support networks within and between schools and local education authorities.

How can we ensure that some of these developments begin to happen — in

249

spite of, or even alongside, the other pressures on teachers today? Why should they happen anyway?

To answer the second question first. We have stressed throughout the book that PSHE matters because it is concerned with helping young people make sense of the world — and especially of their own individual worlds. At its heart is the notion of empowerment, that is, enabling individuals and groups to develop the skills, knowledge and attitudes necessary for promoting their own health — in whatever sphere. PSHE also has much wider significance, as we showed in Chapters 1 and 2. It is only one of a number of new cross-disciplinary fields to have emerged in an attempt to create a more relevant and balanced curriculum. Yet, while different in detail from these other fields (TVEI, CPVE, Life Skills, Personal and Moral Education, Media Studies, Child Development, and so on), its emphases involve the same commitment to bringing real-world issues into the classroom and approaching them in ways that give students a more active role in their own learning. One important feature of this approach is a strong commitment in PSHE to equal opportunities and the equal valuing of all students as people. This has led to links being forged with wider contemporary pressure groups — especially those that involve people taking responsibility for their own needs.

As with any development, there are counter-pressures, some commanding considerable authority, like the proposed 'National Curriculum' and tests of achievement. However, we should not allow these to dim our enthusiasm. PSHE matters. The prize is too important for us to give up our vision of learning.

How, then, can we begin? These are a few starting suggestions:

1. Talk to at least one colleague about some of your ideas. Later try some team teaching or shared lesson planning for PSHE. Eventually, you might invite colleagues to watch you in action!

2. Contact your local adviser and/or INSET team and enquire about workshops on PSHE, active learning methods, curriculum co-ordination. If they do not exist, ask for them.

3. Find out about local training opportunities and enrol on a course in group work methods.

4. Chase up some of the materials and resources suggested earlier and see which of them you might feel comfortable adapting to suit your present teaching programme, even without a PSHE slot in your school. Which of the teaching approaches you are already using might contribute to PSHE goals with suitable modification?

5. Offer to run a department or even a staff seminar on active learning methods or models of PSHE and the PERM approach. Discuss overlaps with your pastoral colleagues in particular. Use group methods a) to encourage participation and b) as a model for classroom practice.

6. Set up a working party to promote positive health policies in your school.

7. Contact a local support group, either inside your own school or in the

locality. If one does not exist, set one up. Getting started on PSHE is not always a straightforward business. You will be glad of all the personal and professional back-up you can find.

8. Send us any feedback, particularly on the exercises, so that we can improve them for the future. We should also be pleased to hear about any interesting developments in PSHE with which you are involved.

There is perhaps still a long way to go. But, if we believe sufficiently in the importance of the destination, we can surely achieve our goal: to see PSHE firmly established in the curriculum backed by healthy whole-school policies for management and staff development. Good luck!

Appendix 1

ABBREVIATIONS

ACSET	Advisory Committee on the Supply and Education of Teachers
ACSTT	Advisory Committee on the Supply and Training of Teachers
A-level	Advanced level (of GCE examination)
AOT	Adults other than teachers
APU	Assessment of Performance Unit
ATW	Active Tutorial Work (scheme/programme)
B/TEC	Business/Technician Education Council
CATE	Committee for the Accreditation of Teacher Education
CDT	Craft, Design and Technology
CEA	Community Education Association
CEDC	Community Education Development Centre
CGLI	City and Guilds of the London Institute
CLID	Curriculum-led Institutional Development
CPVE	Certificate of Pre-vocational Education
CRAC	Careeers Research and Advisory Centre
CSCS	Centre for the Study of Comprehensive Schools
CSE	Certificate of Secondary Education
CSV	Community Service Volunteers
DES	Department of Education and Science
DWTG	Development Work with Tutorial Groups
EEC	European Economic Community
EOC	Equal Opportunities Commission
ESL	English as a Second Language
EWS	Education Welfare Service
FE	Further Education
FEU	Further Education Unit
(formerly **FECDU**	Further Education Curriculum Review and Development Unit)
FPA	Family Planning Association
GCE	General Certificate of Education
GCSE	General Certificate of Secondary Education
GRIDS	Guidelines for Review and Internal Development in Schools
GRIST	Grant-related In-service Training
HCP	Humanities Curriculum Project
HE	Higher Education

HEA	Health Education Authority (formerly HEC)
HEPD	Health Education and Personal Development Team, ILEA
HMI	Her Majesty's Inspector or Inspectorate
ILEA	Inner London Education Authority
ILECC	Inner London Educational Computing Centre
ISDD	Institute for the Study of Drug Dependence
INSET	In-service Education for Teachers
LAPP	Lower Attaining Pupils Project
LEA	Local Education Authority
MACOS	'Man: a course of study'
MODE 3	A school- or college-based form of examination in which the syllabus is set and the papers marked by the teachers and the whole is moderated by the examining board
MSC	Manpower Services Commission
NAPCE	National Association for Pastoral Care in Education
NAYC	National Association of Youth Clubs
NCC	National Curriculum Council
NICEC	National Institute of Careers Education and Counselling
NNEB	Nursery Nurses' Examination Board
NPRA	Northern Partnership Records of Achievement
NYB	National Youth Bureau
OCEA	Oxford Certificate of Educational Achievement
OD	Organisation Development
OTTO	One Term Training Opportunity (INSET)
PAL	Preparation for Adult Life
PSD	Personal and Social Development
PSE	Personal and Social Education
PSHE	Personal, Social and Health Education
PSME	Personal, Social and Moral Education
PTA	Parent-Teachers Association
PVE	Pre-vocational Education
ROSLA	Raising of the School Leaving Age
RSA	Royal Society of Arts
SCDU	School Curriculum Development Unit
SCHEP	Schools Council Health Education Project
SEAC	School Examinations and Assessment Council
SIDE	School-based INSET for Development through Evaluation
SLS	Social and Life Skills
TA	Transactional Analysis
TACADE	Teachers' Advisory Council on Alcohol and Drug Education
T-GROUP	Training Group for Personal Interaction

TRIST TVEI-related In-service Training
TVEI Technical and Vocational Education Initiative
TWL Transition to Working Life (Grubb Institute Project)
UVP Unified Vocational Preparation
YTS Youth Training Scheme

Appendix 2

Action Research: consists in systematic reflection on the practical problems faced by teachers, students or others in schools with a view to deciding what ought to be done about them — and how. It can involve interviews, case studies, participant observation or other forms of data collection but what distinguishes it from other types of small-scale research is that those affected by the planned changes have the primary responsibility for deciding on and then evaluating the strategies chosen for improvement.

Active Learning: implies methods which increase students' awareness of HOW they are learning as well as WHAT. A variety of strategies can be employed (some of which may indeed be physically active!) but they all encourage students to engage more consciously with their own learning.

Aims: are broad statements of educational intent incorporating an attitude to certain values about the purpose of schooling etc.

Andragogy: is a student-centred, self-directed approach to learning in which the learner's own experience and concerns are a central resource.

Appraisal: and target-setting are 'the very essence of managing the school performance of teachers . . . The teacher needs to be aware of three things:
a) responsiblities: a clear understanding of what is required as the basic task, of what its principal accountabilities are, and to whom the teacher is accountable;
b) standards: a clear appreciation of what levels of performance are expected to be reached if the job is to be effectively done;
c) targets: are tasks mutually agreed between the teacher and the appraiser which the teacher accepts over and above the basic task'. Trethowan, 1987.

Assessment: a judgement on what has been learned and achieved.

Attitudes: are dispositions to think or act in a particular way in relation to oneself and to other individuals or groups in society, e.g. tolerance, empathy, honesty, self-confidence.

Authority: refers to the power or influence exercised by legitimate leadership.

Autonomy: means making self-determined, pro-active decisions which are based on personal clarification of the issues and values involved and, some would argue, necessarily involve respecting the autonomy of others.

Basic Skills: Communication, Numeracy, Social and Life Skills and Computer Literacy are the four areas identified in the pre-vocational curriculum.

Collaborative Learning: involves groups of students working together to achieve a common task.

Community: may be thought of as a network of people. The link between them may be where they live, the work they do, their ethnic background or other factors which people have in common. The network may be informal or formal but, for a community to exist, it must have meaning for the individuals concerned.

Complementary Accreditation: is based on use of new assessment schemes, for example, profiling, alongside traditional examination methods.

Concepts: are formed by grouping particular incidents or objects into classes. We conceptualise by classifying. Linking some concepts together and excluding others we can generate 'conceptual systems'. These may be used for predicting behaviour, for interpreting fresh phenomena and data and for perceiving connections between one set of systems and another.

Confluent Education: student-centred learning is confluent when the affective and cognitive domains flow together. While she is thinking, the learner is also feeling; while she is feeling, she is thinking.

Consultancy: offers a form of help based in the main not on diagnosis and prescription but on a process through which the consultant elicits, clarifies and feeds back for comment the issues raised by those consulted. The aim is for the clients to take responsibility for the essence of the work.

Contracts/Contracting: recognise the partnership in education between learner and teacher and the need for co-responsibility which ought to feature in their relationship. Contracting refers to a joint discussion of expectations, hopes and fears which the student has of a course (or element within a course) and which the teacher has of the student.

Counselling: is an enabling process designed to help a person to come to terms with her life as it is or to change it and, ultimately, to grow towards greater maturity through learning to take responsibility and make decisions for herself. It is not meant to denote a process of advice-giving or telling others what to do but rather of trying to provide the conditions under which they can make up their own minds. See Milner in Best *et al.*, 1980.

Course: a planned programme of opportunities to acquire skills, knowledge and experience, often validated by an external body such as RSA or CGLI.

Criterion-referenced Assessments: are those defined and awarded in terms of standards of performance defined in advance and specific to the subject concerned. Candidates are required to demonstrate predetermined levels of competence in specified aspects of the subject in order to be awarded a particular grade. See Broadfoot, 1984.

Critical Incidents: are major tasks which students face, emanating firstly from the organisation of the secondary school and secondly from the adjustments that society demands of adolescents. See Hamblin, 1978.

Cultural Analysis: is a method of curriculum planning which attempts to match the needs of individual children living in a specific society by analysing the kind of society that exists and then mapping out the kind of knowledge and the kinds of experience that are most appropriate. See Lawton, 1983.

Culture: includes 'everything that is man-made in our society — fish and chips and bingo as well as science and mathematics, values and beliefs as well as religion, art and literature; pop culture as well as high culture, and so on'. Lawton, 1981.

Curriculum: refers to the mixture of deliberately planned experiences and activities, including the content and method of teaching, by which the school attempts to socialise its pupils.

Core Curriculum: refers to a number of subjects which are included in the curriculum for all children, including: English, mathematics and science.

Common Curriculum: is a selection from the common culture. It is based on what everyone needs to know or what everyone ought to have access to. It is not a uniform curriculum since different individuals will reach different stages of understanding and appreciation. It concentrates on those aspects of culture which we can demonstrate, as being worthwhile, extremely important in our society and necessary for the whole community. See Lawton, 1981.

Entitlement Curriculum: a curriculum of a distinctive breadth and depth to which all pupils should be entitled irrespective of the type of school they attend or their level of ability or social circumstances. See DES, 1983a (*Curriculum 11–16*).

Curriculum-led Staff Development: implies that its direction, content and organisation should come from the demands that the curriculum makes upon those who are responsible for its organisation and delivery. See FEU/SCDC, 1985.

Developmental Group Work: is concerned with helping people in their growth and development, in their social skills and in the kinds of relationship they establish with other people. Its purpose is to provide individuals with opportunities to relate to others in a non-criticising, supportive atmosphere, to try out new social approaches and to experiment in new roles. See Button, 1974.

Diagnostic Assessment: is aimed at identifying students' progress, their strengths, weaknesses and learning difficulties and so being a guide to future action.

Directed Time: is that element of contractual time in which a teacher can be directed by the Head to attend meetings, undertake INSET, etc.

Discipline: is that part of education which is particularly concerned with growth to personal responsibility. Many factors contribute to this process: the relationships in a school, the degree of participation that is encouraged, the extent to which initiative is recognised, and also the rules, regulations and organisation of the school and classroom.

Education: is concerned with the development of the individual's full range of abilities and aptitudes, with the cultivation of spirital and moral values, with the nurturing of imagination and sensibility, with the transmission and reinterpretation of culture. It is a lifelong process most of which occurs outside of the school as a leisure activity.

Ethos: refers to the prevailing climate or tone of an institution. It can be perceived through hidden-curriculum values, including forms of address, participation in decision making, the fabric and appearance of the school, attitudes to homework and latencss, ctc.

Evaluation: refers to the measuring of students' progress towards the objectives of a particular course and the measuring of their teachers' effectiveness. It is not a final activity but part of a cyclical prcess whereby curriculum development or practice leads to suggestion for modification and improvement which can then be fed back into teaching or development.

Experiental Learning: is designed to encourage learning through first-hand experience, for example, outdoor pursuits, community service, work experience, action research, role play, group work, etc.

Facilitation: is commonly used to indicate an enabling as distinct from an instructional role for the teacher. It includes developing a suitable learning climate, providing a framework of activities, encouraging diversity of outcomes and reporting back observations on progress.

Feedback: refers to the messages teachers convey to students (or vice versa) about their progress in a particular activity, on the basis of which weaknesses can be corrected or errors removed.

Formative Assessment: is a process involving discussion between teacher and student about the student's progress which determines the future course to be followed and goals to be aimed at.

Golden Rule: Do unto others as you would wish them to do unto you.

Graded Tests: consist of series of tests at progressive levels of difficulty designed to be taken by students only when they have a high probability of success. Each test is closely linked to the curriculum for the relevant level, which clearly specifies the tasks to be mastered.

Group Work: 'invites the teacher to see his whole student group as a collection of subgroups of various size and composition in which lies great learning potential. It is carefully structured and will call for sensitive management by the teacher'. Hopson and Scally, 1981.

Guidance: is concern — 'but concern for the total life the pupil is living now and will live in the future'. Rowe, 1971. Typically, in schools, guidance has three aspects: vocational, personal and educational. How guidance is used will be determined by the cultural tradition in which it operates.

Hidden Curriculum: involves the non-teaching aspects of the school day: how the school organises its breaks and lunch-times, what clubs there are, how discipline is maintained, what relationships are like between teachers and students, teachers and teachers, students and students, and so on. It may well be a more potent source of learning than anything which is planned in the classroom deliberately.

Holistic: is an explicit concern to consider the whole person rather than separate parts. Thus, confluent education is holistic.

Humanistic: having a concern for human interests or those of the human race in general.

Ideology: refers to a manner of thinking about social phenomena characteristic of particular classes or individuals. One of the most debated concepts in sociology, its has been used in three distinct senses:

a) to refer to very specific kinds of beliefs, e.g. marxism, fascism;

b) to refer to beliefs that are in some sense distorted or false in the view of the writer;

c) to refer to any set of beliefs, irrespective of whether it is true or false, which is socially determined. See Meighan, 1981.

Locus of Control: refers to a concept originally used by Rotter (1966). It distinguishes between people who feel they are masters of their own fate (internals) and those who feel they have little control over what happens to them (externals).

Micro-politics: refers to the power relations between different individuals in the teaching hierarchy and their mutual influence over each other. See Ball, 1987.

Modular Banking: refers to a series of free-standing modules which may be slotted into or out of a course at short notice in response to demand. See Warwick, 1987.

Module: a unit of learning, usually lasting from six weeks to half a year. Modules may relate to each other as follows:

Complementary, in which performance in one is related to performance in another.

Sequential, in which a set of modules may be taken in any order but, because of their content or skill relationship, the outcome of one cannot be independent of the outcome of another.

Articulated, in which modules form a hierarchy and must be sequenced in time.

Monitoring: keeping under close review both student progress and the progress of the course as a whole.

Needs: have several dimensions:

Normative needs are those defined by an expert or professional according to her own standards. Some normative needs, e.g. food hygiene regulations, are prescribed by law.

Felt needs are those which people themselves feel — i.e. what they want.

Expressed needs are what people say they need.

Relative needs are defined by comparison with similarly placed individuals or groups. See Ewles and Simnett, 1985.

Negotiation: is a process of discussion between student and teacher, either to draw out and review a significant experience or achievement from the past or to plan some future course of action or learning. It presupposes open relationships betwen students and teachers, without undue pressure or prejudice being exerted by one party over the other and where due allowance is made for inexperience or inarticulateness. See Weston, 1979.

Networks: are people talking to each other, sharing ideas, information and resources. They exist to foster self-help, to improve productivity and work life and to share ideas and materials.

Norm-referenced Assessment: is a system under which grades are allocated to predetermined proportions of the candidate-entry for the subject concerned or of some other defined proportion such as the whole age cohort. Thus, the grade awarded to a student depends not only on her own performance but also on how well the other students have performed.

Objectives: are a translation of aims into statements which convey some idea of the practicalities they embody and some idea of how these practicalities might be achieved. For example, if a school were translating into objectives the aim 'to develop in students the ability to act and think independently', one objective might be to teach children to organise some of their work on their own.

Oracy: the ability to express oneseslf verbally and to understand speech (analogous with literacy and numeracy).

Organisation Development: is both a conceptual framework and a practical strategy aimed at helping schools (or other institutions) to become self-correcting, self-renewing systems of people who are receptive to evidence that change is required and able to respond with innovative programmes and integrated arrangements. OD attempts to facilitate the release of latent energy for creativity by helping schools learn productive ways of working on their problems. See Schmuck *et al.*, 1977.

Outcomes: depend on aims, objectives and methods. They might include changes in students' personal awareness, their knowledge, attitudes or behaviour or changes in the school or wider community. In detail, they are different for each student.

Para-curriculum: refers to all those aspects of school life which are not part of the formal curriculum or of the pastoral system. It includes the hidden curriculum and extra-curricular activities.

Pastoral Care: refers to the non-instructional aspects of teachers' roles. It is an umbrella term covering the activities of the school counsellor, careers teacher, house and form tutors. Typically, pastoral care is reactive and normative in its orientation and is specifically concerned with welfare. See Best *et al.*, 1980.

Pastoral Casework: refers to the one-to-one relationship between teacher and student-in-need. It usually involves liaison with other teachers, with parents and with agencies outside of school in an attempt to provide appropriate support, adjustment or control. Nominally concerned with 'helping' the individual, it is often just as much concerned with propping up the system.

Pastoral Curriculum: includes those items on the shopping list of students' needs which are deemed essential for the personal growth of individuals and for their learning rather than those which form part of the logic of a subject. See Marland in Land and Marland, 1985.

Person-centred Learning: implies that:

· the leader must be sufficiently secure in herself and in her relationships to trust in the capacity of others to think and learn for themselves, and to share responsibility for the learning process;

· the student develops her own programme of learning, alone or in collaboration with others, using the structures and resources provided by the leader. Evaluation of the learning process is primarily by the learner herself. See Rogers in Lee and Zeldin, 1982.

Power: is the ability to influence intentionally what happens to us in relation to other people and the physical world. To empower is to get in touch or help someone else to get in touch with these abilities. When people are depowered they feel helpless, apathetic and alienated. See Hopson and Scally, 1981.

Profiles: are methods of displaying the results of an assessment, not in themselves methods of assessment. They may be numerical, verbal or graphical. Used loosely, the term is a catch-all for records and reports on students' achievements and experiences.

> **Profiling**: offers an opportunity of monitoring learning through regular discussion, assessment and feedback as a result of which students can negotiate new learning objectives. The actual profile may be completed by either the student or the teacher — or both. See Hitchcock, 1986.

Record of Achievement: is a school-leaver's document which may include the results of a variety of examinations, graded tests and other assessments as well as other information, including internal records compiled by students and teachers. It covers the total educational progress of the student.

Reflection: is the process of looking back on experience, seeing what went well and what went wrong, why things turned out as they did, what conclusions can be drawn about individual/group strengths and weaknesses, etc. Reflection also involves making connections between one experience and another — looking for common characteristics, evidence of progress and so on.

Reviewing: a process in which student and teacher consider progress made by the student to date and negotiate the next steps. See Pearce, 1981.

School-centred INSET: is a form of INSET which falls virtually exclusively within the professional control of teachers. It implies a high level of responsibility and self-consciousness over the determination of individual and collective needs and a high level of collaborative teamwork in the dissemination and monitoring of innovation.

School-focused INSET: involves trainers and teachers working in partnership in such a way as to meet the identified needs of the school, to raise standards of teaching and learning in the classroom. See Bolam, 1982.

Skills: are specific abilities which can be learnt and enhanced by practice or through experience. They may be dependent on the possession of certain knowledge or concepts and they may be context-specific or general. Often they form clusters as, for example: communication skills, numerical skills, mechanical skills, observational and visual skills, imaginative skills, etc.

> **Social Skills** are those concerned with interpersonal behaviour. They include the ability to co-operate, to negotiate, to express ideas in a variety of contexts, to consider other people's points of view and to recognise non-verbal communication.
>
> **Life Skills** apply to such areas of life as self, peer groups, family, leisure, community and career.
>
> **Coping Skills** embrace all the bits of information, behaviour and decision

making which are required in order to go about one's daily life. See Hopson and Scally, 1981.

Skill Transfer: the extent to which skills learnt in one context can be used in other contexts.

    Transfer Skills: the skills needed to adapt from one situation to another, e.g. the ability to translate theory into practice, to recognise connections, to conceptualise 'problems' and strategies for their solution.

Socialisation: describes the process whereby people learn to conform to social norms — a process that makes possible an enduring society and transmission of culture between generations.

Spiral Curriculum: is based on the conviction (from Bruner, 1966) that the key concepts in any discipline can be introduced to children initially in an elementary form and then in progressively greater complexity and abstraction. It thus provides the rationale for a deliberately planned sequence of presentations on any particular topic which enables the student to apply the same fundamental ideas and concepts to increasingly complex and sophisticated situations and problems.

Staff Development: embraces not only individual education and INSET, individual appraisal and career enhancement, but also whole-staff development as part of a dynamic and changing organisation. It is more than improving teaching technique within a subject area; it involves the all-round development of the individual or team. See Day and Moore, 1986.

Student-centred Learning: encourages student to understand and be able to deal with their own and others' feelings as well as with the cognitive aspects of learning. It explicitly takes as its starting point the students' present needs, interests or experience rather than the requirements of the subject or discipline. See Brandes and Ginnis, 1986.

Summative Assessment: is any form of assessment, typically an examination or test, which comes at the end of a student's course.

Transmission Teaching: occurs when the teacher imparts knowledge to 'ignorant' pupils by telling them what they 'need' to know.

Tutoring: is concerned with the all-round development of the student. It may involve a variety of people, each having a specialised role in relation to students' academic, social, vocational and personal needs. Alternatively one person may have responsiblity for all of these — liaising, as necessary, with specialised staff in and out of school and with parents or employers.

Values: are qualities of worth or desirability in our lives which motivate our thoughts and actions. They may be conscious or unconscious, articulate or inarticulate.

Values Clarification: is concerned with helping students understand the values they hold and the ways in which these are reflected in their behaviour, without any judgement being passed. The focus is on greater self-awareness.

Work Experience: time spent by students in a place of work following a planned programme of experience, aimed to increase their self-confidence, allow them to learn and practice new skills, put school learning into practice and find out about job and training opportunities in a particular area.

Workshop: an activity-based assignment in which students learn by sharing information and skills, as they need them, working at their own pace on agreed tasks. May include some formal input from the teacher and a follow-up plenary session.

Appendix 3

AGENCIES

Action for Governors' Information and Training
Community Education Development Centre
Briton Road
Coventry CV2 4LF
Phone: 0203 44081
Contact: The Information Assistant
(a consortium of organisations which want to establish a national training service
for school governors)

Advisory Centre for Education (ACE)
Victoria Park Square
London E2 9PB
Phone: 01 980 4596
Contact: Advice Service 2.0–5.30 p.m. Monday to Friday
(publishes a range of reports and information sheets for parents and governors,
also the *ACE Bulletin*)

Afro-Caribbean Education Resources Centre
Wyvil Road
London SW8 2JT
Phone: 01 627 2662
(has developed materials for teachers and packs for pupils on all aspects of
multi-cultural teaching)

Association for the Teaching of the Social Sciences
85 Dorchester Road
Solihull
West Midlands
(holds conferences, runs a rescources exchange and publishes the journal, *Social
Science Teacher*)

British Association for Counselling (BAC)
37a Sheep Street
Rugby
Warwickshire CV21 3BX
Phone: 0788 78328/9
Contact: Information Officer
(offers information on the availability of courses and trainers for those who wish to develop counselling and interpersonal skills. Hires out film and videos and runs an accreditation scheme to maintain standards of counselling. Publishes the journal, *Counselling*)

Brook Advisory Centres
10 Albert Street
Birmingham B4 7UD
Phone: 021 643 1554
Contact: Education and Publications Officer
(offer a wide range of teaching materials, including audio cassettes, videos and discussion cards)

Careers Research and Advisory Centre (CRAC)
Sheraton House
Castle Park
Cambridge CB3 0AX
Phone: 0223 460277
Contact: Conference Manager or Course Manager
(runs courses and conferences and publishes a wide variety of books and learning packages in the areas of personal and social education, life skills, pre-vocational education. Also produces a magazine of personal and social education for teachers, *Lifeforce*)

Centre for the Study of Comprehensive Schools (CSCS)
Wentworth College
York University
Heslington
York YO1 5DD
Phone: 0904 414137
Contact: Information Officer
(its data bank provides information on staff development opportunities, fact sheets and examples of 'good' practice)

Commission for Racial Equality (CRE)
Elliott House
Allington Street
London SW1 5EH
Phone: 01 828 7022
(government watch-dog. Publishes the magazine, *New Equals*)

Community Education Development Centre (CEDC)
Briton Road
Coventry CV2 4LF
Phone: 0203 44081
Contact: Resources Officer
(exists to develop, evaluate and provide training for community education nationwide. Publishes the *Journal of Community Education* and the magazine, *Network*)

Community Service Volunteers (CSV)
237 Pentonville Road
London N1 9NJ
Phone: 01 278 6601
Contact: the Advisory Service
(develop and publish resource material and support teachers and youth workers wishing to set up community involvement schemes. Also organise workshops and training sessions. Publish the termly magazine, *School and Community*)

Council of Europe
Publications Section
67006 Strasbourg
France
(publishes reports on behalf of EEC, on subjects including social education of teenagers, youth training and so on)

Counselling and Career Development Unit (CCDU)
The University of Leeds
44 Clarendon Road
Leeds LS2 9PJ
Phone: 0532 450971
Contact: National Programme Co-ordinator
(provides training courses for trainers and teachers; base for the HEC Health Skills dissemination project)

Department of Health and Social Security (DHSS)
Alexander Fleming House
Elephant and Castle
London SE1 6BY
Phone: 01 407 5222
Contact: Information Officer
(responsible for administration of the NHS and for overseeing the personal and social services provided by local authorities)

Economics Association
Temple Lodge
South Street
Ditchling
Sussex BN6 8UQ
(the professional organisation for teachers of economics, presently sponsoring the development of classroom materials for 14 to 16 year olds. Publishes *Economics*)

Education for Capability
Royal Society of Arts
John Adam Street
London WC2N 6EZ
Phone: 01 839 2366
Contact: Janet Jones
(runs a recognition scheme to identify, encourage and publicise creative educational programmes which bridge the gap between education and training)

Equal Opportunities Commission (EOC)
Overseas House
Quay Street
Manchester M3 3HN
Phone: 061 833 9244
Contact: Information Officer
(publishes a wide variety of reports, pamphlets and posters aimed at giving boys and girls equal access to all subjects and to job opportunities)

Family Planning Association Education Unit (FPA)
27–35 Mortimer Street
London W1N 7RJ
Phone: 01 636 7866
Contact: Education Officer
(offers professional training, education and consultation on all aspects of personal and sexual relationships)

Further Education Unit (FEU)
Elisabeth House
York Road
London SE1 7PH
Phone: 01 934 9411/12
Contact: Information Officer
(an advisory, intelligence and development body for further education.
Publishes materials for staff development in areas like tutoring, trainee-centred
reviewing, social and life skills)
from:
Publications Despatch Centre
DES
Honeypot Lane
Canons Park
Stanmore
Middlesex HA7 1AZ
Phone: 01 952 2366 x 503

Grubb Institute, Centre for Explorations in Social Concern
Cloudesley Street
London N1 0HU
Phone: 01 278 2944
Contact: Administrator
(offers research, consultancy and group relations training)

Health Education Authority (HEA, formerly HEC)
78 New Oxford St
London WC1A 1AH
Phone: 01 637 1881
Contact: Education Officer
(responsible for a variety of major curriculum developments and for initial and
in-service training of teachers and health professionals. Offers a resource centre
and publishes reports, videos, leaflets, posters. Publishes the *Health Education
Journal* and *Health Education News*)

HEC Schools Health Education Unit
School of Education
University of Exeter
Heavitree Road
Exeter EX1 2LU
Phone: 0392 264722
Director: John Balding
(runs courses, undertakes research, produces packages for classroom use and
publishes the journal, *Education and Health*)

Institute of Health Education
14 High Elms Road
Hale Barns
Cheshire WA15 0HS
Phone: 061 980 8276
Contact: Secretary
(the recognised professional association for those engaged in health education. Runs meetings, conferences on health issues, provides a comprehensive information sevice and publishes the *Journal of the Institute of Health Education*)

Institute for the Management of Learning
St Martin's College
Lancaster LA1 3JD
Phone: 0524 61966
Director: Andy Smith
(publishes a journal, *Network*, and offers support to trainers and teachers involved in developmental group work)

Lifeskills Associates
51 Clarendon Road
Leeds LS2 9NZ
Phone: 0532 467128
Directors: B. Hopson and M. Scally
(run courses and consultancy projects and publish a wide variety of resource packages for personal and social education and for TVI and CPVE schemes. Also produce the quarterly, *Lifeskills Teaching Magazine*)

Moral Education Centre
St Martin's College
Lancaster LA1 3JD
Phone: 0524 63446 x 228
Director: Michael Cross
(organises in-service training, runs an information and consultancy service for teachers on a whole-school approach to moral education. Publishes the magazine, *Values*, with the Centre for Social and Moral Education at Leicester University)

National Association of Careers and Guidance Teachers
12 Langdale Avenue
Hesketh Bank
Lancashire PR4 6TD
Phone: 077473 4258
(promotes the development of careers education and monitors the effects of
TVEI and other government schemes on young people. Publishes *The Careers
and Guidance Teacher*)

National Association of Governors and Managers (NAGM)
10 Brookfield Park
London NW5 1ER
Contact: Felicity Taylor
(the main membership organisation for people interested in the government of
education, publishes a range of short papers, training packages and guides)

National Association for Pastoral Care in Education (NAPCE)
Deparment of Education, NAPCE/Pastoral Unit
University of Warwick
Coventry CV4 7AL
Phone: 0203 523810
Contact: Peter Lang
(organises national and regional conferences and training events for teachers
involved in pastoral work and PSE, has a data base of 'good practice' and
publishes the journal, *Pastoral Care in Education*)

National Consumer Council (NCC)
18 Queen Anne's Gate
London SW1H 9AA
Phone: 01 222 9501
(concerned with lobbying on behalf of governors, furthering the interest of
parents as consumers and with consumer education in schools)

National Development Centre for School Management Training
35 Berkeley Square
Bristol BS8 1JA
Phone: 0272 303030 x 283
Contact: Information Officer
(conducts and commissions research and training for heads and senior teachers)

National Institiute for Careers Education and Counselling (NICEC)
Harfield Polytechnic
Balls Park
Hertford SG13 8QF
Phone: 0992 558451
Contact: Administrative Officer
(runs a research, consultancy and training programme and, with CRAC, publishes the *British Journal of Guidance and Counselling*)

National Marriage Guidance Council
Herbert Gray College
Little Church Street
Rugby CV21 3AP
Phone: 0788 73241
Contact: Education Officer
(offers training and support for education workers and publishes useful book lists on aspects of group relations, counselling, etc.)

National Organisation for Initiatives in Social Education (NOISE)
ITRC
19 Elmbank Street
Glasgow
Contact: Howie Armstrong, Chairperson
(runs conferences and publishes a journal, *Noise*)

National Youth Bureau (NYB)
17–23 Albion Street
Leicester LE1 6GD
Phone: 0533 554775
(a national resource centre for information, publications, training, research and development for those involved in youth affairs and the social education of young people. Journal, *Youth in Society*)

Oxford Certificate of Educational Achievement (OCEA)
University of Oxford
Delegacy of Local Examinations
Ewert Place
Summertown OX2 7B7
Phone: 0865 54291
(publishes a *Newsletter* and materials for student-centred assessment — including the areas of personal and social learning)

Politics Association
16 Gower Street
London WC1E 6DP
(the professional body of politics teachers in the UK. Publishes the newsletter
Grassroots and the journal *Teaching Politics*. A full list of resources and
services is also available to members from the Politics Association Resources
Bank, 5 Parsonage Road, Heaton Moor, Stockport SK4 4JZ)

Project Trident
The Trident House
Robert Hyde House
48 Bryanston Square
London W1H 1BQ
Phone: 01 723 3281
Contact: Keith Dexter, Director
(supported by both industry and commerce, it provides pupils with out-of-school
experiences which complement and reinforce the work in school: work
experience as part of careers education, voluntary service as part of community
education and residential courses and expeditions)

School Curriculum Industry Project (SCIP)
Newcombe House
45 Notting Hill Gate
London W11 3JB
Phone: 01 229 1234
Contact: National Co-ordinator
(aims to develop better understanding of the economic and industrial world by
developing good practice in schools in fields such as work experience, business
enterprise, teachers into industry, simulated work practice, industrial visits.
Publishes *SCIP News*)

Social Morality Council
23 Kensington Square
London W8
Phone: 01 937 8547
(provides an advisory and development service in the field of PSE. Publishes
the *Journal of Moral Education*)

Society for the Advancement of Games and Simulations in Education and Training (SAGSET)
Centre for Extension Studies
University of Technolgoy
Loughborough LE11 3TU
Phone: 0509 263171 or 0509 266388
Contact: Administrative Secretary

Society for Education in Film and Television (SEFT)
29 Old Compton Street
London W1V 5PL
Phone: 01 734 3211
Contact: National Organiser
(promotes education around all aspects of film, television, photography and the mass media. Publishes the journal *Screen* and the newsletter *Media Education Initiatives* as well as teaching materials)

Tavistock Institute of Human Relations
120 Belsize Lane
London NW3 5BA
Phone: 01 435 7111
Contact: Administrator
(runs a group relations training programme, including courses for teachers, and conducts research and consultancy in the applications of humanistic psychology)

Teachers' Advisory Council on Alcohol and Drug Education (TACADE)
Furness House
Trafford Road
Salford M5 2XJ
Phone: 061 848 0351
Executive Officers: Bill Rice, Jeff Lee and Vivienne Evans
(offers training, consultancy and resources in Health, Personal and Social and Drugs Education. British base for the dissemination of Skills for Adolescence Project. Publishes the journal, *Monitor*)

TVEI Unit
Manpower Services Commission
236 Grays Inn Road
London WC1X 8HL
Contact: LEA TVEI Project Co-ordinator
(provides information on current developments)

University of Surrey, Human Potential Research Project (HPRP)
Department of Educational Studies
Guildford GU2 5XH
Phone: 0483 571281 x 9191
Contact: Administrator
(a major centre for humanistic education and consultancy. Runs a varied programme of courses and workshops, promoting holistic forms of practice and research. Publishes booklets, reports and a distance learning package for trainers and health professionals)

Youthaid
9 Poland Street
London W1V 4DG
Phone: 01 439 8523
(publishes up-to-date information on government legislation and social policy re young people in *Youthaid Bulletin*)

Youth Education Service
14 Frederick Place
Bristol BS8 1AS
Phone: 0272 736323/739744
Directors: Roger White and David Brockington
(produces video and back-up materials for further education staff on aspects of community and social education)

Appendix 4

RESOURCES

The following list contains a brief description of our 'Top 20' teaching packages for PSHE, chosen either for their practical applicability or because they demonstrate a significant theoretical perspective. They are arranged in alphabetical order, according to their title, since this is the form in which they are normally known.

Teaching materials tend to date rapidly but a key feature of the development of PSHE has been the fertile growth of ideas adapted from related work. We have selected as wide a range of packages as possible but, not surpisingly, given major government backing for curriculum development in this area over the past 15 years, there is a preponderance of health education materials. However, most of our examples describe strategies which can be used with or without a health focus. There are of course many other materials, ranging from those associated with the various Schools Council projects to the various leaflets, posters and other publications available from agencies like CSV, the Brook Advisory Centres and Lifeskills Associates. Some of these are listed in Chapter 6; some are in the Bibliography. Others are noted in the references to supporting agencies in Appendix 3.

We wish to reiterate here our concern to encourage reflection and critical analysis of aims and methods. PERMing each resource is a quick way of assessing its approach. We also include a checklist, adapted from Eraut (1977). Used rigorously, this is invaluable as a guide to the suitability of resources. Cost, although an important consideration, is not mentioned here; nor have we included suggestions for primary schools or for students with special educational needs.

LIST OF RESOURCES

Active Tutorial Work for Years 1–5 (1979) Baldwin, J. and Wells, H., Blackwell, Oxford
Active Tutorial Work: 16–19 (1983) Baldwin, J. and Smith, A., Blackwell, Oxford
(A structured programme of exercises for tutor groups with clear age-related aims. Widely used as a core for the pastoral curriculum.)

Choices (1985) Mills, J., Mills, R. and Stringer, L. Oxford University Press, London
(The book is for use with 14+ students. It contains a wide variety of material designed mainly to stimulate communication skills.)

Evaluating Materials

1. Aims and Objectives
a) What are the authors' aims for the materials?
b) Do the authors make explicit the rationale/ideology behind their approach?
c) What do you consider to be the rationale which underpins these materials?
d) What are the objectives of the particular section you are considering?

2. Methods
a) What teaching methods are suggested?
b) Are they congruent with the aims?
c) Do the suggested methods require unusual teaching skills and, if so, is there sufficient guidance for the teacher?
d) Do the suggested methods require particular settings/facilities?
e) What roles are expected of students?

3. Appropriateness
a) How far do the materials take into account the students' own experience/knowledge/skills/age, etc.?
b) To what extent do the materials promote anti-sexist and anti-racist attitudes and challenge other prejudices?
c) Are these materials best used within the pastoral programme, or within subject areas, within personal and social education — or elsewhere?

4. Evaluation
a) What criteria are suggested for evaluating the usefulness of the materials?
b) How do the evaluation procedures for students relate to the aims?
c) Do the methods of evaluation suggested reflect a particular rationale?
(adapted from Eraut *et al.* (1975) checklist used by ILEA HEPD team)

Decisions for Health (1984) Lambeth Health Education Project, ILEA
(A resource pack containing useful trigger material about individual and community responsiblities in health and reflecting anti-racist and anti-sexist concerns.)

Drugwise (1986) Lifeskills Associates/TACADE/ISDD, Leeds
(A thorough approach to drug education for 14 to 18 year olds. This boxed pack contains a curriculum guide, a teachers' manual and learning materials which cover a wide range of drug-taking issues.)

Facts and Feelings about Drugs but Decisions about Situations (1982) Institute for the Study of Drug Dependence, London
(A teacher's manual offering guidance for a short drug education programme. As well as useful background information, the pack provides a rationale for situational analysis, encouraging young people to consider influences on their decisions in realistic situations.)

Free to Choose (1984) Teachers' Advisory Council on Alcohol and Drug Education, Manchester
(A comprehensive pack covering ten aspects of alcohol and drug-taking behaviour. Worksheets and stimulus material can be photocopied for classroom use. There are suggestions for using different teaching strategies and planning a programme.)

Greater Expectations (1986) Szirom, T. and Dyson, S. (The Clarity Collective), Learning Development Aids, Wisbech
(A source book for use with girls and young women. It contains many useful exercises (copyright-free) which encourage reflection on sex stereotyping and offer strategies for combating sexism.)

Group Tutoring for the Form Teacher 1. Lower Secondary School
                                   2. Upper Secondary School
(1981) Button, L., Hodder and Stoughton, London
(A clear, sequential and effective programme to help teachers make positive use of pastoral time. The programme is structured and reflects Leslie Button's theories on developmental group work with young people.)

Health Careers (1982) Dorn, N. and Nortoft, B., Institute for the Study of Drug Dependence, London
(This teachers' manual contains suggestions for tackling health education (drug education in particular) using the concept of the 'health career'. The approach takes 'working life' as its starting point and emphasises a) the false dichotomy between voluntaristic and deterministic approaches, b) the inadequate portrayal of women *vis-à-vis* health issues and c) the diversity of adolescent sub-cultures.)

Health Education 13–18 (1982) Health Education Council, Forbes, London.
(A set of 19 booklets, recommended for different year groups and focusing of particular health issues. The introduction provides a useful health education rationale. Currently under revision.)

Health Matters (1986) Beels, C., National Extension College/Health Education Council, London
(This pack is devised for YTS students and is being disseminated with appropriate training through local YTS Training Centres. The five themes covered are relationships, hygiene, communication, drugs and stress. Clearly presented and adaptable for other contexts.)

It's Your Life (1979) Cheston, M., Religious and Moral Education Press, London
(This short, attractively presented booklet contains many stimulating ideas to use with students on a personal and social education course. The three central themes are 'Yourself', 'Your Surroundings' and 'Your Relationships'.)

Learning from Experience (1985) Barnett, C., Chambers, R. and Longman K., Macmillan Education, Basingstoke
(Billed as a training manual in personal effectiveness for 14 to 19 year olds, this pack covers areas such as communication, co-operating in groups, decision making, evaluating and feeding back information, negotiating, planning and problem solving.)

Learning in a City (1980) ILEA Learning Materials Service, London
(A useful pack with many practical suggestions to encourage students to make use of services available to them and to become more independent young adults.)

Lifeskills Teaching Programmes 1, 2, 3, 4 (1980, 1982, 1985, 1987) Hopson, B. and Scally, M., Lifeskills Associates, Leeds
(These four files contain many exercises designed to increase students' self-empowerment (see *Lifeskills Teaching*, 1981, by the same authors). Particular 'life themes' are explored in detail but teachers can pick and choose according to their student group.

Lifeskills Training Manual (1983) Ellis, J. and Barnes, T., Community Service Volunteers, London
(A training programme which focuses on issues and problems arising from day-to-day situations and on the skills needed to handle them. Compiled for training on youth employment schemes.)

Preparing for Work — The Induction Pack (1983) Carroll, S. and McQuade, P., Framework Press, London
(This pack contains a wide variety of assignments for students on vocational preparation courses in colleges or schools and for YTS trainees.)

Schools Council Health Education Project 5–13 (1977) Nelson, London. *Think Well* (years 9 to 13)
(Although the materials are rather dated, this pack contains a useful discussion of 'health careers', self-concept and health education as decision making. There are eight units covering different health themes.)

Taught not Caught — Strategies for Sex Education (1985) The Clarity Collective, Learning Development Aids, Wisbech
(A programme which emphasises opportunities for the exploration of values and attitudes and the growth of skills necessary to build relationships, communicate and make decisions.)

Values, Cultures and Kids (1982) Bovey, M., Development Education Centre, London
(This handbook provides teaching ideas and resources for courses about Child Development and the Family which recognise and make use of our multi-cultural, interdependent world.)

Bibliography

ACSTT (1974) *In-service education and training*, HMSO, London
—— (1977) *The training of teachers for further education*, Sub-committee Report (Haycocks I), ACSTT, London
—— (1978a) *The training of adult education and part-time further education teachers*, Sub-committee Report (Haycocks II), ACSTT, London
—— (1978b) *Training teachers for education management in further and adult education*, Sub-committee Report (Haycocks III), ACSTT, London
—— (1984) *The in-service educational training and professional development of school teachers*, HMSO, London
Adelman, C. and Alexander, R.J. (1982) *The self-evaluating institution: practice and principles in the management of educational change*, Methuen, London
Allen, I. (1987) *Education in sex and personal relationships*, Policy Studies Institute, London
Anderson, J. (1986) 'Health skills: the power to choose', *Health Education Journal*, vol. 45, no. 1, pp. 19–24
—— (1987) 'A whole school approach', *Times Education Supplement*, 29 May, p. 46
Anzell, R. (1986) 'Getting started', *The Careers and Guidance Teacher*, Summer
Ariés, P. (1962) *Centuries of childhood*, Vintage Books, New York
Armstrong, D. (1985) 'How do we help children learn from their experience in the school organisation?', in Lang, P. and Marland, M. (eds) *New perspectives in pastoral care*, Blackwell, Oxford
Ashton, P., Henderson, E., Merritt, J. and Mortimer, D. (1983) *Teacher education in the classroom and in-service*, Croom Helm, London
Assessment of Performance Unit (1981) *Personal and social education*, HMSO, London
Atherton, J.S. (1986) *Professional supervision in group care*, Tavistock, London
Baldwin, J. and Smith, A. (1983) *Active tutorial work: sixteen to nineteen*, Blackwell, Oxford
Baldwin, J. and Wells, H. (1979, 1980, 1981) *Active tutorial work, books 1–5*, Blackwell, Oxford
Ball, S.J. (1987) *The micro-politics of the school: towards a theory of school organization*, Methuen, London
Balogh, J. (1982) *Profile reports for school-leavers*, Longman for Schools Council, York
Bandura, A. (1972) 'The stormy decade: fact or fiction' in Rogers, D. (ed.) *Issues in adolescent psychology*, 2nd edn, Appleton-Century-Crofts, New York
Barnes, D. (1975) *From communication to curriculum*, Penguin, Harmondsworth
Barnett, C., Chambers, R. and Longman, K. (1985) *Learning from experience: a training manual in personal effectiveness*, Macmillan Education, Basingstoke
Bates, I. *et al.* (1984) *Schooling for the dole? The new vocationalism*, Macmillan, London
Beattie, A. (1984) 'Health education and the science teacher', *Education and Health*, vol. 2, no. 1, pp. 9–16
Beckett, H. (1986) 'Cognitive development theory in the study of adolescent identity development' in Wilkinson, S. (ed.) *Feminist social psychology*, Open University Press, Milton Keynes
Belbin, E., Downs, S. and Perry, P. (1981) *How do I learn?* Longman for the Further Education Unit, York
Bell, D. (1973) *The coming of post-industrial society*, Basic Books, New York

Bell, L. and Maher, P. (1986) *Leading a pastoral team*: *approaches to pastoral middle management*, Blackwell, Oxford

Bell, P. and Best, R. (1986) *Supportive education*: *an integrated response to pastoral care and special needs*, Blackwell, Oxford

Benedict, R. (1934) *Patterns of culture*, Mifflin, New York

Benne, K.D. and Muntyan, B. (eds) (1951) *Human relations in curriculum change*, The Dryden Press, New York

Bernstein, B. (1970) 'Education cannot compensate for society', *New Society*, 26 February p. 344

Best, R. and Ribbins, P. M. (1983) 'Rethinking the pastoral-academic split', *Pastoral Care in Education*, vol. 1, no. 1, pp. 11–18

—— Jarvis, C. and Ribbins, P.M. (eds) (1980) *Perspectives on pastoral care*, Heinemann Educational, London

——, Ribbins, P.M. and Jarvis, C. with Oddy, D. (1981) *Education and care*, Heinemann Educational, London

Bettelheim, B. (1969) *The children of the dream*: *communal child-rearing and its implications for society*, Thames and Hudson, London

Birmingham Youth Volunteers (BYV) (1979) 'What is social education?' in Brown, C. et al. (1986) *Social education*, Falmer, Lewes

Blackburn, K. (1983) *Head of house, head of year*, Heinemann, London

Blos, P. (1962) *On adolescence*, Collier-Macmillan, London

Bolam, R. (1982) *School-focused in-service training*, Heinemann Educational, London

Bolam, R. and Medlock, P. (1985) *Active tutorial work*: *training and dissemination — an evaluation*, Blackwell for the Health Education Council, Oxford

Bond, T. (1986) *Games for social and life skills*, Hutchinson, London

Brandes, D. (1982) *Gamesters' handbook two*, Hutchinson, London

—— and Ginnis, P. (1986) *A guide to student-centred learning*, Blackwell, Oxford

—— and Phillips, H. (1979) *Gamesters' handbook*, Hutchinson, London

Brennan, T. (1981) *Political education and democracy*, Cambridge University Press, Cambridge

Broadfoot, P. (ed.) (1984) *Selection, certification and control*, Falmer, Lewes

—— (ed.) (1986) *Profiles and records of achievement*: *a review of issues and practice*, Holt, Rinehart and Winston, London

Brockington, D., Pring, R. and White, R. (1985) *The 14–18 curriculum*: *integrating CPVE, YTS, TVEI*, Youth Education Service, Bristol.

Brown, C., Harber, C. and Strivens, J. (eds) (1986) *Social education*: *principles and practice*, Falmer, Lewes

Bruner, J. (1960) *The process of education*, Harvard University Press, Cambridge, Mass.

—— (1966) *Toward a theory of instruction*, Harvard University Press, Cambridge, Mass.

—— (1971) *The relevance of education*, Norton and Co., New York

—— Goodnow, J. and Austin, G. (1956) *A study of thinking*, Wiley and Sons, London

Bulman, L. and Jenkins, D. (1987) *The pastoral curriculum*, Blackwell, Oxford

Burgess, T. (ed.) (1986) *Education for capability*, NFER/Nelson, London

—— and Adams, E. (1980) *Outcomes of education*, Macmillan, Basingstoke

Bush, T., Glatter, R., Goodey, J. and Riches, C. (eds) (1980) *Approaches to school management*, Harper and Row, London

Butterworth, C. and Macdonald, M. (1985) *Teaching social education and communication*: *a practical handbook*, Hutchinson, London

Button, L. (1974) *Development groupwork with adolescents*, Hodder and Stoughton, London

—— (1981) *Group tutoring for the form teacher*, Hodder and Stoughton, London

——— (1983) 'The Pastoral Curriculum' in *Pastoral care in education*, vol. 1, no. 2, pp. 74–82

——— (1987) 'Development group work as an approach to personal, social and moral education' in Thacker, J. *et al.* (eds), *Personal social and moral education in a changing world*, NFER/Nelson, Windsor

Campbell, G. (ed.) (1984) *Health education and youth: a review of research and developments*, Falmer, Lewes

——— (ed.) (1985) *New directions in health education*, Falmer, Lewes

Canfield, J. and Wells, H.C. (1976) *100 ways to enhance self-concept in the classroom*, Prentice Hall, Englewood Cliffs

Cantor, L. and Roberts, I. (1983) *Further education today*, Routledge and Kegan Paul, London

Carr, W. and Kemmis, S. (1986) *Becoming critical: education, knowledge and action research*, Falmer, Lewes

Carroll, S. and McQuade, P. (1985) *The staff development manual*: vol. 1, *Delivering the curriculum*; vol. 2, *Staff development in action*, (1986), Framework Press, Lancaster.

Central Statistical Office (1985) *Social trends no. 15*, HMSO, London

City and Guilds (1985) *Profiling systems — assessment handbook 5*, CGLI, London

City of Salford Education Department (1983) *Schools looking at themselves*, Salford

Clarity Collective (1985) *Taught not caught — strategies for sex education* (British edn Dixon, H. and Mullinar, G.), Learning Development Aids, Wisbech, Cambs.

Clarke, B. (1984) 'Introducing social and personal education in a large upper school', Pastoral Care in Education, vol. 2, no. 3, pp. 197–201

Claxton, G. (1984) *Live and learn: an introduction to the psychology of growth and change*, Harper and Row, London

Cleaton, D.R. and Foster, R.J. (1981) *Practical aspects of guidance I: careers education*, Careers Consultants Ltd, Richmond, Surrey

Clemett, A.J. and Pearce, J.S. (1986) *The evaluation of pastoral care*, Blackwell, Oxford

Cohen, P. (1986a) *No kidding: project report 1983–6*, Post-sixteen Centre, Institute of Education, London

——— (1986b) 'No kidding — it's really useful knowledge?', *Social Science Teacher*, vol. 16, no. 1, pp. 18–25

Coleman, J.C. (1974) *Relationships in adolescence*, Routledge and Kegan Paul, London

——— (1979) *The school years*, Methuen, London

——— (1980) *The nature of adolescence*, Methuen, London

Collins, N. (1986) *New teaching skills*, Oxford University Press, London

Community Service Volunteers (1979) *Lifeskills training manual*, CSV with MSC, London

Conger, J.J. and Petersen, A. (1984) *Adolescence and youth*, 3rd edn, Harper and Row, New York

Cooper, L.C. (1984) *The pastoral curriculum: a challenge for the urban comprehensive*, MA Dissertation, King's College, London

Coopersmith, S. (1967) *The antecedents of self-esteem*, Freeman, San Fransisco

Cowley, J., David, K. and Williams, T. (eds) (1981, 2nd edn 1987) *Health education in schools*, Harper and Row, London

Cox, K. and Lavelle, M. (1982) *Staff development through teacher interaction: a school-based case study*, Department of Educational Management, Sheffield City Polytechnic

Cox, K. and Lavelle, M. (1983) *Learning from experience: problems and principles of developing an INSET course*, Department of Educational Management, Sheffield City Polytechnic

Crick, B. and Porter, A. (eds) (1978) *Political education and political literacy*, Longman, York

Cuff, E.C. and Payne, G.C.F. (eds) (1985) *Crisis in the curriculum*, Croom Helm, London

Dale, R. (ed.) (1985) *Education, training and employment: towards a new vocationalism?*, Pergamon for Open University, Oxford

Darley, C. and Helsby, G. (1984) 'Evaluation of current in-service provision' in *14–19 curriculum development unit, bulletin no. 11*, St Martin's College, Lancaster

Darley, C. and James, T. (1984) 'An assessment of current initiatives and their in-service implications' in *14–19 curriculum development unit*, St. Martin's College, Lancaster

David, K. (1983) *Personal and social education in secondary schools*, Longman for Schools Council, London

—— and Charlton, A. (1987) *The caring role of the primary school*, Macmillan, Basingstoke

—— and Cowley, J. (1980) *Pastoral care in schools and colleges: with specific reference to Health Education, and drugs, alcohol and smoking*, Edward Arnold, London

—— and Williams, T. (eds) (1987) *Health education in schools*, 2nd edn, Harper and Row, London

Davies, B. (1979) *In whose interests? From social education to social and life skills training*, National Youth Bureau, Leicester

—— (1986) *Threatening youth: towards a national youth policy*, Open University Press, Milton Keynes

—— and Gibson, A. (1967) *The social education of the adolescent*, University of London Press, London

Daws, P. (1976) *A good start in life: a personal review of the beginnings of counselling in English education during the decade 1964–74*, CRAC/Hobsons Press, Cambridge

Day, C. and Moore, R. (eds) (1986) *Staff development in the secondary school*, Croom Helm, London

Deal, T.E. and Nolan, R.R. (1978) 'Alternative schools: a conceptual map' in Lee, V. and Zeldin, D. (eds) (1986) *Planning in the curriculum*, Hodder and Stoughton for the Open University, London

Dennison, W.F. and Shenton, K. (1987) *Challenges in educational management*, Croom Helm, London

Denys, J. (1980) *Leadership in schools*, Heinemann Educational, London

Department of the Environment (DOE) (1984) *Training for jobs*, HMSO, London

DES publications alphabetically by title:

DES (1979) *Aspects of secondary education in England: a survey by HM Inspectors of Schools*, HMSO, London

DES (1985a) *Better schools*, HMSO, London

DES (1977a) *Curriculum 11–16 (working papers by HM Inspectorate: a contribution to current debate)*, HMSO, London

DES/Welsh Office (1983a) *Curriculum 11–16: towards a statement of entitlement: curriculum reappraisal in action*, HMSO, London

DES/HMI (1985b) *Curriculum 5 to 16*, HMSO, London

DES (1985c) *Education for all* (the Swann Report), HMSO, London

DES (1983b) *Educational and economic activity of young people aged 16–19 years in England and Wales from 1973–74 to 1981–82*, Statistical Bulletin 2/83, HMSO, London

DES/HMI (1987a) *Good behaviour and discipline in schools*, HMSO, London

DES (1977b) *Health education in schools*, HMSO, London

DES/HMI (1986a) *Health education from 5 to 16*, HMSO, London

DES (1978a) *Making INSET work: in-service education and training for teachers: a basis for discussion*, HMSO, London

DES/Welsh Office (1987b) *The national curriculum 5–16: a consultation document*, HMSO, London

DES (1977c) *A new partnership for our schools* (the Taylor Report), HMSO, London

DES (1982) *The new teacher in school*, HMSO, London

DES (1984a) *Parental influence at school: a new framework for school government in England and Wales*, HMSO, London

DES/Welsh Office (1984b) *Records of achievement: a statement of policy*, HMSO, London

DES/Welsh Office (1981a) *The school curriculum*, HMSO, London

DES (1981b) *Schools and working life: some initiatives*, HMSO, London

DES/Welsh Office (1985d) *Science 5–16: a statement of policy*, HMSO, London

DES (1978b) *Special educational needs* (the Warnock Report), HMSO, London

DES/HMI (1986b) *A survey of the lower attaining pupils programme: the first two years*, HMSO, London

DES (1972) *Teacher education and training* (the James Report), HMSO, London

DES/Welsh Office (1983c) *Teaching quality*, HMSO, London

DES (1977d) *Ten good schools: a secondary school enquiry*, HMSO, London

DES (1981c) *West Indian children in our schools* (the Rampton Report), HMSO, London

DES (1983d) *Young people in the eighties*, HMSO, London

Donoughue, C. *et al.* (1981) *In service: the teacher and the school*, Kogan Page, London

Dorn, N. and Nortoft, B. (1982) *Health careers*, Institute for the Study of Drug Dependence, London

Douglas, T. (1984) *Groupwork practice*, Tavistock, London

Downey, M. and Kelly, V. (1978) *Moral education: theory and practice*, Harper and Row, London

Draper, P. (1980) 'Three types of health education', *British Medical Journal*, 16 August, pp. 493–5

Dufour, B. (ed.) (1982) *New movements in the social sciences and humanities*, Maurice Temple Smith, London

Dweck C.S. (1986) 'Motivational processes affecting learning', *American Psychologist*, vol. 41, no. 10, pp. 1040–8.

Easen, P. (1985) *Making school-centred INSET work: a school of education pack for teachers*, Open University with Croom Helm, London

Eichenbaum, L. and Orbach, S. (1983) *What do women want?* Michael Joseph, London

Eichenbaum, L. and Orbach, S. (1985) *Understanding women*, Penguin, Harmondsworth

Elder, G.H. (1968) 'Adolescent socialisation and development' in Borgatta, E. and Lambert, W. (eds), *Handbook of personality theory and research*, Rand McNally, Chicago

Elkind, D. (1967) 'Egocentrism and adolescence' in *Child Development*, vol. 38, pp. 1025–34

Elliott, G. and White, D. (1986) *Parents, teachers and the guidance process*, Manpower Services Commission, London

Elliott, J. (1982) 'The idea of a pastoral curriculum: a reply to T.H. McLaughlin', *Cambridge Journal of Education*, vol. 12, no. 1, pp. 34–60

——— and Pring, R. (1975) *Social education and social understanding*, University of London Press, London

Elliott, G. and White, D. (1986) *Parents, teachers and the guidance process*, Manpower Services Commission, London

Eraut, M. (1977) 'Some perspectives on consultancy in in-service education', *British Journal of Inservice Education*, vol. 4, no. 1, pp. 95–9

Eraut, M., Good, L. and Smith, G. (1975) *The analysis of curriculum materials*, University of Sussex Education Area Occasional Paper, Falmer, Sussex

Erikson, E.H. (1968) *Identity: youth and crisis*, Faber and Faber, London

Evans, M. (ed.) *Health education in secondary schools: 10 case studies*, TACADE, Manchester

Ewles, L, and Simnett, I. (1985) *Promoting health, a practical guide to health education*, John Wiley, London

Fiehn, J. (1986) 'The silent P — politics in PSE', *Clio*, vol. 6, no. 2, pp. 4–6, ILEA, London

Flavell, J.H. (1962) *The developmental psychology of Jean Piaget*, Van Nostrand, New York

Fletcher, C. (1983) *The challenges of community education: a biography of the Sutton Centre 1970–82*, Department of Adult Education, Nottingham University
—— and Thompson, N. (1980) *Issues in community education*, Falmer, Lewes
—— Caron, M. and Williams, W. (1985) *Schools on trial: the trials of democratic comprehensives*, Open University Press, Milton Keynes
Ford, J., Mongin, D. and Whelan, M. (1982) *Special education and social control*, Routledge and Kegan Paul, London
French, J. and Adams, L. (1986) 'From analysis to synthesis: theories of health education, *Health Education Journal*, vol. 45, no. 2, pp. 71–4
Freud, A. (1937) *The ego and the mechanisms of defence*, Hogarth Press, London
Further Education Unit (FEU) (1980) *Developing social and life skills*, Longmans for the FEU, York
—— (1979) *A basis for choice* (the Mansell Report), HMSO, London.
—— (1892a) *Profiles*, DES, London
—— (1982b) *The changing face of FE*, Longman for the FEU, York
FEU/SCDC (1985) *Supporting TVEI: FE and the development of technical and vocational curricula*, DES, London
Gagné, R.M. (1977) *The conditions of learning*, 3rd edn, Holt, Rinehart and Winston, London
Galloway, D. (1981) *Teaching and counselling: pastoral care in primary and secondary schools*, Longman, Harlow
—— and Goodwin, C. (1987) *The education of disturbed children: pupils with learning and adjustment difficulties*, Longman, Harlow
Galton, M. and Moon, B. (eds) (1983) *Changing schools . . . changing curriculum*, Harper and Row, London
Gershuny, J. (1983) *Social innovation and the division of labour*, Oxford University Press, London
Gessell, A., Ilg, E.G. and Ames, L.B. (1956) *Youth: the years from ten to sixteen*, Harper and Row, London
Gibson, R. (1986) *Critical theory and education*, Hodder and Stoughton, London
Gibson, T. (1979) *People power: community and work groups in action*, Penguin, Harmondsworth
Gilligan, C. (1982) *In a different voice: psychological theory and women's development*, Harvard University Press, Cambridge, Mass.
Gipps, C. (ed.) (1986) *The GCSE: an uncommon examination*, Bedford Way Papers No. 29, Institute of Education, London
Grainger, A.J. (1970) *The bullring*, Pergamon Press, Oxford
Grey, G. and Hill, F. (1988) *Health action pack*, National Extension College for the Health Education Authority, Cambridge
Guthrie, I.D. (1979) *The sociology of pastoral care in an urban school*, MA Dissertation, Kings College, London University
Hadow, H. (1926) *Report of the Consultative Committee under the chairmanship of Sir Henry Hadow on 'The education of the adolescent'*, HMSO, London
Halsey, A.H., Heath, A. and Ridge, J. (1980) *Origins and destinations*, Oxford University Press, London
Hamblin, D. (1978) *The teacher and pastoral care*, Blackwell, Oxford
—— (1980) *Problems and practice of pastoral care*, Blackwell, Oxford
—— (1981) *Teaching study skills*, Blackwell, Oxford
—— (1983) *Guidance: 16–19*, Blackwell, Oxford
—— (1984) *Pastoral care — a training manual*, Blackwell, Oxford
—— (1986) *A pastoral programme*, Blackwell, Oxford
Handy, C. (1985) *The future of work*, Blackwell, Oxford
—— and Aitken, R. (1986) *Understanding schools as organizations*, Penguin, Harmondsworth

Hanko, G. (1985) *Special needs in ordinary classrooms*, Blackwell, Oxford

Harber, L., Meighan, R. and Roberts, B. (eds) (1984) *Alternative educational futures*, Holt, Rinehart and Winston, London

Hargreaves, D. (1982) *The challenge for the comprehensive school: culture, curriculum, community*, Routledge and Kegan Paul, London

Harlen, W. and Elliott, J. (1982) 'A checklist for planning or reviewing and evaluation' in McCormick, R. (ed.) *Calling education to account*, Heinemann with Open University Press, London

Havighurst, R.J. (1972) *Development tasks and education*, McKay, New York

Healey, M. (1984) 'Developing a social education programme: a case study', *Pastoral Care in Education*, vol. 2, no. 2, pp. 93–7

Heller, H. (1984) *Helping schools change*, CSCS, University of York

Hicks, D. and Townley, C. (eds) (1982) *Teaching world studies: an introduction to global perspectives on the curriculum*, Longman, Harlow

Hirst, P.H. (1982) 'Ideas into action: development and the acceptance of innovations', *International Journal of Education Development*, vol. 1, no. 3, pp. 79–102, quoted in Dennison, W.F. and Shenton, K. (1987) *Challenges in educational management*, Croom Helm, London

—— and Peters, R.S. (1970) *The logic of education*, Routledge and Kegan Paul, London

—— and Woolley, P. (1982) *Social relations and human abilities*, Methuen, London

Hitchcock, G. (1986) *Profiles and profiling: a practical introduction*, Longman, Harlow

HMSO (1976) *Manual of nutrition*, London

HMSO (1983) *People in the '80s — a survey*, London

Holly, P. (1986) 'Guidelines for undertaking internal development through evaluation' in Reid, K. *et al.* (1987) *Towards an effective school*, Blackwell, Oxford

Holt, M. (1983) *Curriculum workshop: an introduction to whole curriculum planning*, Routledge and Kegan Paul, London

Hopkins, D. and Widen M. (1984) *Alternative perspectives on school improvement*, Falmer, Lewes

Hopson, B. and Hough, P. (1976) 'The need for personal and social education in secondary schools and further education', *British Journal of Guidance and Counselling*, vol. 4, no. 1, pp. 16–27

Hopson, B. and Scally, M. (1980, 1982, 1985, 1987) *Lifeskills teaching programmes I, II, III, IV*, Lifeskills Associates, Leeds

Hopson, B. and Scally, M. (1981) *Lifeskills teaching*, McGraw-Hill, Maidenhead

Horton, T. and Raggatt, P. (eds) (1982) *Challenge and change in the curriculum*, Hodder and Stoughton for the Open University, London

Houston, G. (1984) *The red book of groups*, The Rochester Foundation, London

Hovey, A. (1987) *Governing a healthy school*, Health Education Authority, London

Hoyle, E. (1986) *The politics of school management*, Hodder and Stoughton, London

Hunt, D.E. (1980) 'How to be your own best theorist', *Theory into Practice*, vol. 19, no. 4, pp. 287–93

Hunt, J. and Hitchins, P. (1986) *Creative reviewing, groundwork*, Groundworks, Grange-on-Sands, Cumbria

Hustler, D. and Ashman, I. (1985) 'Personal and social education for all' in Cuff, E.C. and Payne, G.C.F. (eds) *Crisis in the curriculum*, Croom Helm, London

Inner London Education Authority (ILEA) (1977) *Keeping the school under review*, ILEA, London

—— (1983a) *Effective learning skills*, ILEA, London

—— (1983b) *History and social sciences at secondary level: social sciences*, ILEA, London

—— (1984a) *Improving secondary schools* (the Hargreaves Report), ILEA, London

—— (1984b) *Religious education*, ILEA, London

—— (1985a) *Educational opportunties for all* (the Fish Report), ILEA, London

———— (1985b) *Implementing the ILEA's anti-sexist policies*, ILEA, London

———— (1986) *The teaching of controversial issues: advice from the Inspectorate*, ILEA, London

Irving, A. (1984) *Study skills across the curriculum*, Heinemann Educational, London

Jacques, D. (1984) *Learning in groups*, Croom Helm, London

Jenks, J. (1984) *The role of health education in the integration of personal and social education in the secondary school*, unpublished paper, ILEA, London

———— (1986) 'Report to the Chief Inspector's Working Party on INSET. A co-ordinated response to needs, priorities and resources', unpublished paper, 19 November

Johnson, D.W., Johnson R.T., Tiffany, M. and Zaidman, B. (1984) 'Cross-ethnic relationships: the impact of intergroup co-operation and intergroup competition' in *Journal of Educational Research*, vol. 78, no. 2, pp. 75–9

Jones, A. (1987) *Counselling adolescents: school and after*, 2nd edn, Kogan Page, London

Jones, K. (1986) 'The survival of the blackest', *Guardian*, 25 February

Jones, N. (1985) 'School welfare and pupils with special educational needs' in Ribbins, P. (ed.) *Schooling and welfare*, Falmer, Lewes

Joyce, B. and Weil, M. (1980) *Models of teaching*, Prentice Hall, New York

Kelmer-Pringle, M. (1980) *The needs of children*, Hutchinson, London

Kirk, R. (1987) *Learning in action: activities for personal and group development*, Blackwell, Oxford

Kirkwood, B. and Clements, S. (1986) 'A strategy for school-based staff development' in Day, C. and Moore, R. (eds) *Staff development in the secondary school*, Croom Helm, London

Knowles, M.S. (ed.) (1984) *Andragogy in action*, McGraw-Hill, Maidenhead

Kohlberg, L. (1971) 'Stages of moral development as a basis for moral education' in Beck, C., Crittendon, B. and Sullivan, E. (eds), *Moral education interdisciplinary approaches*, University of Toronto Press, Toronto

———— (1984) *The psychology of moral development: the nature and validity of moral stages*, Harper and Row, London

Kraftwohl, D., Bloom, R. and Masia, B. (1964) *The taxonomy of educational objectives*, Longman, York

Kyriacou, C. (1986) *Effective teaching in schools*, Blackwell, Oxford

Lambert, K. (1986) *School management: materials and simulations for in-service training*, Blackwell, Oxford

Lang, P. and Marland, M. (eds) (1985) *New directions in pastoral care*, Blackwell, Oxford

Langeveld, W. (1979) *Political education for teenagers*, Council of Europe, Strasbourg

Latey (1967) *Report of the committee on the 'Age of Majority'*, HMSO, London

Law, B. (1984) *The uses and abuses of profiling*, Harper Education, London

Lawton, D. (1981) *An introduction to teaching and learning*, Hodder and Stoughton, London

———— (1983) *Curriculum studies and educational planning*, Hodder and Stoughton, London

———— (1986) *School curriculum planning*, Hodder and Stoughton, London

Lee, R. (1980) *Beyond coping: some approaches to social education*, FEU/Longman, London

Lee, V. and Zeldin, D. (eds) (1982) *Planning in the curriculum*, Hodder and Stoughton for the Open University, London

Leviton, H. (1975) 'The implications of the relationship between self-concept and academic achievement' in *Child Study Journal*, vol. 5, pp. 25–35

Lewin, K. (1939) 'Field theory and experiment in social psychology: concepts and methods', *American Journal of Sociology*, vol. 44, pp. 868–97

———— (1951) *Field theory and social science*, Harper and Row, London

Likona, T. (ed.) (1976) *Moral development and behavior*, Holt, Rinehart and Winston, New York

Lindner, B. (1987) 'State, control and "community involvement"', *Journal of Community Education*, vol. 5 no. 4, pp. 17–20

Lindsay, G. (ed.) (1983) *Problems of adolescence in school*, Croom Helm, London

Loevinger, J. (1976) *Ego development*, Jossey-Bass, San Francisco

Lukes, J. (1979) 'School sociology and social studies in Humberside', *The Social Science Teacher*, vol. 9, no. 2, December, quoted in Lee, R. (1980) *Beyond coping*, FEU, London

McCormick, R. (ed.) (1982) *Calling education to account: a reader*, Heinemann for Open University, London

—— and James, M. (1983) *Curriculum evaluation in schools*, Croom Helm, London

McGuiness, J.B. (1982) *Planned pastoral care: a guide for teachers*, McGraw-Hill, Maidenhead

Macintosh, H.G. and Hale, D.E. (1981) *Measuring learning outcomes*, Open University Press, Milton Keynes

McLaughlin, T.H. (1982) 'The idea of a pastoral curriculum', *Cambridge Journal of Education*, vol. 12, no. 1, pp. 34–60

McMahon, A., Bolam, R., Abbot, R. and Holly, P. (1984) *Guidelines for review and internal development in schools: a secondary school handbook*, Longman for Schools Council, York

McMahon, T. (1986) *Developing tutor skills*, FEU, London

McNiff, J. (1985) *Personal and social education: a teachers' handbook*, CRAC/Hobsons Press, Cambridge

McPhail, P. (1982) *Social and moral education*, Blackwell, Oxford

—— Ungoed-Thomas, J.R. and Chapman H. (1972) *Moral education in the secondary school*, Longman, Harlow

Manchester City Council (1986) *Alternative curriculum strategies*, Manchester

March, G. (1981) *Starting points*, Careers Office, Wiltshire County Council, Trowbridge

Marland, M. (1974) *Pastoral care*, Heinemann Educational, London

—— (1980) 'The Pastoral Curriculum' in Best *et al*. (eds) *Perspectives on pastoral care*, Heinemann Educational, London

Martin, I. (1986) 'Education and community: reconstructing a relationship', *Journal of Community Education*, vol. 5, no. 3, pp. 17–23

Martini, R., Myers, K. and Warner, S. (1984) *Is your school changing? a pack for teachers to use in their schools to monitor progress towards sex equality*, ILEA, London

Maslow, A. (1968) *Towards a psychology of being*, Van Nostrand, New York

Mead, M. (1928) *Coming of age in Samoa*, Morrow, New York

Meighan, R. (1981) *A sociology of educating*, Holt, Rinehart and Winston, London

Miller, D. (1976) *The age between: adolescents in a disturbed society*, Cornmarket/Hutchinson, London

Miller, J. (1982a) *Training in individual guidance and support*, MSC, London

—— (1982b) *Tutoring*, FEU, London

—— Taylor, B. and Watts, A.G. (1983) *Towards a personal guidance base*, FEU, London

—— Turner, C. and Inniss, S. (1987) *Preparing for change: the management of curriculum-led institutional development*, Longman for FEU, York

Miller, J.B. (1976) *Towards a new psychology of women*, Penguin, Harmondsworth

Millman, V. and Weiner, G. (1985) *Sex differentiation in schooling: is there really a problem?* Longman for SCDC, York

Ministry of Agriculture, Fisheries and Food (1976) *Manual of nutrition*, HMSO, London

Moon, B. (1986a) 'Exploring the future: prerequisites for staff development' in Day C. and Moore R. (eds), *Staff development in the secondary school*, Croom Helm, London

—— (1986b) 'Managing the wild horses of the curriculum', *Journal of Community Education*, vol. 5 no. 3., pp. 9–11

—— (1987) *Modular curriculum: remaking the mould*, Harper and Row, London

Musgrave, P.W. (1978) *The moral curriculum: a sociological analysis*, Methuen, London

Naisbitt, J. (1984) *Megatrends*, Macdonald and Co., New York

NAPCE (1986) *Preparing for pastoral care: in-service training for the pastoral aspect of the teacher's role*, Blackwell, Oxford

Nielsen, L. (1987) *Adolescent psychology*, Holt, Rinehart and Winston, New York

Nottingham, B. and Cross, M. (1981) 'Moral Education across the curriculum', in *Brown Paper II*, St Martin's College, Lancaster

Nuttall, D. (1981) *School self-evaluation: accountability with a human face*, Longman for Schools Council, York

—— (1986) *Assessing educational achievement*, Falmer, Lewes

OCEA (1987a) *The personal record component*, Oxford University Press, London

OCEA (1987b) *Student reviewing and recording*, Oxford University Press, London

Offer, D. and Offer, J. (1975) *From teenage to young manhood*, Basic Books, New York

Oldroyd, D., Smith, K. and Lee, J. (eds) (1984) *School-based staff development activities: a handbook for secondary schools*, Longman for SCDC Publications, York

Open University (1983) *Course E204 Purpose and planning in the curriculum: Block 1. Unit 2. Educational ideologies*, Open University Press, Milton Keynes

O'Sullivan, D.J. (1987) *From pastoral care to personal and social education*, MA Dissertation, King's College, London

Pearce, B. (1981) *Trainee-centred reviewing*, MSC, London

Peel, E. (1971) *The nature of adolescent judgement*, Staples Press, London

Pepper, B., Myers, K. and Coyle-Dawkins, R. (1984) *Sex equality and the pastoral curriculum — a pack of activities to use in tutor time*, ILEA, London

Peters, R.S. (1981) *Moral development and moral education*, Allen and Unwin, London

Pfeiffer, J.W. and Jones J.E. (1974–83) *A handbook for structured experiences for human relations training*, University Associates, La Jolla, California

Phares, J.E. (1976) *Locus of control in personality*, General Learning Press, New Jersey

Phenix, P.H. (1964) *Realms of meaning*, McGraw-Hill, Maidenhead

Piaget, J. (1932) (trans. Gabin, M.) *The moral judgement of the child*, Penguin, Harmondsworth

—— (1971) (trans. Coltmer, D.) *Science of education and the psychology of the child*, Longman, London

Porter, A. (ed.) (1983) *Teaching political literacy*, Bedford Way Papers No. 16., Heinemann, London

Pring, R. (1984) *Personal and social education in the curriculum*, Hodder and Stoughton, London

—— (1987) 'Implications of the changing values and ethical standards of society' in Thacker, J. *et al.* (eds) *Personal, social and moral education in a changing world*, NFER-Nelson, Windsor

Purnell, C. (1983) 'Towards a personal and social development programme for an open access sixth form', *Pastoral Care in Education*, vol. 1, no. 3, pp. 180–8

Quicke, J. (1985) 'Charting a course for personal and social education', *Pastoral Care in Education*, vol. 3, no. 2, pp. 91–9

Raymond, J. (1982) 'How form tutors perceive their role', *Links*, vol. 7, no. 3, pp. 25–30

—— (1985) *Implementing pastoral care in schools*, Croom Helm, London

Reid, K., Hopkins, D. and Holly, P. (1987) *Towards the effective school: the problem and some solutions*, Blackwell, Oxford

Rennie, J., Lunzer, E.A. and Williams, W.T. (1974) *Social education: an experiment in four secondary schools*, Evans/Methuen Educational, London

Reynolds, D. (ed.) (1985) *Studying school effectiveness*, Falmer, Lewes

Ribbins, P. (ed.) (1985) *Schooling and welfare*, Falmer, Lewes

—— and Ribbins, P. (1986) 'Developing a design for living course at "Deanswater":
an evaluation', *Pastoral Care in Education*, vol. 4, no. 1, pp. 23–37

Rice, B. (1981) *Informal methods in health and social education*, TACADE, Manchester

Richardson, E. (1973) *The teacher, the school and the task of management*, Heinemann,
London

Richardson, R., Flood, M. and Fisher, S. (1980) *Debate and decision-making in a world
of change*, One World Trust, London

Rodmell, S. and Watt, A. (eds) (1986) *The politics of health education*, Routledge and Kegan
Paul, London

Rogers, B. (1984) *Careers education and guidance*, CRAC/Hobsons Press, Cambridge

Rogers, C. (1983) *Freedom to learn for the eighties*, Charles E. Merrill, Columbus, Ohio

Rogers, D. (ed.) (1983) *Issues in adolescent psychology*, 2nd edn, Appleton-Century-Crofts,
New York

Rosenberg, M. (1965) *Society and the adolescent self-image*, Princeton University Press,
Princeton

Rotter, J.B. (1966) 'Generalised expectancies for internal versus external control of reinforcement', *Psychological Monographs*, vol. 80, no. 1

Rowe, A. (1971) *The school as a guidance community*, Pearson Press, Hull

Ruddock, J. (ed.) (1982) *Teachers in partnership: four studies of in-service collaboration*,
Longman for Schools Council, York

Rutter, M., Graham, P., Chadwick, O. and Yule, W. (1979) 'Adolescent turmoil: fact or
fiction?' in Rogers, D. (ed.) *Issues in adolescent psychology*, 2nd edn, Appleton-Century-
Crofts, New York

Rutter, M., Maughan, B., Mortimer, P. and Ouston, J. (1979) *Fifteen thousand hours:
secondary schools and their effects on children*, Open Books, London

Ryder, J. and Silver, H. (1985) *Modern English society*, 3rd edn, Methuen, London

Sachs, D. (1982) 'How to distinguish self-respect from self-esteem', *Philosophy and Public
Affairs*, vol. 10, Fall

Salmon, P. (1980) *Coming to know*, Routledge and Kegan Paul, London

—— and Clare, H. (1984) *Classroom collaboration*, Routledge and Kegan Paul, London

Saylor, J.G., Alexander, W.M. and Lewis, A.J. (1981) *Curriculum planning for better
teaching and learning*, 4th edn, Holt Saunders International, New York

Schmuck, R.A., Runkle, P.J., Arends, J.J. and Arends, R.I. (1977) *The second handbook
of organisation development in schools*, Mayfield Publishing Co., Palo Alto, California

Schools Council/Health Education Council (1977) *Schools Council health education project
5–13*, Nelson, London

—— (1980) *Schools Council health education project 13–18: developing health education
– a co-ordinator's guide*, 2nd edn, Forbes, London

Schools Council/Nuffield Foundation (1970) *The humanities project*, Heinemann, London

Seedhouse, D. (1986) *Health: the foundations for achievement*, John Wiley, London

Seligman, M.P. (1975) *Helplessness: on depression, development and death*, Freeman and
Co., San Francisco

Selman, R.L. (1976) 'Social-cognitive understanding: a guide to educational and clinical
practice' in Lickona, T. (ed.) *Moral development and behaviour*, Holt, Rinehart and
Winston, New York

Settle, D. and Wise, C. (1986) *Choices: materials and methods for personal and social
education*, Blackwell, Oxford

Shaw, H. and Matthews, D. (1980) *Working together, No. 2. A handbook for leaders working with parent groups*, Christchurch, New Zealand (distributed by Lifeskills Associates,
Leeds)

Silver, H. (1980) *Eduation and the social condition*, Methuen, London
—— (1983) *Education as history*, Methuen, London
Skilbeck, M. (1984a) *School-based curriculum development*, Harper and Row, London
—— (ed.) (1984b) *Readings in school-based curriculum development*, Harper and Row, London
Slaughter, R.A. (1986) *Futures across the curriculum*, Department of Educational Research, University of Lancaster
—— (1987) *Futures, tools and techniques*, Department of Educational Research, University of Lancaster
Smith, D. and Wootton, R. (1986) *Exploring enterprise: school and business perspectives*, Longman for SCDC, York
Smith, J. Southworth, M. and Wilson, A. (1985) *A course in political education for 14–18 year olds*, Longman, York
Smith, M. (1981) *Creators not consumers*, NAYC, Leicester
—— (1984) *Questions for survival*, NAYC, Leicester
Smith, P.D. (1986) *Simulations for careers and life skills: a practical lesson guide*, Hutchinson, London
Starkey, H. (1982) *Social education for teenagers: aims, issues and problems*, Council of Europe, Strasburg
Stenhouse, L.A. (1970) 'Handling controversial issues in the classroom', *Education Canada*, vol. 9, no.4
Stevenson, M. (1984) 'The balanced curriculum: some perspectives on the current debate', *Curriculum*, vol. 5 no. 2, pp. 22–9
Stewart, B. and Brownlow, J. (1985) *Myself: a descriptive report*, Northern MIND, Gateshead
Stibbs, J. (1987) 'Staff care and development', *Pastoral Care in Education*, vol. 5, no. 1, pp. 36–9
Stoner, F. (1986) 'Managing the school: the role of the head at a time of rapid change' in Day, C. and Moore, R. (eds) *Staff development in the secondary school*, Croom Helm, London
Stradling, R. (1986) *Political education: a handbook for teachers*, Edward Arnold, London
Stronach, I. (1984) 'Work experience: the sacred anvil' in Varlaam, C. (ed.) *Rethinking transition*, Falmer, Lewes
Szirom, T. and Dyson, S. (British edition by Slavin, H.) (1986) *Greater expectations: a sourcebook for working with girls and young women*, Learning Development Aids, Wisbech
Tambini, M. (1985) *Working with parents: a pilot study*, ILEA HEPD Centre (unpublished)
Tanner, J.M. (1962) *Growth at adolescence*, Blackwell Scientific, Oxford
Thacker, J., Pring, R. and Evans, D. (eds) (1987) *Personal, social and moral education in a changing world*, NFER-Nelson, Windsor
Thomas, E.J. (1968) 'Role theory, personality and the individual', in Borgatta, E. and Lambert, W. (eds)
Toffler, A. (1970) *Future shock*, Bodley Head, London
—— (1980) *The third wave*, Morrow, New York
Tones, K. (1986) 'Promoting the health of young people — the role of personal and social education', *Health Education Journal*, vol. 45, no. 1., pp. 14–18
Trethowan, D. (1987) *Appraisal and target-setting: a handbook for teacher development*, Harper and Row, London
Turner, C. (1978), *Inter-personal skills in further education*, Futher Education Staff College, Bristol
TVEI Unit (1985) *TVEI related in-service training (TRIST)*, MSC, London
Varlaam, C. (ed.) (1984) *Rethinking transition*, Falmer, Lewes

291

Vuori, H. and Ripela, M. (1981) 'Development and impact of the medical model', *Perspectives in Biology and Medicine*, Winter

Wake, R.A., Marbeau, V. and Peterson, A.D.C. (1979) *Innovation in secondary education in Europe*, Council of Europe, Strasbourg

Wakeman, B. (1984) *Personal, social and moral education: a sourcebook*, Lion Books, London

Wall, W.D. (1977) *Constructive education for adolescents*, Harrap, London

Wallace, R.G. (1985) *Introducing technical and vocational education*, Macmillan, Basingstoke

Warwick, D. (1987) *The modular curriculum*, Blackwell, Oxford

Watkins, C. (1985) 'Does Pastoral Care = Personal and Social Education?' *Pastoral Care in Education*, vol. 3, no. 3, pp. 179–82

—— and Wagner, P. (1987) *School discipline: a whole school appraoch*, Blackwell, Oxford

Watkins, P.R. (1987) *Modular approaches to the school curriculum*, Longman for SCDC, York

Watts, A.G. (1983) *Education, unemployment and the future*, Open University Press, Milton Keynes

—— and Kant, L. (1986) *A working start: guidance strategies for girls and young women*, Longman for SCDC, York

Watts, J. (ed.) (1977) *The Countesthorpe experience*, Allen and Unwin, London

Webb, N.M. (1984) 'Sex differences in interaction and achievement in co-operative small groups', *Journal of Educational Psychology*, vol. 76, no. 1, pp. 33–44

Wellington, J.J. (ed.) (1986) *Controversial issues in the curriculum*, Blackwell, Oxford

Weston, P. (1979) *Negotiating the curriculum: a study in secondary schooling*, National Foundation for Educational Research, Slough

White, R. and Brockington, D. (1978) *In and out of school: the ROSLA community education project*, Routledge and Kegan Paul, London

White, R. and Brockington, D. (1983) *Tales out of school*, Routledge and Kegan Paul, London

White R., Pring, R. and Brockington, D. (1985) *The 14–18 curriculum: integrating CPVE, YTS, TVEI?*, Youth Education Service, Bristol

Whitfield, R.C. (1971) *Disciplines of the curriculum*, McGraw-Hill, Maidenhead, Berks

Whyld, J. (ed.) (1983) *Sexism in the secondary curriculum*, Harper and Row, London

Williams, T. (1985) *School health education in Europe: profiles of 15 European countries*, HEC Health Education Unit, Department of Education, University of Southampton

—— (1986) 'School health education 15 years on', *Health Education Journal*, vol. 45, no. 1, pp. 3–7

—— (1987) 'Health education in secondary schools' in David, K. and Williams, T. (eds) *Health education in schools*, Harper and Row, London

—— and Williams, N. (1980) *Personal and social development in the school curriculum, SCHEP 13–18 co-ordinators' handbook*, Forbes, London

Williamson, D. (1980) 'Pastoral care or pastoralization?' in Best, R. *et al.* (eds) *Perspectives on pastoral care*, Heinemann Educational, London

Wilson, C. (1979) 'The development of self' in Coleman, J. (ed.) *The school years*, Methuen, London

Wilson, J. (1967) *Introduction to moral education*, Penguin, Harmondsworth

Winnicott, D.W. (1971) *Playing and reality*, Tavistock Publications, London

Wooster, A. (1985) 'Personal and social development in the primary school', *Pastoral Care in Education*, vol. 3, no. 3, pp. 183–8

—— and Hall, E. (1986) *Communication and social skills – a course guide*, University of Nottingham

Index